ESSEX
in History

Audley End

ESSEX
in History

Kenneth Neale

Phillimore

1997

Published by
PHILLIMORE & CO. LTD.
Shopwyke Manor Barn, Chichester, West Sussex

ISBN 1 86077 051 7

Printed and bound in Great Britain by
BOOKCRAFT LTD.
Midsomer Norton

Contents

List of Illustrations

Frontispiece: Audley End

Acknowledgements

The publishers and author wish to express their thanks to the following for supplying and granting permission for the reproductions of illustrations in this book: Basildon Development Corporation, 85; British Airports Authority (Stansted), 88; Cambridge University Collection of Air Photographs, 19; Colchester Archaeological Trust, 8; Colchester Museums, 6; Essex County Council (Archaeology Section), 5, 9, 81; Essex County Council (Essex Record Office), 22, 29, 35, 39, 46, 50, 52, 59, 70, 71, 73, 76, 78; Peter Froste, 6, 26; Harlow Development Corporation, 84; Director of the National Army Museum, 80; K.P. Neale and A. Royall, 82, 83; Lord Petre, 45, 49; Port of London Authority, 77; Reuters, 86; University of Essex, 11; Jeffery W. Whitelaw, 87.

Foreword

The history of the county from the earliest times to our own day is one of which Essex people can be proud. In this book Kenneth Neale has described how national and international events have affected Essex and how the county and its people have been involved in them. He tells us too about the lives of Essex people in town and country, in peace and war, through hard times and periods of prosperity. It is a book about people, change, challenge and achievement.

Today, Essex still derives its identity from the loyalty and the aspirations of the people who live here. The book reflects that in its historic setting. It will, I am sure, help to encourage those traditions and values that have always enriched the life of the county.

Readers will enjoy the story that it tells. They will learn too, much about the county and the richness of the Essex heritage which is happily ours and must be preserved for our posterity.

Essex has an amazing diversity, not only in the countryside but also in its towns, villages and environment. There are considerable differences in lifestyle and occupation which make the County particularly fascinating. There is also a most extensive coastline varying between beautiful estuaries, and not so beautiful oil terminals and power stations. Essex is a county of exceptional interest. Kenneth Neale has done a magnificent job in capturing the spirit of our County. We are most grateful to him.

September, 1997
Audley End

Brayhooke.

LORD LIEUTENANT OF ESSEX

Preface

(1st Edition, 1977)

'All history is local history'

It has been remarked, with conviction and truth, that all history is local history. Nowhere in England is interest in local history stronger than in Essex, This has been largely due to the dedicated work of the local and county historical and archaeological societies and the excellence of the Essex Record Office to all of whom this book is in some way a tribute.

A definitive single-volume history of the county has yet to be written. This book, I hope, will meanwhile help to fill the gap between the compendious *Victoria County History* and the broad general treatment of the subject in the other recent histories that I have discussed in the reference note. For most of my life I have been devoted to Essex and its history. In writing *Essex in History* I have therefore tried to present the county in the historical perspective and narrative form that I would have found helpful when I first embarked on the subject. It is but a modest offering to those who require an introduction to Essex history and a source of general reference. I would like to think that it will also give pleasure to those who read history for enjoyment and nourish a special interest in Essex. It is in no way a substitute for the *V.C.H.* or the original sources to which the serious student must have recourse. But it may be found useful as a thematic interpretation of Essex history and thus contribute in some measure to a better understanding of the evolution of the county and the continuity and quality of Essex life.

The source material on which this book relies is too vast for me adequately to list or acknowledge. Suffice it to say that I am generally indebted to the whole company of Essex historians and topographers whether they have dug, delved, or written for the benefit of county history. Specially am I grateful to Dr. F.G. Emmison, county archivist until 1969, whose encouragement and inspiration have sustained my work and interest through many years of endeavour. To him, and to Mr. K.C. Newton, the county archivist, I am indebted also for their expert suggestions for the Tudor and Medieval chapters, periods in which they have unrivalled knowledge of the county.

WEST CHILTINGTON, SUSSEX.   KENNETH NEALE

Preface

(Second edition 1997)

It is now twenty years since *Essex in History* was first published. Since then, recent events and modern developments in the county have entered the historical record. In the field of archaeology new scientific techniques, additional resources and the priority given to archaeological investigation has resulted in a significant increase in knowledge and more reliable interpretation. Major discoveries like those at Elms Farm Heybridge, the 'rescue' work at Stansted, further evaluation of the important complexes at Mucking, renewed interest in Camulodunum and, more generally, the field work and coordinating role of the County Archaeological Section at Chelmsford have given Essex archaeology fresh impetus.

Beyond that, there has been a massive growth in public and educational interest in local and county history. More historical work is being published by local societies, new standards of presentation are evident in the county's museums; and there is a constant demand for lectures and talks around the county. The 'industry', for that is almost what it is, thrives. In an age when this public appetite for knowledge and understanding of the past seems to be a natural and desirable response to the instability and challenges of contemporary life, historians have a valuable contribution to make. That seemed to justify a second edition of *Essex in History* and I have gladly undertaken the revision. In doing so I have tried to reflect the developments I have referred to. Thus, those chapters that are primarily based on archaeological research and that describe the recent past in the county have been considerably enlarged and generally re-written. The remaining chapters have all been enhanced by reference to recent academic works.

I hope that this book, as well as interesting those who cherish the county and enjoy its history, will encourage them to join their local history societies and to support the county organisations like the Friends of Historic Essex, the Essex Archaeological and Historical Congress, the Essex Society for Archaeology and History and the Essex Society for Family History. To all of those I am grateful for what they do for Essex history and for the friendships and support I have received from them over many years.

It remains for me to thank the publishers, Phillimore and Company and especially Noel Osborne their Managing Director and Nicola Willmot, Production Manager, for unfailing help and courteous cooperation with this revision and, of course, with the previous publications they have accepted from me.

GREAT SAMPFORD, ESSEX.   KENNETH NEALE

Chapter One

ဆာငၑ

ROMAN ESSEX AND THE PREHISTORIC BACKGROUND

'Colonia Victricensis'

It is two thousand years since the people of Essex first glimpsed the legionary eagles of
the invading Romans. None could have foreseen that 400 years of Roman authority
would be experienced before other invaders, in their turn, dispossessed the Romano-
British communities that grew up in the imperial province. Yet for all the panoply of
power and material splendour of the empire the imprint of the Roman centuries on the
subsequent life and face of Britain was comparatively slight. Apart from the military
roads, the siting of some of our towns and the visible remains of Roman military architecture, as at Colchester, there is not much of significance to remind us of their presence.
Culturally and linguistically we have received almost nothing direct from the long
occupation. Topographically, and from the evidence of philology, the British landscape
owes far more to the Saxon usurpers of Roman Britain and to the earlier tribal communities
upon whom Roman military government was imposed. Yet it is impossible to ignore the
period during which most of Britain belonged to a great and enduring empire, and
received, temporarily, the benefits of a higher civilisation. All this is as true of the Roman
experience in Essex as it is generally of England. But before describing Roman Essex we
ought first to examine the pre-Roman eras for the integrity of no age excludes the legacy
of posterity. Indeed, much of the structure of pre-Roman society survived and the quality of life of the Romano-British communities seems to have broadly reflected much that
can now be seen, culturally and in daily life, to have been rooted in prehistoric experience.

Our knowledge of Britain before the Romans is derived almost entirely from the
products of archaeology and the vivid, if sometimes subjective, records of Roman
historiography. The annals of Caesar and Tacitus, the son-in-law of Agricola, clothe
with history and human personality the visible evidence of lifeless ruins, earthworks,
artefacts and coinage. But these limited though invaluable accounts expose only the
margins of prehistory and it is to archaeology, in all its scientific dimensions, that we
must turn for a reconstruction of the receding ages of remote antiquity. These are the
realms of anonymous people whose times we can only describe by the remains of their
settlements and the materials they used. Often they are known only by the sites or the
form of the articles they made. It is not easy to visualise the Windmill Hill tribes of
neolithic Britain, the Beaker people of the Bronze Age, or those of the Clactonian flake-
culture who settled on the primeval channel of the Thames where now is the foreshore
of the county's summer resorts. But they were nevertheless people with desires and
aspirations comparable with those of succeeding ages.

The sharply indented coastline and major estuarine localities of modern Essex are
significant features in the geology and geography of the county. They are of fundamental
importance too for its ethnic characteristics and history.

1

Beyond the coastal and riverine areas the landscape of the undulating Boulder Clays and chalklands is the result of successive glaciations and climatic changes. Over time the landscape assimilated the surface veneers imparted by the impact of human activities. Beneath the ground lies a story to which there is no known beginning and which has only been broadly recovered by geological and archaeological investigation and analysis. Modern science and inter-disciplinary approaches, like the study of fossilised pollens that date from the inter-glacial periods, are disturbing what were the established geological and archaeological chronologies. However, it remains clear that there were viable human communities in Britain long before Essex enters the archaeological story of mankind sometime during the inter-glacial period before about 400,000 B.C. But there has not, as yet, been any evidence recovered in the county for that. The earliest palaeolithic site yet known in Essex is along the foreshore of the West Beach at Clacton-on-Sea and the nearby Lion Point at Jaywick. There, a fossil channel, marking a prehistoric channel of the Thames, was found to contain a series of stone tools and other artefacts of a definable culture and technology. This Clactonian assemblage has been dated to about 400,000 B.C. and has been very important to the study of the palaeolithic period generally in Europe. At this site has thus been identified a palaeolithic culture, coeval with mammoth, rhinoceros and hippopotamus, of people who fashioned their tools and weapons by a flaking technique.

Among the artefacts recovered from these sites have been scrapers, pointed tools made on anvils of stone, spear-tips and rough chopping implements, for the hand-axe does not appear to have been manufactured by the Clactonians. The flints were worked roughly in two ways. Some can be seen to have been broad-flaked and others laboriously trimmed by chipping all round to make what are called by archaeologists, core tools. Perhaps the most remarkable of these Clactonian discoveries was the only wooden palaeolithic artefact so far found in Britain, a yew wood spearhead dated to the period 350-400,000 B.C. All these are the products of the primitive technology practised by the earliest identifiable people of Essex.

As would be expected along the Thames valley especially, but over Essex in general, in the terraced river gravels there is a wealth of palaeolithic evidence. Despite the losses that have resulted from quarrying in the terraced areas around Grays and on the Tilbury marshes Acheulian hand-axes, Levallois flakes, Clactonian artefacts and numerous palaeoliths have been found. Other traces of palaeolithic life in the county have also been revealed along the watersides of the old river valleys of the Colne, the Lea, the Roding and on the higher surface gravels. The riverine dwellers of the Old Stone Age hunted wild boar, elk and reindeer with their crude weapons. A fossilised antler found on a palaeolithic floor at Thurrock suggests that animal horns too were used as tools or weapons. A quarry at Purfleet has yielded a series of Acheulian flints, and an axe-head of this period was found at Pimp Hall, Chingford. At Marks Tey, in a depression in the Boulder Clay filled with silt of a fresh-water lake left by the retreating ice, is an important palaeolithic site. Similar lake sites have been located at Kelvedon, Witham and Tiptree. In the lower gravels at Wanstead and Purfleet there are vestiges of this remarkable period. Interesting artefacts, now in the museum at Southend-on-Sea, come from a rich palaeolithic site at Barling Magna just to the north-east of the town. A hand-axe of the period comes from Tilbury on Thames-side. Work on the M11 motorway at Woodford revealed part of the palaeolithic floor of south-west Essex.

Archaeologists working in this period expect to find more and thus enlarge our understanding of these earliest of the known cultures of Essex.

The people of the Old Stone Age lived, as we have seen, mainly along the river valleys of the south. (The use of the familiar 'three-age system'–Stone, Bronze, Iron–is perhaps now obsolescent or at least unfashionable in some quarters in view of the new techniques available to archaeologists which now enable them to date material with much greater precision. I am using these terms, however, as they are convenient and understood by the general reader for whom this book is largely intended. Furthermore they still represent the only age classification for most of the material to which I have referred and are still in general use.)

The people of the Middle Stone Age began, in about 12,000 B.C., to occupy the heaths and moorlands of the southern, eastern and central areas of England. For upwards of 10,000 years these scattered bands of roving hunters colonised and cultivated the newly-won lands. Their stone hoes and primitive digging sticks show that England was for the first time being farmed. Hitherto, fish, game and wild plants provided the larder for mesolithic communities. But towards the end of this period the soils of Essex were being turned to receive the seed of the first generation of farmers. Plant geneticists now believe that this transition from communities of gatherers and hunters into a farming society through the domestication of wild plants may have happened over a comparatively short period of time, perhaps not more than a hundred or two hundred years. It has been compared with the dramatic effect on human experience of the mastery of fire. The problem for archaeologists is that, if the change was a transient sequence of short duration, there is not likely to be much remaining evidence for that progression in human development. Nevertheless, however long it took, the mesolithic period was one in which essential foundations of all future civilisations were laid.

In Essex the archaeological evidence for the mesolithic period is based upon the analysis of a few significant assemblages of flint tools and scattered isolated finds which are difficult to interpret within a reliable chronology or typology. However, the distribution of these finds is widespread throughout the county although mainly concentrated on coastal sites such as Walton-on-the-Naze and along the eastern rivers, the Crouch, the Colne and the Blackwater, that drain into the North Sea. There are other concentrations in the chalky sub-soils of the north-west, in the Epping Forest area and on Leaside. The curious rarity of artefacts from this period along the Thames, as compared with the palaeolithic, is thought to be the consequence of a probably low level of contemporary population in the area, still unexplained, and the technical difficulty of recognition and identification I have indicated above.

The neolithic period was marked by a significant advance in manual techniques, although the art of using metals had not then been mastered. This was the period in which were developed new skills in grinding and polishing stone implements with greater refinement than ever before in this island; there were, too, widespread forest clearances and the period is also notable for conspicuous field monuments which were erected throughout Europe. Stonehenge in Wiltshire is the most impressive of these and advanced radiocarbon technology has dated its construction to the third millennium B.C. It is convincing testimony to the existence of a structured and orderly neolithic society in southern Britain.

In farming, a simple rotational system was achieved by the practice of periodic moves of the areas under cultivation. This system of shifting agriculture is still practised in some parts of Africa, although there, as in neolithic Europe, it could survive only while there remained available a superabundance of land and ample rural labour. The people of the time also practised animal husbandry and there is some evidence of trading. From this time date the earliest surviving earthworks of Britain, the so-called causewayed camps on the chalk ridge of southern England, of which those at Combe Hill and Whitehawk in Sussex are typical examples. The timeless migration of peoples from the continent–by then separated from Britain by the North Sea–which ended with the Scandinavians some 3,000 years or more later, continued with the arrival of the Windmill Hill tribes. From the remains of their circular hut dwelling sites have come relics, more plentiful than for preceding periods, from which this picture of a developing culture has been built up. Such remains demonstrate the extension of human settlement to the chalklands of Sussex and Wessex, the light soils of East Anglia and along the limestone belt that stretches from the south-west to Lincolnshire and Yorkshire. Pottery, with its typical banded decoration of incised chevron and lozenge design, weapons and tools have been found on a number of occupation sites in Essex. There is also the evidence of burials, although continuous farming has obliterated numerous barrows that once marked the settlement areas.

In Essex the neolithic period is still not satisfactorily understood although there is increasing, but as yet largely unco-ordinated, evidence from numerous sites. The only causewayed enclosures so far identified in Essex are those at Orsett on the Thames Terrace, which has three concentric discontinuous ditches, and the late neolithic example at Springfield Lyons near Chelmsford. At Tye Field, Lawford, a late neolithic enclosed settlement has been established and others, as at Lamarsh, where there is believed to be a double enclosure, have been identified by cropmarks. Important sites of the period are known at Clacton, Dovercourt, Walton-on-the-Naze and Hullbridge. Curious monuments, somewhat enigmatic features enclosed by parallel earthen banks with quarry ditches on either side, have been tentatively identified by aerial photography at Lawford, Great Holland, Wormingford, Little Horkesley and Dedham. The best known in Essex, however, is the Springfield Cursus on the gravel terrace above the flood plain of the River Chelmer. Some 700 metres long and 50 metres wide, it is a major feature similar to others known on Salisbury Plain and first, though spuriously, designated in the 18th century by the antiquarian William Stukeley who 'surveyed the wonderful works of Cunobeline' at Colchester. It implies that there was by the late neolithic period a sufficiently large and organised population to provide the labour for this major monument which is assumed to have had a ceremonial or ritualistic purpose. It seems to have remained in use over a period of several centuries.

Metal, as fire and the cultivation of seeds had previously done, was to raise the levels of human existence from the plateau on which it had languished during most of the long and dreary millennia of the Stone Ages we have briefly surveyed.

಼ಞಣ

In visualising the life of the nomadic communities of Britain's prehistory it is important to remember that the climatic conditions in which they lived were markedly different from those we experience today. In the middle of the second millennium

B.C.–from which the Bronze Age may be regarded as beginning, though these ages naturally overlap to a considerable degree–it was certainly warmer than it is now, and the rainfall considerably less. It was during the late Bronze Age, around 1000 B.C., that climatic change to cooler and wetter conditions meant settled agriculture and regular cultivation. Thus were created the first field systems of small, irregularly shaped areas with curvilinear boundaries and cross-ploughed with primitive equipment, which had a permanent effect on the landscape of Britain. This led to densely settled and intensively cultivated areas and the establishment of extensive tracts of the upland areas on which sheep and cattle were grazed. Throughout this period migration from the continent continued to people the land and invigorate the population.

From about 1700 B.C. the Beaker people, so designated from the drinking vessels found in their tombs, began to arrive in Britain from the areas of Holland and the Rhineland. Ethnically related to the island tribes, they brought new skills to enhance the quality of metal work in bronze, copper and gold which was already being carried out at a folk level in Bronze Age Britain. They established themselves among the people of the south-west, in Wessex, the highlands, East Anglia and in the vicinity of the Thames. Their beakers have been recovered along the North Sea coast. They have appeared, too, in the north-west of Essex at Great Chesterford, on the gravels and in minor concentrations along the eastern limits of the county. The remains of a Bronze Age pile dwelling have also been discovered near Southchurch, and other relics at Clacton, thus demonstrating a continuity of settlement in this archaeologically rich district.

In Essex the distribution of Bronze-Age sites and finds presents a complicated pattern, not easily reconciled with a coherent picture of the various phases of the period and the evolution of the social and economic aspects of life at the time. Early Bronze-Age sites are found along the rivers and the coast. The eastern river systems, north of the Thames and the coastline between Harwich and Clacton, are the principal areas for the early Bronze Age. This did not change all that much in the middle Bronze Age although there are many examples of ring ditches, barrows, cremation cemeteries and evidence of metal working. Interestingly, in view of future history, there seems to have been a significant development of population and social resources in the vicinity of Colchester. Braintree and the nearby Rayne and Panfield are the sites of isolated axe finds and, in the latter places, hoards which included imported artefacts. Large Bronze-Age cemeteries have been proven at Alphamstone, Ardleigh and White Colne. Bronzefounders' hoards were discovered along what is thought might have been an organised supply system used by the bronzesmiths on a routeway from Grays Thurrock via Aveley, Fyfield, Clavering and Elmdon. A large group of ring ditches excavated in the Brightlingsea peninsula in 1989, as a result of apparently multi-period crop markings, resulted in the recovery of large numbers of Bronze-Age burial urns. These included bucket, barrel and globular forms of the middle Bronze-Age typology with interesting decorative features well established in southern England.

In recent years there has been an emphasis on excavations at late Bronze-Age sites in Essex which have revealed several settlement enclosures. Most significant are those at Mucking, Springfield and Great Baddow. The North Ring at Mucking yielded evidence of post-built houses of sub-circular form with porches; the South, double-concentric rings which contained a central round house also with a porch. The Chelmer valley sites at Springfield and Baddow and the fertile soils of the general vicinity there are thought to have considerable archaeological potential. The excavation of the enclosure ditch at Springfield Lyons produced the largest collection of mould fragments from any late Bronze-Age site in England. Many were considered to be for moulding swords and therefore suggest, as I have already indicated, a site of some political or administrative significance. The enclosure site seems to have been abandoned in the late Bronze Age, although a more precise date is not known, and it was not re-occupied until the Saxons arrived in Essex. Contextual evidence, however, supports the view that the surrounding areas were farmed continuously throughout the intervening period.

More specifically, a few more examples of the evidence for Bronze-Age life in Essex help to demonstrate the richness of this seminal period in the story of the county. At Shoebury in 1891 was discovered a rare and interesting penannular armlet decorated with a fine hatched diagonal design. Other work of the period has been taken from the ground in a hoard at Hatfield Broad Oak, at Saffron Walden, High Roding, Arkesden and elsewhere in north-west Essex. In the Thames-side parishes representative material, celts, spearheads, adzes, sickles, knives and other implements have been found in various localities. Swords have been unearthed at Barking and Thurrock, spear heads from the marshes around Plaistow and a dagger from the river at Bow Bridge. A bronze bowl excavated at Walthamstow is a fine example of the domestic utensils of the age. A late Bronze-Age hoard dated to *c.*800 B.C. of almost 300 items, one of the finest in Essex, came from Vange. It included axes, swords, knives, tools, sickles and a rare adze of continental provenance. The late Bronze-Age settlement at Lofts Farm, Heybridge has provided evidence, from domestic items, tools and the carbonised remains of plants, of a pastoral economy and continental trade via the Essex estuaries which were important as natural routeways into southern England from Europe.

Reverting to the general theme it is not surprising that the nature and pace, by prehistoric criteria, of change and progress in this period has led to it being described as 'the first golden age of Europe'. The eponymous bronze is a bright, shining alloy of copper and tin, sufficiently strong to permit the fabrication of durable metal artefacts. Some of these are of high artistic quality and exhibit a remarkable technical

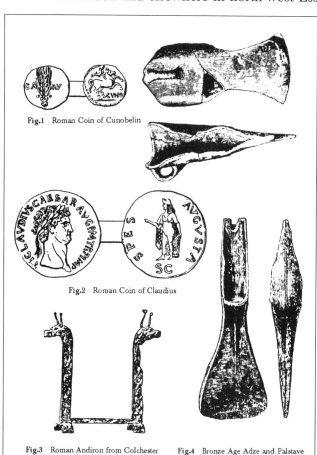

Fig.1   Roman Coin of Cunobelin

Fig.2   Roman Coin of Claudius

Fig.3   Roman Andiron from Colchester   Fig.4   Bronze Age Adze and Palstave

1   *Coins and artefacts*

capacity to work in this metal. Its use promoted the development of the first industrial societies and the beginnings of an international trading system that had tremendous implications for regional dependencies and the subsequent political histories of the great European civilisations. Among the previously scattered agrarian communities sprang up comparatively large, complex towns, prestigious buildings such as palaces and fortified citadels along with the development of water-borne transport on the sea and rivers of Europe where the main sources of metal were located. Cultural and artistic standards based on the new metallurgy were significantly enhanced. From then on human experience was to be enriched by manufacturing, international trade and the exploitation of valuable raw materials. The impact of the Bronze-Age period in Essex, consistent with and as part of the general European experience, makes it one of pivotal importance in the county's prehistory.

ଽଠଓଵ

Archaeologically the Iron Age divides into three cultural periods, early, middle and late. For the historian the period from about 500 B.C. to the Roman conquest divides more conveniently into two parts. The first archaeological periods of the Hallstatt and La Tène cultures, taken together, was the longer. A span of some 400 years saw the improvement of farming, the introduction of the ox-plough team, the cultivation of cereals and the domestication of animals for meat, wool and hides. The Iron-Age peoples of Essex lived in round timber-framed houses with high conical thatched or hide-covered roofs and walls of wattle and daub. The larger population that resulted from continuing immigration and the development of agriculture led to social changes, too. Tribal group-ings became more coherent and, under the leadership of a chiefly class, based their organisation and security on hill forts or, in the flat lands, fortified areas defended by ditches and ramparts, traces of which are still visible in the landscape of Essex. With the advent of a new wave of European migration about 100 B.C. a second Iron-Age phase can be identified historically. Archaeologically less complicated than the earlier peri-ods, the later period, of the tribes covered by the generic term Belgae, is that for which we can rely also on the works of the Roman historians. The Belgic invasions were first directed at what are now Kent, Essex and Hertfordshire. Later, these aggressive and well-organised tribes penetrated Sussex, Berkshire and parts of Hampshire. The most powerful grouping was that of the Catuvellauni who occupied a large area of Hertford-shire and Essex, posing a serious threat to the security of the Trinovantes whose terri-tory extended eastwards to the North Sea. The Trinovantian domain, although it is difficult to define as its boundaries were fluid under pressure, was centred on *Camulodunum* (Colchester).

The more highly developed society of the invading Belgae introduced into Britain the first wheeled vehicles, the rotary quern, a more efficient potter's wheel that raised the production of pottery above the purely domestic level, and a coinage minted in gold, silver and bronze. On the land the irregular pattern of the arable and pastures of preceding ages gave way to fields more regular in shape and with straightened boundaries. These rectilinear field systems have been clearly identified in the Chelmer valley at Little Waltham and in the vicinity of Braintree. The arable was worked by iron-shod ox-drawn ploughs able to cope with the heavier soils of the claylands. If not established in the Iron Age these farmlands were certainly consolidated and cultivated in that period throughout most of mid-Essex and the northern reaches of the county. Modified forms of this rectilinear landscape appear later in the planned developments of the Roman period. Over virtually the whole of Essex there is evidence of settlement or human activity in the Iron Age.

The newcomers preferred to concentrate their major settlements within fortified enclosures surrounded by defensive ditches with high ramparts. The earthworks north of St Albans, the Devil's Dyke at Wheathamstead and the western defences of *Camulodunum* are good examples of the military engineering of the Iron Ages. The development of *Camulodunum*–the fort of the Celtic war god *Camulos*–by the Belgae marked a shift of the centre of gravity of tribal power in pre-Roman Britain from the Hertfordshire-Essex borders to the Trinovantian capital.

The development of *Camulodunum* may be attributed to the tactical and strategic value of the site. The general area of modern Colchester embraces a plateau of more than 10 square miles protected on its northern bounds by the River Colne, and to the south it is shielded by the tributary called the Roman River. The overland approach on the west of the peninsula was guarded by an elaborate system of linear earthworks reminiscent of the controversial ditches south of Chichester. Though largely ploughed down they can still be traced. Furthest west was Gryme's Dyke which was supported by the Triple Dyke and the Lexden and Berechurch Dykes. These earthen dykes, some 24km long and up to 8m high, were then formidable barriers. As such they were the largest of their kind of that early date in Britain. That alone underlines the strategic and political importance of *Camulodunum*. They do not seem to have been constructed to any overall plan and their complexity suggests a process of piecemeal enhancements. The earliest stretch of the defences is Heath Farm Dyke, the latest is Gryme's Dyke. At the heart of the complex, just north of the Roman River and shielded by Kidmon's Dyke, was the original Trinovantian settlement at Gosbecks which later, as the centre of the Catuvellaunian Cunobelin's domain, was of significance before and during the Roman occupation.

The oppidum in which the Belgic capital appears to have been concentrated was situated near Sheepen Farm just to the south of the main coast road. North of the dyke system is Pitchbury Ramparts, a semi-bivallate oval hillfort which appears to have remained in use into the late Iron Age. This extensive complex was an extremely important trading and manufacturing centre for the Iron-Age settlements in the area and into the Romano-British period. The whole fortified area was sufficiently large to include the arable farmlands and pasturage required to meet the needs of the settlement. But its situation on the Colne and proximity to the sea also made it an important communication centre for trade with the continental homelands of the settlers. There is evidence that a fairly extensive export trade in slaves, corn, hides and British hunting dogs, which were much valued, was carried on in return for continental luxuries such as wine, jewellery and fine glassware. In the Colchester museum may be seen the mutilated relics of the funerary furniture entombed with the cremated remains of an important personage. Some believe that the large and impressive tumulus at Lexden, the richest late Iron Age grave in Britain, was the burial place of Cunobelin himself.

Elsewhere in Essex there are other earthworks of secondary importance, but visible reminders of the inter-tribal rivalry of the Iron-Age Britain on which the Roman legions descended. The best-known are perhaps the hill forts now embedded in Epping

Forest. That at Ambresbury Banks, along-side the main Cambridge Road just south of Epping, still exhibits clearly a defined oval area of about 12 acres enclosed by ditch and counterscarp. Loughton Camp lies further to the east; and though it is not so large occupies a more commanding site. These two forts, together with Wallbury Camp at Great Hallingbury and Ring Hill Camp which overlooks the Cam west of Saffron Walden, date from the second century B.C. They probably formed part of the western frontier defences of the Trinovantes. Other Iron-Age hill forts in Essex are at Danbury, where the bank and

2 *Ambresbury Banks: an Iron-Age camp in Epping Forest*

ditch surrounded the present churchyard area, and the Pitchbury Ramparts near Little Horkesley already mentioned.

When the Belgic colonists first began to move into Britain the population was probably no more than about 250,000. At the time of the Roman invasion it could hardly have risen higher than 350,000-400,000, despite the Belgic settlement over the south-east and south midlands, where their heavier wheeled ploughs enabled them to cultivate the loams which had been inaccessible to the implements of the earlier set-tlers. In Essex the tribal capital at *Camulodunum,* as we have seen, had been intensively occupied for some time before the Roman invasion. And the Romans had for long been interested in the mineral wealth of Britain. There was tin in Cornwall, copper, iron ore and gold in Wales, and silver was produced from lead by a process of cupellation. But there were political factors, too. Roman policy was expansionist, and inter-tribal strife in Britain made the island a tempting target. Essex was to the Romans, as Ptolemy tells us in his *Geography*, the land of the Belgic Trinovantes 'in whose territory is the town of Camulodunum'. This tribe, probably the first to have formal agreements with the Roman authorities, was to be an important factor in the political and military as-pects of the invasion launched by Julius Caesar.

The tribal background to the Caesarean raid of 55 B.C. is complicated. We learn from Caesar's *de Bello Gallico,* a politically motivated memoir, sometimes tendentious and burdened with personal vanity, but nevertheless an austere and broadly reliable narrative, of the history of the expansion of Roman rule by aggressive military cam-paigning. Caesar himself in this account of the Gallic Wars describes how, favoured by fair weather, winds, and tide, he assaulted the British coast. Attacking with cavalry, charioteers and infantry led by the standard bearer of the 10th Legion, the Romans, after a sharply contested struggle routed the British tribesmen. But a mishap to his seaborne reinforcements encouraged Caesar's adversaries to resume hostilities after they had sued for peace and left their hostages in his hands. The crisis overcome, the Romans desolated the lands of the offending tribe and returned to the continent to prepare a new campaign. This was launched the following year, 54 B.C.

During their approach to the Thames the Legions were confronted by the Catuvellauni under Cassivellaunus. Caesar's commanders were approached by

3   *William Stukeley's plan of Roman Colchester*

Mandubracius, a young prince of the Trinovantes seeking Roman protection from the Catuvellauni. This was granted in return for hostages, a regular Roman practice in such circumstances, supplies and a vague alliance with the Romans. Mandubracius' father had been killed by the Catuvellauni and, after their defeat by the Romans, possibly on the Devil's Dyke at Wheathamstead in Hertfordshire, Mandubracius returned as king of the Trinovantes. Historians are not entirely agreed on the chronology of subsequent events. However, it seems that from about 17 B.C. the Trinovantes were dominated in turn by Tasciovanus the Catuvellaunian king and the Trinovantian Addedomaros. The latter was succeeded by Dubnovellaunus and then in A.D. 5-10 by Cunobelin who managed to extend his realm to *Verulamium* (St Albans) and by A.D. 25 he had annexed Kent from the Cantii. This by then powerful ruler was dead by A.D. 42 but, as *Rex Britannorum*, had held sway over virtually all of southeast Britain. It was his sons Caratacus and Togodumnus who divided his kingdom between them. They, hostile to Rome, fought and were defeated by the Romans under Aulus Plautius in A.D. 43, his primary purpose being the capture of *Camulodunum,* the acknowledged centre of tribal authority and the richest town in pre-Roman Britain.

It is necessary to enlarge a little on this major event in British history. On the eve of the Roman conquest, the kingdom of Cunobelin was the most important in Britain. To the west his brother, Epaticus, ruled an area from the Weald to Salisbury Plain. East Anglia and the fens were dominated by the Iceni, the far west was Dobuni territory, and the Brigantes controlled the country along and north of the Humber. In Rome, Caligula had been murdered in A.D. 41 and his successor, Tiberius Claudius, unexpectedly occupying the imperial throne, looked to a foreign adventure to buttress his prestige. And so, in A.D. 43, the legions, after the most thorough preparations and some delay embarked at Boulogne, under Aulus Plautius, with the object of securing Britain for the Empire. Four legions, the 2nd Augusta, the 9th Hispana, the 14th Gemina and the 20th Valeria, with their auxiliaries, were put ashore in the bridgehead established at Richborough. Among the legionary commanders was Vespasian, the future emperor. The force of some 40,000 men was far too strong for the British tribal armies opposed to them. From their Kentish base the Romans made rapid and spectacular progress. The momentum of their victory on the Medway carried them over the Thames and into Essex where they captured and destroyed *Camulodunum*, thus securing control of the whole of the south-east. Togodumnus was slain and Caratacus forced to flee to the west where he continued his resistance for a while from the highlands of Wales. His dignity and bearing after being taken captive to Rome has achieved legendary fame. Perhaps surprised by the speed and success of their advance, the legions were forced to await the arrival of Claudius, who had been summoned so that the ill-fated emperor–he was ultimately poisoned by his wife Agrippina– might himself take possession of *Camulodunum*. Led into the ruined stronghold by armoured elephants and in the presence of the Praetorian Guard, Claudius received the formal submission of the British Kings–surely the most poignant moment of the most ancient town of Essex in all its long history. Here surrendered Cogidubnus of the southern Regni, and probably Prasutagus whose people, the Iceni, were to shatter Roman power in the old British capital less than 20 years hence. But the relatively poor by Roman standards and by then wasted town was not suitable for the capital of the new Province in which Plautius was installed as the first Governor. And so, a fine new city, with a temple dedicated to Claudius, who was worshipped there as a deity, was built on the hill to the south-east of the oppidum to serve as the seat of government until *Londinium* was developed and fit to assume its role as the future capital of Britain.

೮೦೮೫

Before we examine more closely the extent of the Roman settlement in Essex it will be interesting and relevant to consider the nature of the Roman army that subdued and occupied this country. That it was highly professional needs hardly be said, and it is generally understood that it was the best equipped and most efficient fighting force that the world had until then known. It

4 *Marcus Favonius: Centurion of the XXth Legion*

is not always appreciated that the bulk of its soldiers were not Romans in the strict sense, but Romanised Europeans and mercenaries of varied origin. During the occupation six legions, on which the striking power and mobility of the Roman army relied, served in Britain. Usually there were three, based at Caerleon, York and Chester. There were never more than four at any one period. A legion was commanded by a legate and divided into 10 cohorts of 480 infantrymen, except in the case of the lst Legion, which comprised 960 men. The cohorts were sub-divided into smaller units in the charge of centurions, the subalterns of the Roman army. The total was thus rather less than 6,000 men, though they were supported by cavalry and large numbers of auxiliary troops. Each legion also had its engineers, architects, doctors, farriers, cooks and a signals unit. Clad in protective helmets and light armour, and armed with sword and javelin, the infantry were trained to fight at close quarters with the support of artillery and mounted units. But they were not invincible, as we shall see.

It was men retired from their service with the legions who were settled as an act of policy at *Camulodunum* to establish the Roman *Colonia*, which was the principal Roman town of Essex. I propose to return to Roman Colchester later in this chapter. Here, I should like, before resuming the narrative of events in Roman Essex, to discuss briefly the pattern of settlement that has been revealed by archaeological research. Broadly speaking an archaeological 'dig' results from speculative deduction or chance and sometimes a combination of both. Literary references or conjectural reconstruction from known evidence may indicate the likely presence of a road or building at a particular point. With recent advances in geo-physical surveying by the use of electric probes, computerised recording equipment and other technical devices, more precise evaluations can be made before a decision is taken to excavate. Traditionally, before undertaking extensive excavations, a trial trench was dug in an effort to pinpoint the object of discovery. Alternatively the chance results of a constructor's excavation or of deep ploughing may reveal evidence that can be matched with historical or archaeological knowledge or indicate for the first time the location of early remains. Archaeologists do not dig 'blind'. Usually their excavations follow a planned pattern of recovery; less often, and less satisfactorily, a 'rescue dig' is necessary to prevent the obliteration for ever of previously unknown evidence. Nor does the archaeological process end with the excavation. This is but the preliminary to lengthy, complicated and highly technical procedures. By these are established more accurate typologies and elaboration of the preliminary assessments of a site by examination of the 'finds' and the study of 'plots', in which computerised data and other scientific information is used to enhance results.

As one would expect, there is a marked concentration of Roman remains along the route to the *Colonia* at Colchester from London, especially at Chelmsford and Kelvedon and in the vicinity of Colchester itself. Great Dunmow, Braintree, Harlow, Heybridge and various scattered villa sites in Essex have also yielded important evidence of Roman ocupation. In the north-west there is the former walled town at Great Chesterford. The county was not more intensively developed by the Romans because of the difficult and thickly-wooded terrain and the needs of the Roman strategy, which envisaged Essex as a base, with radial and lateral communications to other strategic centres rather than as an area of economic development.

The Roman route from London to Colchester is, on the whole, well established. For long the subject of controversy, still not finally resolved, is the location of the

Roman *mansiones*, or military stations, along the route. That Chelmsford, the county town today, was the principal station *Caesaromagus* is clear. However, we know from the Antonine Itinerary (*Itinerarium Antonini Augusti*) that there were two other intermediate posts sited at approximately equal intervals along the road. On the evidence of other Roman military routes, there may indeed have been more, but there is nothing to support that possibility. One of the known stations was *Canonium* in the area of Kelvedon and Rivenhall. Kelvedon, which is on the direct alignment of the route, seems to be the more likely location of the staging post, but the exact course of the old road has yet to be fully proved. Excavations a mile from the direct line at Rivenhall have produced evidence of Romano-British occupation on a sufficient scale to have given rise to the suggestion that this was the site of *Canonium* itself. The site of the other post, *Durolitum*, still defies solution, although serious efforts have been made to establish its location. Gidea Park at Romford, which satisfies what little evidence there is, has, until recently, attracted support as the most probable area, but remains conjectural. Other possibilities are Chigwell (Little London), Romford and Passingford Bridge near Abridge, but none has yielded tangible results. Along this road, which now carries the east coast holiday traffic, the Roman legions and *viatores* (travellers) tramped and rode for more than three centuries. It is a road steeped in the history of Roman Essex, much of it, alas, irrecoverable. But it requires no great effort of the imagination, with the benefit of all we know from other sources, to visualise the ordered and efficient control that the Roman authorities exercised over this important line of communications and the Romano-British communities that were settled along it.

It is surprising that the archaeological status of Chelmsford seems to have taken so long in being established. *Caesaromagus* (Caesar's market place) was, on the place-name evidence alone, clearly of importance. Recent archaeology shows that it was more so than any other Roman town in Essex except that at Colchester. No other Roman settlement in the whole of Britain bore the emperor's name. The focus of the Roman settlement there was to the south of the modern centre and the River Can at Moulsham. Essex archaeologists, as we have seen in reference to Springfield and other prehistoric sites in the vicinity, have demonstrated the administrative and economic importance of this part of Essex. The Romans built the military post at Chelmsford to secure and control the route from London to Colchester. The town, built without a defensive wall, developed as a civilian centre, its role as a trading and industrial base being quite different from that which the Romans, and indeed their tribal predecessors, required at Colchester. Its military and defensive phases were relatively brief and intermittent; its important civilian functions have persisted to this day in its role as the county town and centre of modern industrial enterprises. The size and extent of the excavated structures—the *mansio* is the largest in Britain—suggest that initially a much more important role was envisaged for *Caesaromagus* which did not mature for reasons we can only conjecture.

Elsewhere in Essex, Roman influence, as opposed to administrative authority, spread slowly, never striking deeply into the large undeveloped areas of the county. Although there are traces of some Roman occupation in most districts, there were few significant settlements off the line of the military roads. A small Roman town of some consequence was what is now Great Chesterford, which lies to the north-west by the River Stort. Its Roman name is lost in antiquity and it is the silent ruins alone that

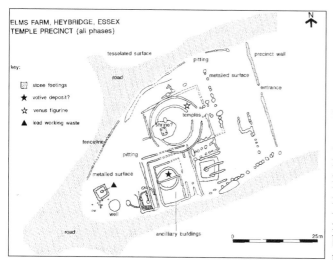

ELMS FARM, HEYBRIDGE, ESSEX
TEMPLE PRECINCT (all phases)

key:

▦ stone footings
★ votive deposit?
☆ venus figurine
▲ lead working waste

5 *Plan of excavation of the Roman town at Elms Farm, Heybridge.*
© *Essex County Council*

pronounce its provincial origins. That it was larger in area than *Caesaromagus* seems quite clear from the proven course of the fourth-century vallation. Great Chesterford was, in its Roman context, locally important at the junction of Roman routes running north, south to *Londinium* and eastwards to Colchester. In its class it was well-defended and excavations have revealed a range of industrial, commercial and domestic buildings which indicate its versatile roles in the Roman system of provincial administration. Furthermore, although the defences have now disappeared, within the walls have been identified the remains of a Roman temple as well as a Romano-British cemetery and metal workings of the period.

The most recent major excavation in Essex is that which has been carried out at Elms Farm, Heybridge near Maldon since 1993. Here, much of a Roman town and an extensive late Iron Age round-house settlement have been discovered. Earlier occupation remains and subsequent Saxon evidence demonstrate a continuous sequence of some 2,500 years at this very important site for Essex archaeology. Some indication of its archaeological interest was realised during the construction of a railway embankment in the late 19th century. The finds are so large in number and significant in quality that the evaluation of the site is not yet complete. Hundreds of thousands of pottery sherds and thousands of metal objects are in process of identification and assessment as I write. Already archaeologists have defined the topography of the Roman town, its street systems and buildings of industrial, administrative and religious significance. The pattern of the town's commercial and industrial functions is beginning to emerge, including its links with continental traders. Pewter bowls made from tin mined in Cornwall, Samian ware from Gaul, a rare Gallo-Belgic stater and part of a clay figurine of Venus are among the exciting finds from this Roman town by the Blackwater estuary.

Another important Roman site in Essex is at Harlow where the new town has now been built in the old frontier zone of the Catuvellaunian and Trinovantian domains. Its position was thus of some political significance and in Roman times it was within the influence of *Verulamium* (St Albans) rather than of the Colonia at Colchester. When the presence of Roman buildings was first appreciated in 1764 they were considered to indicate the site of one of a series of staging posts along the Stort valley. That they were more significant than that was not realised until Miller Christy, that indefatigable Essex historian and writer, excavated the area in 1927. The full chronology of the site was established by the excavations of the West Essex Archaeological Group, directed by Dr. N.E. France, in 1962-8 and in subsequent archaeological investigations. We now know that an earlier Belgic settlement was re-occupied in the early years of the Roman period. The site, on a slight eminence called Stanegrove, appears always to have had some religious significance and among the Roman villa-farms in the general area a

6 *Roman theatre at Gosbecks: reconstruction by Peter Froste*

temple was found. In its earliest form it appears to have been one of a known Romano-Celtic type such as the temple at Caerwent or that, sited as at Harlow at a distance from the settlement, on Chanctonbury in Sussex. Of an essentially simple structure, with mortar and flint walls and tesselated pavements, the Harlow temple was similar to those excavated elsewhere in Essex at Colchester (Gosbecks Farm), Kelvedon and Great Chesterford. The discovery of part of a cult statue of the Goddess of Healing and Warfare, Minerva, has led to the belief that the Harlow temple was a shrine where she was worshipped. About A.D. 200 it was reconstructed and enlarged within a walled courtyard, the last of a number of rebuildings. The numismatic evidence suggests that it was allowed to decay either during or after the reign of Constantine; that is to say during the early part of the fourth century. Other coins found on site have their provenance in the reigns of eminent Roman emperors such as Claudius, Vespasian and Aurelius Caesar.

Gosbecks Farm at Colchester, already mentioned, is now being developed as an archaeological park, a welcome initiative which will make accessible to the public some of the riches of Essex archaeology. It is a part of the complex at *Camulodunum* which was the first great prize of the Roman conquest. After the capture of the tribal capital, the settlement at Gosbecks was reserved to the native population as a major market facility. It had been the fortress of Cunobelin and his important Belgic predecessors. Here can be seen the largest of the four Roman theatres discovered in Britain. The semi-circular structure, reminiscent of Hellenic architecture, could seat up to 5,000 people. Two of these theatres were at St Albans and Canterbury. Also at Gosbecks is the Sanctuary, a sacred area which included a Romano-Celtic temple. It all lies behind the great dykes that defended *Camulodunum* and as such is one of the most interesting and important Roman sites in Britain. Its survival as a native sanctuary, especially after the Boudiccan disaster, reflects considerable tolerance by the Romans, or at least, inspired by prudent political motives, the recognition of the importance of native rights and traditions.

Apart from the main Roman stations and settlements in Essex, lesser evidence of the long occupation is widespread. In some parts of the county in almost every village there can be found some traces of the period; be it in the use of Roman materials, tiles in the walls of a church, a plinth in the foundations of a medieval house, the recurring testimony of the plough or the result of the increasing use of metal detecting equipment. The evidence, though often slight, is there. At Felsted, Henham, Finchingfield, Great Sampford, Lindsell, Stisted, Langenhoe or Fyfield and numerous other villages of rural Essex such tokens of the imperial province serve to remind us of the era when the recorded history of the county began. The important discoveries at the airport site of Stansted led to a rich haul from two burial sites which included beautiful Roman vessels and tableware. In 1959 an interesting discovery arose from a series of aerial surveys in south Essex that revealed sites which would demonstrate the continuity of occupation and define sequences of changing land use that can still be traced in various parts of the county. In some fields at Mucking, now destroyed by quarrying, was identified by the colourations of ripening barley an integrated pattern of rectangular and circular crop-marks. Excavation showed that the area contained hut circles, iron-working hearths and graves with a chronological sequence from neolithic to Roman times. These fields had thus been farmed from remote antiquity into our own age.

It was not at first realised how important to European archaeology this site was to prove. There were no obvious boundaries or related earthworks to identify or establish its status until gravel working exposed ancient artefacts such as axes and spear heads. Subsequent archaeological excavation gradually uncovered the wealth of early settlement that lay hidden in the ground. The site is perhaps more important for its neolithic and particularly Saxon periods and I shall return to the latter in the next chapter. For the Roman period it proved valuable for understanding the structure of the Roman military supply system in relation to Essex and the Thames estuary. The strategic value of the elevated Mucking site is evident. A first-century enclosure excavated there and the recovery of metal items of Roman military equipment associated with buildings of the period suggested its use as a supply base. Other evidence for settlement in the Roman period included ceramics, keys, brooches, seal boxes, fragments of glass vessels which had been blown or moulded, and figurines made of pipeclay.

Far and wide across the county are the faded remnants of this unparalleled age. Colchester, like Roman Chichester, was a port. Its site had been continuously occupied from at least the Iron Age and it became one of the most important Roman towns in Britain. At Fingringhoe and at Heybridge on the Blackwater were Roman military depots. A Romano-British town was established on the south-facing slope of Chapel Hill at Braintree, where previously there had been Celtic and Belgic settlement. Under the High Street a twisted bronze and silver wire bracelet of the Roman period was found. The saltings on the coastal fringes near Bradwell now cover most of the site of

A View of the Hills near Ashdon, in Essex, raised over y bodies of those slain in a Battle fought there.

7   *The Bartlow 'Hills' burials near Ashdon*

the Roman fort of Othona. Although the precise original purposes of the Roman coastal defences are unclear, it is thought that Othona was constructed, along with other fortifications, to guard what became known as the Saxon Shore during the declining years of the Roman occupation. At the time the responsible Roman officer, the Count of the Roman Shore (*Comes Littoris Saxonici*) was Carausius. It is his name that is identified with Othona, of which very little now remains to be seen on the creeks and marshes of the Essex shoreline.

Along Thames-side at Tilbury, Grays Thurrock and Canvey there is further evidence of the time. In the museums of Essex we can see, in their glass sepulchres, the mute symbols of Roman Essex. Bronze fibulae from Marks Tey, a terra-cotta figurine from Arkesden, an onyx cameo on a gold finger-ring from Othona and a bronze brooch in the form of a crouching panther found at Harwich. A fine Roman scythe comes from Great Chesterford and a garnet gem stone set in a finger-ring inscribed with the god of war, Mars from Gosbecks. Glass, bronze and ceramic vessels and *paterae* from cremation burials are also among the Roman treasures recovered from Essex soil. There were baths too—no Roman inventory would be complete without them—and mosaic pavements. The latter not, it is true, of the classical quality of those we can now relish at Fishbourne or Bignor, except possibly those sadly destroyed at Wanstead. Nor must we forget the intriguing Bartlow Hills burials of the north-west and the Red Hills of the coastal margins.

The results of archaeology in the county thus enable us to conjure a picture of generations of Romano-British farmers, tilling their ancient fields, basking in the apparent security of an exotic culture and their Roman citizenship. The material comforts of life, derived from political stability and the economic prosperity of Roman society, were readily available. We may discern also, in the domestic equipment and personal ornaments recovered by the spade, the tangible evidence of the good life. Paying their respects to the Roman war gods, and in latter days nominally Christian, these complacent communities were safe, or so they thought, in the hands of the imperial legions. So they were for most of the four centuries during which Roman Britain existed. But there were two major crises, both survived, before the inexorable tides of history finally engulfed the life of Roman Britain.

ಯ)ೞ

The Romans established the *Colonia* at *Camulodunum* in A.D. 49, according to Tacitus, in order to introduce the natives to the arts of civilised life. During these early years of the occupation the former Belgic capital served as the centre of Roman authority, but in A.D. 60 it was consumed in the flames and fury of the Boudiccan rebellion. At the time of the Claudian invasion the Iceni of East Anglia were ruled by Prasutagus, who submitted to the Roman conquerors and accepted the indignity of client-kingship. At his death in about A.D. 59 his inheritance passed to his daughter, Boudicca, and her two daughters, the Icenian princesses. The Romans unwisely allowed their greed to move them to excesses. The Queen herself was brutally flogged, the princesses outraged and the treasures of the Icenian dynasty seized. The wrath and indignation of the affronted Britons overflowed. The revolt that flared in the Icenian heartland was joined by the Trinovantes to the south in the area of the *Colonia*, who had their own grievances to assuage.

The *Colonia*, the first objective of the rebels, was overwhelmed by the surprise and ferocity of the assault that was launched against it. The well-kept secrets of the rising had lulled the complacent Roman community into a false sense of security. In the event there was no time to evacuate women, children or the sick. The makeshift defences were totally inadequate. When the statue of Victory collapsed, the prescient Britons had taken it as a sign of impending disaster. The Romans no doubt attributed it to a technical failure. Fire and sword razed the *Colonia* to the ground. No one was spared. Only in the temple of Claudius, an object of special vengeance for those whose taxes had financed its construction, was any resistance sustained by the doomed defenders. It soon shared the fate of the remainder of the town which was given over to destruction and atrocity. Archaeological excavation has shown that there were very few areas of the Roman Colonia that escaped the Boudiccan conflagration.

The 9th Legion, led by Petilius Cerialis, was hurried from Lincoln to the relief of the imperilled Roman communities in south-east England. But it was overborne somewhere in the fenlands by the momentum of the rebellion. *Verulamium* and *Londinium*, like the *Colonia* and *Caesaromagus* in Essex, were shattered by fire and rapine. The charred underground layers of soil, now valuable strata for archaeological reconstruction, symbolise one of the most bitter and hideous episodes in British history. But the cruel tide of the revolt was eventually stemmed and its force spent against the broad shields of Suetonius Paulinus's 14th and 20th Legions which were recalled from Anglesey and delivered the decisive counter-stroke at an unknown battleground on which perished a large part of the rebel force and its camp followers. Boudicca herself ended her life in despair and by her own hand. The scene of this historic drama has yet to be determined. Argument continues. Some historians have placed these events at Kings Cross, others at Chester. In

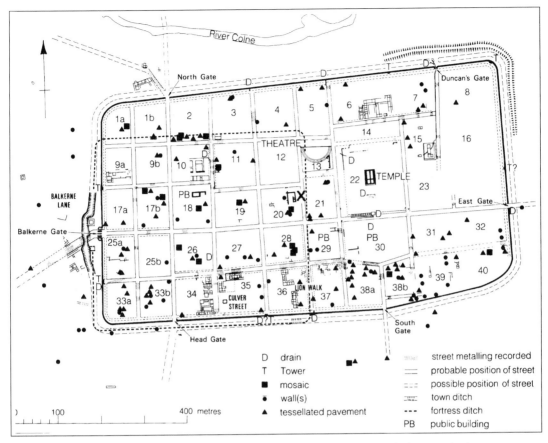

8 *Plan of Roman Colchester: a grid of streets divided the town into rectangles known as insulae.*

Essex Ambresbury Banks, near Epping, and Hayes Green, by Layer Marney, have been advanced as possible venues. Most would opt for High Cross, near Towcester, in the Midlands. So far as the Essex sites are concerned the historical and circumstantial evidence is minimal. The archaeological evidence is negligible. But the people of Essex and its greatest Roman centre were at the heart of this grim affair and it must therefore be recorded as one of the major events in the county's history.

The period after the Boudiccan revolt of A.D. 60-61 saw the consolidation of Roman power in Britain and the evolution of an integrated provincial society conveniently called Romano-British. At the *Colonia* the old street grid-pattern was re-established and the town walls built possibly, as they are early (A.D. 65-80) in Roman experience, to ensure or demonstrate the determination of the Romans to sustain their authority. Soon after Roman rule had been fully re-established in south-east Britain, *Londinium* superseded the *Colonia* as the seat of the provincial government, but the Essex settlement continued to be an important centre of Roman life and culture. So complete and rapid was the restoration of Roman power in Britain, despite the heavy blows they had sustained at the hands of the Icenian and Trinovantian hordes, that in little more than a decade they could contemplate further expansion. In the western campaign from A.D. 74-77 Frontinus completed the conquest of Wales. While the Romanisation of southern Britain was being carried out with thoroughness and speed, Agricola reduced the north, and by A.D. 84 stood towards the line of the Tweed. Hadrian built his famous wall in A.D. 122 and the Roman frontier was taken further north, to the Antonine wall that linked the Clyde with the Forth by an immense earthwork, in A.D. 139. But history was to demonstrate that the most northerly Roman defences were already advanced beyond the limits that Rome's inadequate sea-power could sustain. The conquest of the whole island was beyond the strategic resources of the over-stretched empire, and, although the pressure from the Picts and Irish was contained until the disaster of A.D. 367, the Roman presence in the north was frequently challenged and seriously extended.

⁋C∞

The demands of Essex history as well as the importance of the town as a basic element in Roman society make it necessary to describe in some detail the settlement that was established at Colchester. As with London, Chester, Chichester and York elsewhere, Colchester provided the base of power and wealth on which the prosperity of the area in Roman times depended. A number of factors governed the choice of the site as the first capital of Roman Britain. Doubtless the prestige of *Camulodunum*, as the centre of Belgic power, led to the establishment there, after its capture, of the base of the 20th Legion. Later, the development of the settlement from A.D. 49 was inspired by similar motives as the adoption of the cognomen of the 20th Legion suggests. The *Colonia Claudia Victricensis*–the victorious colony of Claudius–was the name bestowed upon the town, it is believed, by the legate of Britain, Publius Ostorius Scapula. There is some reason, however, to think that it was originally designated *Colonia Claudia* and that *Victricensis* was added after the defeat of the Boudiccan rebellion. There were naturally strategic reasons also, like those that motivated its earlier inhabitants and governed the selection of the site. It stood at the highest navigable point of the River Colne, on workable gravels, some eight miles or so inland on ground protected by natural river defences. It was also a viable focus of inland communications and seawards to the western shores of the continent and the mouth of the Rhine.

The colony founded by Publius Ostorius before he embarked on the final campaign that overthrew Caratacus was not fortified nor a garrison town as was, for example, York. But it was intended to provide a reservoir of trained reserve manpower power as it was settled by retired veterans of the 20th Legion who were allocated plots of land for their private use. It was expected, too, that their sons would in due course be recruited into the Roman army. Similar settlements were made later by Flavius at Lincoln, at York and at Gloucester under Nerva. The Roman populations of the *Coloniae* enjoyed full Roman citizenship and a charter of rights under which the settlements were administered according to Roman law. Although of military origin, as time passed, people of largely British ancestry eventually formed the majority of their populations and the character of the *Coloniae* gradually changed until they came to resemble other large and important towns in the province.

Some relics of its imperial heyday may still be seen in Colchester today, though they provide no more than a glimpse of the fine and prosperous town created by the Romans. After the destruction wrought by Boudicca's avenging host in A.D. 60, the town was rebuilt, being one of the first to be enclosed by a defensive wall. Built mainly of septaria, quarried from the sea cliffs of the Essex coast, and banded with typical Roman tile courses, it was nine feet thick and backed with earth except along the north side. It may have risen to a height of about 20 feet. Today the highest remaining fragment is about 13 feet high. Along the top of the circumvallation was a rampart walk with watch-towers set at tactical intervals. It is not known exactly when it was built, but it was certainly one of the first Roman towns in Britain to be walled, and the original structure probably dates from before the second century. The circumference of the wall measured about one and three quarter miles and enclosed an irregular parallelogram some 108 acres, which may be compared with the area within the London walls of about 330 acres, and at *Verulamium* of 200 acres. The remains of the main entry on the west side of the town, the Balkerne Gate, are some of the most interesting surviving Roman structures in the town. Reconstructed pictures of the gate show it to have been one of the finest in Britain in its time and comparable with that at Lincoln. There were four portals, two of modern road width with side entrances for pedestrians, spanned by bold semi-circular stone arches, leading directly to the forum. This splendid gateway, more than 150 feet wide, bore a name of obscure origin, but it is worthy of the oldest recorded town in Britain. Other significant stretches of the old wall may be seen today on Balkerne Hill and in Priory Street.

Within the walls of the *Colonia* the streets, which were re-planned after the Boudiccan disaster, were arranged to intersect at right-angles which, after the Roman fashion divided the town into about forty blocks, called *insulae*. The pattern is still apparent in the layout of the modern street plan of the county's most distinguished town. The central feature of the town had been the great colonnaded temple that was violently destroyed in the revolt. Erected in about A.D. 50, it was dedicated to the Emperor Claudius and served as a focus of the emperor-worship cult in Britain. Regarded as a symbol of oppression by the natives of *Camulodunum,* it was one of the most imposing edifices in the Roman province. After its destruction in A.D. 60 it was rebuilt and again became the most prominent building in the *Colonia* until its final decay. The lower stage of the structure of the temple provided a massive and firm base for the castle erected by the Normans 1,000 years later. When, in 1683, a Colchester ironmonger named John Wheeley unsuccessfully tried to demolish the castle for building materials he uncovered its Roman base. It was not until Sir Mortimer Wheeler examined the site in 1919 that its true importance was appreciated. In a systematic survey of the structure he realised that the vaulted podium of the Claudian temple had been used to construct the vaults of the Norman keep. The dimensions of the octa-style temple of Claudius, which stood on a base of 80 feet by 105 feet within a spacious precinct, indicate its significance as the most important building in the *Colonia.*

Recoveries from the Roman cemeteries alongside the roads leading from the *Colonia* and the coin collections now in our museums have added personality to the silent witness of the stones of the city. Among the amphorae, pottery, tesserae, glass vessels and urns has been located a plethora of coins. In the various strata lay the *denarii* of the great Roman administrator, Hadrian, and of Severus Alexander. Here too were the *antoniniani* of Nero, Carausius and Allectus. Humbler Romans have been identified by their tombstones. A particularly fine representation of a Roman soldier was a monument to M. Favonius Facilis, a centurion of the 20th Legion. Another was the duplicarius

Longinus, a trooper of the Thracian cavalry. There was the grave, too, of a young woman of Roman Colchester bearing the name Considia Veneria. A bronze head, found in 1907 in the River Alde near Saxmundham, is thought to have been taken by Boudicca's marauding supporters and carried away from the town as loot. The archaeological world was excited in 1996 by the discovery at Stanway just outside Colchester, of a Roman board game, *Latrunculi* (little soldiers), laid out for play. It was part of the grave goods of an important British personage buried there just prior to the Claudian invasion of A.D. 43. As the modern town is developed so more of the secrets of the *Colonia* are being uncovered. One of them was a tile-built burial chamber rich in Roman pottery, glass and metalwork. Much of great interest must still remain, pending further opportunities to delve into the soil of the ancient capital.

ଈୠ

Interesting topographical features of Roman Essex are the prominent conical barrows near Ashdon, known as the Bartlow Hills, and believed to be the burial mounds of Romanised British farmers of substance. Originally there were seven; now there are four, the others having been cleared away for agricultural purposes. There are also the so-called 'Red Hills' of which several hundreds have been identified in the coastal areas of the county, notably between the Colne and the Blackwater, along Thames-side and on Canvey Island. Usually on or near the saltings of the estuaries, they are variable in size and composed of reddish burnt earth, the remains of salt production by the evaporation of sea-water. The salt-making process of the Red Hills may have dated from as early as *c.*50 B.C., possibly having been introduced by immigrant Belgic tribes. It apparently continued into the second century of the Roman period. Indeed the Roman occupation stimulated the production of salt on the Essex coast. Its scale seems to have been beyond that required for local consumption and may thus be regarded as a marketable product. It has been conjectured that *Camulodunum*, which was geographically proximate to the salt producing areas of the Red Hills, was a trading centre for this commodity. However, there is no documentary evidence for this and only flimsy archaeological support. Nevertheless the now extensive archaeological investigation of this industry has shown that it was carried out on a scale sufficient to merit a place in the evaluation of the economy of Roman Essex.

Topographically the hallmark of the Roman period, the general impression of which has survived the development of the landscape, was the great all-weather strategic road system that laced Britain with communications that were not equalled until the Victorian railways were laid and the motorway routes developed in modern times. Perhaps our earliest recollections of Roman history in the classroom include names like Watling Street, Ermine Street, Stane Street and the Fosse Way, that can still be traced on the ground today. Apart from the main military routes, of which the Antonine Itinerary listed 16, a network of subordinate roads of commercial importance, particularly in the south, was also developed. In Essex the principal routes were the military road from London to the *Colonia* and Stane Street, still a main lateral route, which connected the *Colonia* with East Anglia and westwards to *Verulamium*, crossing the Essex-Hertfordshire border at what is now Braughing. Other important road communications linked Stane Street, at Great Dunmow, with the military road and Great Chesterford with Cambridge.

9   *Roman Villa at Chignall St James. © Essex County Council*

Another familiar feature of Roman topography is the villa and its associated farm-lands which overlay the irregular patterns of the prehistoric landscapes and trackways. The Romans introduced new tree species such as sweet chestnut, plum, and walnut onto the villa farms. The invention of the mould-board plough in the later phases of the Roman period changed and lengthened the shapes of the old rectilinear field systems. Although 'villa' is a useful if sometimes misunderstood term, the Roman villas are not easily defined. They were really farmhouses with frequently a further range of buildings that varied greatly in size, role and amenity. Some were no larger than a small house with modest decoration and minimum services. Others, such as Bignor in Sussex, Lullingstone in Kent, or Chedworth in Gloucestershire, were large well-appointed and handsome mansions some of which were the foci of local Roman administration. In the buildings a range of living rooms, decorated with painted plaster walls and mosaic floors, was centrally heated from the hypocaust through which was circulated warm air directed from a furnace. The bath suite, with its progression of communal facilities, the *caldarium* (hot room), *tepidarium* (warm room) and *frigidarium* (cold room), was the essential luxury of Roman society and latterly the prosperous native landowning class. The fine tesselated pavements that remain in the ruins of the villas depict the dramatic scenes of Roman mythology or exhibit the much-favoured polychromatic designs of the mosaicists.

In Essex, Roman villas were not especially numerous. Nor were they as large and sumptuous as elsewhere. This was due to a number of geographical and economic factors and the effects of the Boudiccan rebellion. Most of the villas in the county were built within the general vicinity of Colchester, though there was also a significant group in the Stort valley. They were notably absent on the Essex side of the Thames and in the immediate proximity of London. On the whole they were mainly located in the northern half of the county. At Finchingfield, Halstead, Pebmarsh and Gestingthorpe there were examples of villa sites that archaeologists have shown to have been developed on earlier Belgic farms. Others are now being identified from crop markings visible to aerial photography and have yet to be excavated. Ridgewell, to the north-east of Braintree, was the site of a villa from which considerable numbers of Roman relics, such as coins and domestic equipment, were recovered. There were villas, too, at Chelmsford, Chignall St James, Boreham, Rivenhall, Gosfield and Felsted. In the north-west they have been excavated at Hadstock, Bricksteads at Finchingfield and on Chennell's Farm by Chapel Green at Wendens Ambo. Excavations, as at Beauchamps Farm, Wickford, have demonstrated a typically continuous chronology. A settlement in the Iron Age of perhaps the fifth or fourth centuries B.C. was farmed throughout the period until sometime in the Roman-British era when a villa with its associated out-buildings was developed, only to be destroyed by fire and abandoned in the latter part of the fourth century A.D., almost 1,000 years later. The scale and quality of the Essex villas are a good indication of the degree of Romanisation that took place and the geographical and economic constraints that governed this. Important though it was strategically, Essex was never developed by Roman society to the same extent as the more favourable regions south of the Thames.

⚜

The general stability and comfortable prosperity that Roman Britain enjoyed through three and a half centuries from its recovery after the trauma of the rising of A.D. 60-61 to the final abdication was punctured at intervals by pressure from without. In A.D. 211 Caracullis, his exiguous supply lines over-stretched, was forced to abandon the provincial territory north of the Hadrianic frontier. Towards the end of the third century Saxon marauders began to make the first tentative probes that eventually led to their colonisation of the island province. A chain of coastal defences from the Wash to Sussex was established, as already indicated, along the Saxon Shore. So long as the resources to man and defend the seashore forts were available, the incoming Saxons could be excluded from the eastern estuaries of the Blackwater, the Stour and the Orwell. Commanding the mouths of the Colne and the Blackwater was the Essex fort of Othona, or Ithanceaster, a little to the north-east of Bradwell-on-Sea. Now largely engulfed by the encroaching sea, it once played an effective role in defending the seaward approaches to Roman Britain. During the early fourth century Pictish and Irish invaders were repulsed. But later came a disaster that, as did that three centuries earlier, brought the Roman province to the brink of ruin.

In A.D. 367 the emperor Valentinian was confronted along the entire northern limits of the Roman Empire in Europe by warring tribal forces. In Britain combined armies of Picts, Scots and Saxons launched a powerful onslaught against the Roman defences at various points on the long coastline and the northern barriers. These simultaneous assaults exposed the limitations of the reserve forces available to the Roman commanders in Britain. The great northern wall was penetrated and overrun. Fullofaudes, the *Dux Britanniarum,* was defeated and it would seem captured by the invaders. On the coast the Count of the Saxon Shore, Nectaridus, was killed. When the attackers stood at the gates of *Londinium* itself the province was on the point of disintegration. The emperor Valentinian sent from Gaul a man, Theodosius the Elder, of Spanish birth and a tried administrator, to stem the tide. Landing at *Rutupiae* (Richborough) in Kent with two legions he was forced to await reinforcements. But as soon as he was ready he advanced, with speed and resolution, to the relief of the capital. With difficulty the situation was restored and he pursued a victorious campaign until the whole country was again pacified. Hadrian's wall was rebuilt. Many who had deserted the Roman army returned to the colours and peace returned. Although the threat of external aggression was not wholly eliminated the consequences of the violent episode that the province had survived were limited. Strong government, supported by victorious and jubilant troops, ensured recovery and a further period of prosperity and security. It was not until Rome itself was overwhelmed that Britain became untenable.

Towards the end of the fourth century the empire was under intolerable pressure from the Huns, Vandals, Visigoths and other tribes. Further Pictish attacks were launched against the northern frontier in Britain. Irish invaders occupied parts of Wales and the defences of the island, reorganised by Stilicho, a Vandal by origin, were again under pressure, but the final stages that led to the end of Roman Britain are obscure. In A.D. 305 Constantine, the first Christian Roman emperor, had been proclaimed at York. The last to be proclaimed in Britain, in A.D. 407, was Constantine III. In A.D. 410 Honorius sent his imperial rescript saying that Britain could no longer look to Rome for support. Already the Saxons were at the doors of the province. As a result of the desperate decision taken by Honorius it appears that the Roman garrisons withdrew from the then almost defenceless island. Nothing could thus prevent the Anglo-Saxon settlement and the establishment of the English kingdoms of which Essex, for so long the scene of Roman life, was one.

It has been the task of Essex archaeologists and historians, slowly and methodically to re-create, by patient excavation and interpretation with modern sophisticated devices for evaluation, the events and nature of life in the county during the long millennia of its prehistoric and Roman experience. Colchester, the modern successor to *Camulodunum* and the *Colonia Victricensis,* is the most remarkable and evocative symbol of these periods. With the coming of the Anglo-Saxons the shadow of the so-called 'Dark Ages' fell peremptorily over the county; when it was eventually lifted little of Roman Essex remained.

Chapter Two

୫୦ୠ

THE EAST SAXONS

'Thought the harder, heart the keener, courage the greater'

It is from the time of the Anglo-Saxons that we recognise the origin of much in our national institutions and the character of our people. The political and social organisation of Britain derives ultimately from these hard-fighting, hard-living pagan colonists. To them also we owe the English language that, enriched as were our people too, from alien sources, has developed into the principal medium of world communication and has indeed now been taken to the lunar landscape by the trans-Atlantic descendants of these intrepid and restless people. From their continental homelands in the area of Schleswig-Holstein and the north German rivers, the land-hungry Teutonic tribes to which the Angles, Saxons and Jutes belonged had been extending their territory towards and along the North Sea coast for many generations before they turned seriously to the colonisation of Britain. The nature and chronology of the invasion is difficult to establish with any precision, but it is clear that it was not a co-ordinated or speedy process. This most important event in British history may be compared with the advance of the American colonists as they rolled back the frontiers of the new America westwards across the Appalachians and the prairies of the hinterland. It bore no resemblance to the highly professional military operations of the Claudian legions in A.D. 43 or Duke William's Norman knights in 1066. As so often thereafter the Anglo-Saxons 'muddled through' on the strength of their courage, tenacity and resource.

So far as Essex is concerned we are, notwithstanding the excavation of important habitation and burial sites at Mucking and Wicken Bonhunt, in some difficulty in buttressing the still fragile evidence offered by the archaeology of the period. With the notable exception of St Peter's-on-the-Wall and notwithstanding relics of the period in many Essex churches and the definitive 'long and short work' at Priors Hall, Widdington, a house that presumably had an ecclesiastical origin, there remains hardly anything substantial. The relative paucity—excepting Mucking—of Saxon burials and other extant evidence of the period so far discovered in the county emphasises the insecurity of the archaeological foundations on which we must erect a picture of the course of events from the fifth century. However there is the valuable testimony of the surviving names of the towns and villages of Essex. For the later phases of the period we enter historical territory illuminated by the books, charters and epic poems of a literate society. In these now priceless records we enjoy the Anglo-Saxon equivalent of Roman literature and epigraphy. Thus the historian may rely, though the problems of interpretation and assessment are of great complexity, on the scholarship and integrity of Bede, the literature of Gildas and Nennius, the Alfredian chronicles and the exhilarating heroic poetry of the age. But, one may ask, if the philology of Essex and the documentary evidence demonstrates so convincingly the basic characteristics of this Saxon county, why is it that the tangible evidence of this otherwise well attested truth is so frustratingly sparse? Various reasons have been advanced. It is suggested that the forests and marshes discouraged early settlement, though this view is not wholly consistent with other evidence. Nor is the view that postulates the survival of a strong Romano-British society convincing. There is, however, reason to think that quite soon after the settlement the Saxons in Essex abandoned the old pagan custom of cremation for inhumation without the ritualistic burial of weapons and other grave goods with their dead. The most likely theory, therefore, it seems, is that which attributes the disappointing return from the archaeologist's spade in Essex to funerary practice and fortuity. Buildings were, of course, largely made of timber and thatch and would not have survived except in the shadowy sub-surface imprints that archaeologists must locate, expose and define through the various techniques now available to them.

Let us examine briefly the philological evidence for the fundamental Saxon character of the county. The almost total absence of Celtic place-names and the rarity of names of Scandinavian provenance, despite the fact that Essex became part of the Danelaw seem to be decisive in establishing the dominant position of the Saxons in Essex. Even the Norman Conquest which resulted in the intrusion of a number of French derivatives does not seriously alter the pattern for such are often combined with earlier Saxon place-names. Choose any diameter of Essex and trace a route by road, or on the map, via the ancient villages from the sea or river boundaries across the county. The way will lie through villages and country towns whose names include elements such as 'field', 'hurst', 'ford', 'ley', 'don', 'ham' or the significant 'ing' that advertise their Saxon origins. Only occasionally shall we encounter the Danish 'thorpe' or 'by'; more prevalent are Norman patronymics.

The so-called 'ingas' names in Essex are common and may generally be taken to indicate an early Saxon settlement. This element, which may also occur medially as well as at the end of a place-name, can also be interpreted to mean the 'people of' or the 'dwellers at', depending on the other element(s) in the compound which may have personal or geographical connotations. The occurrence of these names follows a pattern consistent with the geographical factors of the early years of the Saxon colonisation of Essex. Thus they will be found along the coastal margins as in Wakering, Fobbing, Corringham, and Mucking, or on the river-lines of the county. The best example of this is the group of nine Roding villages–or more correctly Roothing–that mark the territory of 'Hrotha's' people. The pattern may also be seen in Margaretting, Fryerning, Mountnessing, and Ingatestone where the derivation is from 'ginges', in relation to the River Wid and in Feering, Messing and Bocking along the Blackwater. On the Chelmer and its tributaries are Cressing, Ulting, Terling, and Patching. Such names are widely distributed in the county as Hedingham, Tillingham, Barling, Nazeing, Epping, Barking, and Havering also demonstrate. Any Essex topographer will name without hesitation a score of 'ingas' names in the county from heart. It is impressive evidence of the establishment of a strong Saxon community in the earlier, if not the first, phases of the great migration.

As the forest clearances proceeded and more lands were brought into agricultural use, the 'field' and 'ley' or 'leigh' names were born. So we find Finchingfield, Wethersfield, Bardfield, Purleigh, Hockley, Hadleigh, and Rayleigh. The Saxon gods are present, too, in name if not in spirit in the first element of Widdington and in the field-names of Wodnesfeld and Wedynsfeld. The god of thunder, Thunor (or Thor), appears in the name of the Thurstable Hundred and in Thundersley and Thunderley Hall, near Wimbish. The few Celtic survivals are often attached to rivers, as in the Thames, the Lea, or the Pant–the 'valley' river–that flows from north-west Essex to become the Blackwater at Bocking. Here and there Scandinavian names such as Thorpe-le-Soken and Kirby-le-Soken will be noted. The Norman French compounds are readily identified in such as Woodham Ferrers, Stondon Massey, Berners Roding, and Theydon Garnon, which all bear names derived from the Norman baronage. Before we leave this intriguing aspect of Saxon Essex I must refute the misinterpretation of the name of the county's oldest town that even some modern authorities still seem to accept. The name of Colchester is quite certainly not a compound form from the '*Colonia*' and the Old English 'ceaster' (a fort). The first element, of Celtic provenance, derives from the River Colne on which the town stands and the name will be found in the Anglo-Saxon chronicle as 'Colneceaster' in the early part of the 10th century. It is a challenging thought that all the towns and villages I have mentioned in these passages, and numerous others in Essex, bear names that testify to more than 1,000 years of continuous history.

৪৩੦৪

Agreeable as it is to speculate on the philology of Essex we must again turn our attention to history and resume from the point where we left the narrative at the end of the previous chapter. It is a matter of considerable difficulty to draw convincing conclusions from the inadequate and conflicting knowledge that we have about the coming of the Anglo-Saxons. All one can say is that the colonisation assumed serious dimensions sometime between the rescript of Honorius in A.D. 410 and A.D. 446 when the Britons again appealed in vain to Rome for help. Recent archaeology suggests that a date towards the end of this period is more likely. By A.D. 477 the Saxons were ensconced in Sussex, and in A.D. 495 secured a foothold further west on Southampton water. They were checked in A.D. 516 at Mons Badonicus, an unknown battle-ground, by the defenders of Arthurian Britain. But the westward advance was soon resumed and Salisbury was occupied in A.D. 552. A Saxon victory at Dyrham in A.D. 577 secured Gloucester and Bath for the invaders, and in the north Catterick was won in A.D. 590. During the same period East Anglia and Essex were settled, though here, too, we are in difficulty about the chronology of this process. The inhospitable nature of the forest terrain and the marshlands of the river valleys was one factor in delaying the settlement in eastern England. Furthermore, the heavily silted estuaries impeded navigation, the Thames only offering an inviting inland route for the long clinker-built craft that were rowed across the North Sea by the Anglo-Saxon immigrants. One theory accepts that the first landings in Essex occurred in A.D. 527 under the leadership of a chief called Aescwine. Other evidence points to a landing by Sleda and his people in A.D. 587, but it would be surprising if this was the first. It may, indeed, be that the first arrivals in Essex were Anglian and took place at the end of the fifth century, although they were soon superseded by Saxon settlement, and the Stour marked an ethnic and linguistic frontier as well as a political boundary. Essex has ever since generally had closer cultural affinities with London, Kent and even Wessex than with East Anglia. Beyond the present county boundaries the shape and extent of the East Saxon kingdom varied over time. We do not know exactly how much territory was controlled by the East Saxon kings. Nor is the nature of the East Saxon kingdom's relationship with the neighbouring kingdom of Saxon Middlesex precisely clear. We do know that the East Saxon kingdom extended into Kent and that Surrey–the southern district–was contested with the Saxon Kings of Mercia and Wessex. It is a diffuse and mobile picture.

As to the indigenous populations it is clear that these people were subjected to Saxon authority. There is evidence, however, particularly in the significant relationship of early Anglo-Saxon cemeteries to Roman sites, as for example at Great Chesterford, Bradwell, and Colchester, of tolerance and co-existence after the first impact of the settlement. By A.D. 600 a number of Anglo-Saxon kingdoms had arisen throughout England. Bede tells us that by A.D. 604 the East Saxon kingdom, peopled by settlers of the old Saxon race, was ruled over by Sabert, who owed allegiance to Aethelbert of Kent, to whom he was related. Although the East Saxon dynasty was never of national importance, it flourished for a while, extending its influence to most of Hertfordshire, Middlesex, London, and Surrey. It was usually subordinate to Mercia, Kent, or Wessex. The dynasty was unique in Anglo-Saxon England in acknowledging descent from the native god Seaxneat rather than to Woden. Sabert died in c.A.D. 617, and was succeeded by his sons, Saweard and Seaxred, whom we shall see in conflict with the Christian church. By A.D. 653 Sigebert, the East Saxon king, was under Northumbrian influence, but by the time of Sebbe, who abdicated in c.A.D. 693 to be succeeded by his sons, Sigeheard and Swefred, Wessex was the dominant power in Essex. Mercian supremacy was re-established in A.D. 704 only to give way to Egbert of Wessex in A.D. 825 on the defeat of Beornwulf at Ellendun, just south of Swindon. After that there is no record of an East Saxon kingdom. The last of the kings of the East Saxon line, Swebriht, Selred, Swithred, Sigeric and Sigered, maintained the curious alliterative sequence that began with Sabert 200 years before.

ჩႬჩ

In retrospect the ever-changing pattern of political supremacy in Anglo-Saxon England postulates an instability and lack of social coherence hardly compatible with the development of enduring national qualities and values. Yet this was not so. In the crucible of the age a nation was born and its vital elements have survived the vicissitudes of time. Not least of the remarkable achievements of the age was the conversion of the heathen English peoples to Christianity, one of the permanent and dominant factors of our subsequent history. The new faith never enjoyed the monopoly of spiritual allegiance in Roman Britain, and it was almost 600 years after Paul baptised the world's first Christian ruler in Cyprus, the Roman proconsul Sergius Paulus, that an English king acknowledged Jesus Christ.

In A.D. 597 Pope Gregory took one of the definitive decisions in English history when he despatched the modest and somewhat reluctant Augustine to Britain. This formidable undertaking was launched in Kent where the king, Aethelbert, whose wife was a Frankish Christian, received the faith. Augustine first established himself at Canterbury, thereafter the principal seat of English Christianity, before turning his attention to London and the East Saxon kingdom where paganism was more strongly entrenched than in Kent. From Bede's great ecclesiastical history, written in the eighth century in the famous northern monastery at Jarrow, we learn of Augustine's appointment of Mellitus to the episcopal see of London with responsibility for gathering the East Saxons into the demanding embrace of the new religion. Although the ground had been prepared, the task was to prove beyond his powers. Son of Ricula, the sister of his overlord, Aethelbert of Kent, Sabert, the East Saxon king, needed little persuasion and was soon counted among the royal converts. This initial success was to prove a false dawn. Little further progress was made and after Sabert's death his sons drove Mellitus from the kingdom and he was forced to flee to France. The sons were pagans and the prospects for Christianity in Essex were obviously poor but, according to Bede, the immediate cause of the expulsion of Mellitus was his refusal in St Paul's to give them 'that white bread' which they had seen their father receive from the bishop. Soon afterwards both brothers were killed in fighting with the West Saxons, but the pagan elements in Essex were too strong to allow of Mellitus returning to his diocese. Bede tells us that he consequently stayed at Canterbury where in A.D. 619 he became archbishop in succession to Lamentius. It was to be left to the Celtic church, through the immediate influence of another Anglo-Saxon king, to rekindle the torch extinguished at Sabert's death.

Again we rely on the scholar of Jarrow for an account of the circumstances in which Christianity finally took root in Essex. During a visit to the powerful Oswiu, king of Northumbria, Sigebert 'the Good' of Essex was baptised at Lindisfarne by Bishop Finan. Encouraged by Oswiu, Sigebert sought the aid of the Celtic church in converting his people. Cedd, English by birth and the brother of St Chad, was brought from Mercia where, says Bede, in preaching the word of God he had been 'gladly heard'. Before leaving Holy Island he was consecrated Bishop of the East Saxons and forthwith set out in A.D. 653 for his pagan diocese. Although political factors prevented him from going to London he set about his mission in Essex with energy and conviction. His drive and authority were equal to the task and he succeeded in establishing Christian communities at Ythanceastre (Bradwell) on the Blackwater, and at Tilaburg (Tilbury) on the Thames. From those two places Celtic Christianity radiated throughout the East Saxon kingdom. The murder of Sigebert was a sad blow to the bishop, but he baptised the king's successor, Swithhelm, at the East Anglian royal court at Rendlesham and the crisis passed. Even after the synod of Whitby in A.D. 664, which Cedd attended in the Celtic party, many people in Essex again turned to their pagan gods and altars when plague threatened the kingdom. The church was by then firmly rooted.

Shortly afterwards Barking Abbey was founded by Eorcenwald, and Cedd died of the plague at Lastington, a monastery in Yorkshire. Barking, which achieved fame and authority as a nunnery, became one of the principal monastic foundations in England and, as I have described in *Discovering Essex in London*, an important influence in Essex. Under its powerful abbesses, and well endowed by the East Saxon aristocracy, it played a major part in bringing the Celtic missions into the church of Rome following the historic decisions at Whitby. Almost the only traces that remain of the success of the Celtic missionaries in recovering the spiritual ground lost by Mellitus in Essex are the dedications of some Essex churches to Celtic saints and the sad but inspiring relic at Bradwell.

A visit to Cedd's humble little church of St Peter at Bradwell is a deeply moving experience. Its simple piety is symbolic of the compassion and spirituality of the heroes of the conversion. It was built in *c.*A.D. 654 probably during the early months of Cedd's mission, largely from the Roman masonry quarried from the decaying coastal fortress of Othona, one of the nine forts of the Saxon Shore. In its original form it comprised an apsidal nave and narthex, and for centuries lay neglected as a farm building until its re-consecration by the Bishop of Chelmsford in 1920. In its lonely

10   *St Peter's-on-the-Wall at Bradwell*

field on the edge of the North Sea it remains, once more in Christian care, an evocative symbol of one of the great events of the county's history. After its founder's death, Wine was appointed as bishop of the East Saxons to be succeeded in turn by the founder of Barking, which had by then assumed the mantle of church leadership from the Celtic missions. That event epitomised the transference of ecclesiastical power from the pious humility of the Celtic church to the dynamic majesty of Rome.

೮೦ಛಿ

Compared with the scale and results of Roman archaeology in Britain the Anglo-Saxon field is neglected and disappointing. Leaving aside the wholly exceptional wealth and significance of the ship-burial at Sutton Hoo, the material at our disposal is relatively meagre. Except in numismatics much of the major work on this period has been left to historians. Essex, as I have already suggested, offers no relief from this generally parlous situation. In Essex we must be content, apart from the very rich find at Broomfield, with modest recoveries of hand- and wheel-made pottery, glass, minor pieces of jewellery, weapons, and implements. Generically the archaeological material of Saxon Essex belongs with that of Sussex and Wessex rather than to the Anglian range in the north, Mercia and East Anglia, although there are limited affinities with Kentish work of Jutish origin. The relics of cremation burials have been recovered at

Colchester, Kelvedon, Feering, Shoebury, Great Chesterford, Heybridge, and Mark's Tey. From the archaeological evidence for Saxon Colchester, a few sunken huts, a little pottery and some funerary objects, we can only deduce that the population, and consequently social and economic activity, was at a low ebb compared with the period before the collapse of Romano-British administration in the town. Not until the mid 10th century did Colchester resume its precedence as a town of some importance with a regional status. The Feering excavation was specially interesting because of the association of Saxon and Romano-British evidence. Other Saxon cemeteries have been excavated at Saffron Walden and Prittlewell, the material recovered from the latter in 1923 being like that of the impressive Broomfield burial of Kentish type. Very little of the Saxon provenance came from the excavations at Stansted prior to the building of the airport and even at Elms Farm, Heybridge the Anglo-Saxon settlement was sparse and seems to have been of short duration. However Anglo-Saxon ironworkings at Little Totham are of interest and fairly extensive.

The Anglo-Saxon jewellers produced work of a very high quality and exhibited particular skill in the use and setting of rare stones in personal ornaments. They also developed the use of plaited gold and silver wire with considerable success. Their artistic expression, although tempered with characteristic reticence, possessed a vitality and resourcefulness that excelled anything produced in Europe during that period. An interesting example of a bird brooch of rare design, set with garnets, was found at Walthamstow and is now in the British Museum. At nearby Forest Gate a jewelled ornament, that apparently belonged to part of a larger piece, was worked in gold with inset garnets and blue glass. Other Anglo-Saxon jewellery has come from sites in the north of the county: a gold ring from West Bergholt, another from Colchester, and a twisted gold wire finger-ring from Coggeshall. From Brightlingsea there is a fine bracelet. Perhaps the most splendid object of all was a fine glass drinking horn found in 1937 at Gerpins Farm, Rainham, that is now in the British Museum. There have been, too, the splendid glass claw beakers recovered at Mucking, though of continental provenance.

Mucking is, indeed, so far as its archaeological status is concerned, a unique Anglo-Saxon site and justifiably famous internationally as an example of a major early fifth-century migration settlement. Over 200 sunken hut dwellings were excavated there and about fifty other later surface buildings as well as large quantities of ceramic items and artistic metalwork of high quality. The Saxon cemetery at Saffron Walden referred to above is to be seen in the context of a settlement in the area of Abbey Lane in the modern town and, later, a Saxon habitation site west of the High Street. The earthworks of the so-called Battle Ditches, or the 'great fosse' at that site once thought to be post-conquest, are now believed to be of Saxon origin. Little now remains to be seen of the ramparts of the old Saxon burgh at Witham which was sited in a strategic situation overlooking the valley of the river Brain.

ಬಂಣ

During the eighth century the minatory power of the Vikings cast its shadow across European Christendom. These marauding seafarers, 'the men of the viks (fjords)', had at first no political ambitions. The object of their expeditions was plunder, but it would be a mistake to think of them merely as barbarians. Ruthless and cruel they certainly were, but the level of their technical competence in the arts of peace as well as war was high. The sword and axe were their favourite weapons, and these were often beautifully ornamented. The Vikings loved, too, the luxury of fine embroidered and brocaded clothes, and in their ships exhibited much technical and artistic skill. The highly painted and carved prows of their ships together with their coloured sails, often bearing the dreaded raven, must have been a stirring sight. The remains of their clinker-built craft have been found in the river at Lea Bridge and at the site of the Lockwood reservoir. But the Saxons of Britain and their fellow-sufferers in Europe could hardly have been appreciative of the cultural achievements of their pitiless assailants. For them the raven symbolised war, death and destruction.

In Britain the first blow fell upon the undefended island monastery of Lindisfarne which was sacked and burned in a savage attack in A.D. 793. The effect was traumatic. The assault upon Holy Island struck terror in men's hearts as it was clear that no mercy would be shown by the marauders whoever their victims might be. This was merely the beginning of a long, bloody and costly struggle with the northmen that was to dismember the English kingdoms. But in the end a united and stronger nation was to emerge.

Essex was not a rich area and it seems probable that this is the explanation of why it was spared from the Vikings until A.D. 851 when the northern shores of the Thames were ravaged before the raiders turned to Kent. By that time Viking sea-power had made itself felt along much of the Atlantic coast, the northern littoral of the Mediterranean, Russia, Iceland and even north America. These superb seamen and brilliant navigators, in their large, fast, and seaworthy ships, had decisive advantages over their victims whose forces were irregular, immobile and concerned to maintain their families and their lands. Until the general confrontation between Alfred and the Danish armies the invaders appeared to be invincible.

In A.D. 865 the Danes launched a massive and well co-ordinated attack on the English kingdoms. The Great Army landed in East Anglia where it over-wintered while its forces were concentrated for the offensive of A.D. 866. The first thrust carried them to York which they stormed, and then pursuing and destroying the remnants of the Northumbrian forces put an end to Anglian rule in the north. Turning south again the Great Army established itself at Nottingham and Mercia sued for peace. By A.D. 868 the Danish host was back in East Anglia in winter quarters at Thetford, having burnt and destroyed Peterborough on the way. By December A.D. 870 heavily reinforced, the Danes were ready to attack Wessex. The vast heathen army made its base at Reading and moved on to the chalk hills of Wessex where it suffered an unexpected defeat. On the Berkshire Downs at Ashdown the West Saxons, with spirit and valour, rolled back the tides of the invasion. For the first time in an equal contest the confident and hitherto victorious Danish army was routed with severe losses after bitter hand-to-hand fighting. Wessex had been saved and Alfred, not strong enough to press his victory, was, nevertheless, in a position to conclude a tactical peace with the Danes that gave his kingdom a respite of five years. But the invaders still dominated the whole of eastern England, including Essex, north of the Thames.

The next phase of Alfred's long and heroic struggle against the Danes had decisive consequences for the county. Under pressure from renewed Danish attacks in A.D. 876-8 the defences of Wessex collapsed, and Alfred was forced to retreat to the marshlands of Athelney in Somerset, from where he rallied the English forces for the counter-attack. When he was once again strong enough to mount an offensive, he was greeted with rapture by the West Saxons who flocked to the standards of their great leader. The courage and panache of Alfred's forces carried them to another great downland victory over their old enemies at Aethandune. This decisive contest made it possible for the frontiers of Alfredian Wessex to be advanced almost to the Lea, which in A.D. 886 became the boundary between Saxon England and the Danelaw. Alfred's generous treatment of Guthrum and the Danish leaders after their defeat laid the foundations for the eventual unity of the two warring Nordic races. But it left Essex, as Saxon as anywhere in Britain, in Danish hands.

Although Essex witnessed a naval engagement at the mouth of the River Stour in A.D. 884 in which Alfred's newly-formed navy destroyed a Danish flotilla, the Peace of Wedmore ensured stability and general peace for more than a decade. But after Guthrum's death in A.D. 890 the Danes resumed their assault on Alfred's kingdom. By A.D. 892 massive Danish forces were on the move, spearheaded by Haesten's powerful force in Kent. The strategic problem that confronted Alfred was to prevent the converging Danish armies from meeting and thus presenting him with overwhelming odds. Landing from a fleet of 250 ships a large Danish force was poised to join in a vast co-ordinated attack. Alfred, with all his old powers of decision, and despite a Danish diversion in the west, struck quickly and hard. His son, Edward, who was eventually to liberate Essex, led the Saxon fyrd to victory over the Danes at Farnham and pursued them into Essex. At Benfleet Haesten had built a fort on the low-lying land by the Thames. With a daring thrust into Danish territory Edward marched to Benfleet where he stormed the Danish stronghold which he looted and destroyed before returning to London with the women and children, including Haesten's own wife and son. The captured Danish ships, lying in a creek off Canvey Island, were taken away to London and Rochester. Haesten, absent at the time, fell back to the Danish fort at Shoebury, which lay within the present garrison site there. Alfred, with his usual chivalry and magnanimity, restored to Haesten his wife and child, though the campaign was not yet at an end. Railway navvies, working at South Benfleet station during the 19th century, uncovered the charred relics and human remains that bore grim testimony to the bloody encounter in the struggle for the Danish camp.

In A.D. 895 the Danish forces in Essex moved to Mersea Island, an old haunt of theirs, in preparation for a move against London. Towing their ships up the Thames and the Lea they ensconced themselves in fortified positions on the river about 20 miles above the capital. In A.D. 896 Alfred countered this move by covering London with forts on either side of the Lea. His engineers were then set to work to divert the main channel of the river so that the Danish force with its vessels upstream was stranded, immobile and isolated. The Danes were thus forced to withdraw from the area with the loss of their ships to the jubilant Saxons who hauled them into London. Danish sallies from Shoebury into Mercia were also failures, and, after a heavy defeat at Buttington-on-Severn, the Danish host, broken in spirit and severely weakened by its losses, dispersed, the major part of the force returning to France. The Danelaw, however, was still under their authority and it was left to Edward the Elder to wrest Essex from their grasp.

In A.D. 912 Edward, campaigning in the east, annexed the Mercian aldermanry of London and marched on into Essex where he camped at Maldon while a stockaded earthwork was constructed at Witham; in the words of the Anglo-Saxon Chronicle 'wrought and getimbred'. The early Saxon settlement in Maldon, or Maeldune as it was then referred to, does not seem to have been significant. But its role is not in doubt towards the end of the tenth century by which time it was a burh or fortified settlement, one of a series constructed in Essex by Edward the Elder. The purpose of this Saxon outpost in Danish Essex was to cover the Danish stronghold at Colchester while Edward pursued his tactical thrusts deep into the county. A determined Danish attack at Maldon was repulsed, and Edward was able to bring the ancient Roman capital at Colchester under his rule. The Anglo-Saxon Chronicle records how in A.D. 921 another strong Danish force recovered the town, killing all those who were unable to escape. But Edward was by then in the ascendancy and 'before Martinmas' he led the Saxon levies to victory over the Danes who surrendered the town to him and many came over to his side. Edward immediately set about rebuilding Colchester and its defences, for a son of Alfred would not be slow to grasp its strategic importance in eastern England. In fact the town also grew, as already indicated, in civic stature, for in A.D. 931 Athlestan the king is known to have held his Easter Gemot (council) in Colchester. In Aethelraed's reign (978-1013) a local mint was established there as well as at Maldon and later Horndon, Witham, and possibly, Harwich; previously Essex had relied on the London mint for its coinage.

Although its origins are obscure it was during the early 10th century that the Hundred seems to have been established as a territorial unit of local administration. It is not known with any certainty whether the Hundred was based on area, population, or fiscal standards. The Hundredal divisions are unequal in size, which tends to support the view that fiscal or family groupings originally governed the designation of the administrative areas. Essex was divided into 20 Hundreds, and it is clear that they were important as the basis of fiscal, judicial and governmental administration by the latter part of the Anglo-Saxon period. By then a parochial system was also fully developed. The Hundred survived as an element of local government for almost 1,000 years. The parish in its civil form is still functioning as the first tier of local authority today.

The year A.D. 991 marks one of the epic events of Essex history, made immortal in the poetic account, of which an important fragment has survived, of Byrhtnoth's heroic death at the Battle of Maldon. In that year the Vikings, having ravaged Ipswich, made their way to Maldon. Here, according to the extant Anglo-Saxon tradition, they were confronted by the gallant grey-haired old giant, the Saxon Ealdorman of Essex and his loyal followers. Son of Byrthelm, Byrhtnoth had married Aethelflaed, the youngest daughter of Aelfgar, whom he succeeded as Ealdorman of Essex in c.A.D. 953. On the famous day in the high summer of that year, near Northey Island on the River Pant, now the Blackwater below Bocking, the foes came face to face. With misplaced chivalry the ealdorman, outnumbered and without real hope of victory, allowed his opponents to cross a narrow causeway to fight on level terms. Despite the odds he and his thanes fought to the death, his Saxon comrades, Eadweard, Offa, Aetheric, Byrhtwold, and others

11   *Anglo-Saxon text from the epic poem of the Battle of Maldon*

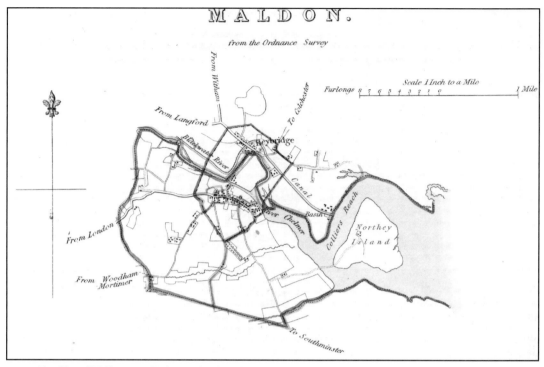

12 *Map of Maldon in 1837 showing Northey Island and the causeway, site of the Battle of Maldon in A.D. 991*

falling at his side. After the battle, which had seen in the words of the old poem such 'grim war-play', the victors, it said, could scarcely man their ships. The battle, recorded in the great Anglo-Saxon verses to which I have referred, was regarded by the Saxons as a supreme example of the code of allegiance that was cherished between leaders and men among the Germanic peoples. Byrhtnoth's body was taken to Ely where the battle was commemorated on a tapestry presented by his widow. In 1769 the decapitated remains were disinterred at Ely Cathedral and the old hero's height was estimated at six feet nine inches.

The story, much cherished, is doubtless a mixture of fact and fiction much disputed by scholars. But in essence its inspirational qualities survive largely thanks to the poem which has embellished the simple reference in the Anglo-Saxon Chronicle with a panache that has carried its message into the heart of Essex historiography. The only original manuscript of the great poem of Maldon was destroyed by fire in Dean's Yard, Westminster, in 1731, but, fortunately, it had been copied not long before. Although the battle has little political significance, the memory of the valour of these men of Essex was treasured as symbolic of Saxon virtues and honour. To leave the field of battle, or desert the sworn leader, meant humiliation and dishonour. In the old warrior Byrhtwold's inspiring words as he brandished his spear in rallying the dead ealdorman's compatriots, 'thought the harder, heart the keener, courage the greater' as their strength and numbers waned.* That eloquent Saxon oration has spiritual resonances that the Englishmen of Elizabeth, of Cromwell, of Nelson, and of Churchill would understand.

ഇരുജ

*A modern scholar, Donald Scragg, has translated the familiar lines 312 and 313 of the Anglo-Saxon poem 'The spirit must be the firmer, the heart the bolder, courage must be the greater'. This is perhaps more satisfactory but the wording I have used is now enshrined in Essex historical tradition.

After Maldon Viking pressure on England increased, and Olaf of Norway, Cnut's father, and Swegen, king of Denmark mounted numerous attacks along the Essex coast and the Thames. In 1016 one of the decisive events in our country's story took place on Essex soil. The site of the battle of Assandun has been disputed by generations of distinguished historians. Thus, much erudition has been devoted to the respective claims of Ashdon, near Saffron Walden, and Ashingdon on the river Crouch which, until recent scholarship that tends to favour Ashdon, commanded most support. We still do not know.

Following the death of Aethelraed in 1016 London acknowledged Edmund Ironside as king, but in Wessex the Danish leader Cnut enjoyed much support. After an indecisive victory over Cnut at Otford, Eadric of Mercia went over to Edmund, but was to prove a treacherous ally. Edmund managed to recover the allegiance of Wessex and relieved London, which had been besieged by Cnut. Another inconclusive battle in Kent left Cnut still in the field, and he moved into Essex making towards Mercia. There he was pursued by Edmund who, deserted by Eadric in the field, was overcome by Cnut on 18 October at Assandun where, says Holinshed, 'after a sore and cruel fight, the Englishmen were beaten down and slaine in heaps'. Among the dead was the renowned Ulfkell Snilling; Edmund himself was a fugitive. No doubt with Byrhtnoth and Maldon in his mind the Anglo-Saxon chronicler records Eadric's betrayal of his lord and the loss of 'the flower of the English nation'. But Cnut's army, too, was exhausted by the tremendous struggle that had taken place in the Essex fields, and on an island on the River Severn he concluded a treaty with Edmund agreeing to divide the kingdom. Wessex and Kent, including London still unconquered, went to Edmund, but Essex and the rest of England were once more firmly under Danish rule. Within a month, on 30 November 1016, Edmund Ironside was dead and Cnut inherited the remainder of the English kingdom and his brilliant reign commenced. He was again in Essex in 1020 attending the consecration of the church by the battlefield at Assandun. He was succeeded by his son, Harold, after his death in 1035.

During Cnut's reign, in which he strengthened the provincial form of government set up by Aethelraed, Essex was associated with East Anglia under Earl Thurkill. Between his banishment in 1020 and the appearance in political history of Harold Godwineson in 1045 the situation is obscure, but his writ ran as far afield as Huntingdon and Cambridgeshire as well as throughout Essex and East Anglia. England having reverted to the old Saxon dynasty on the accession of Edward the Confessor in 1042, Viking attacks were resumed, and Walton-on-the-Naze was raided by the Danes in 1049. Banished in 1051, Harold's earldom was granted to Aelfgar, son of Leofric of Mercia, but Harold returned in 1052 to resume his position. On Earl Godwin's death—his father—in 1053 he succeeded to the earldom of Wessex, and we again find Aelfgar as earl of East Anglia. Later the eastern counties' connection with Harold Godwineson's family was renewed when the earldom of East Anglia was conferred on his younger brother, Gyrth, who was eventually to die with him at Hastings. The same fate awaited Leofwine, another brother, who governed Essex, it having been separated from East Anglia, along with Kent, Hertfordshire, Surrey, and Buckinghamshire.

During the latter years of his reign Edward the Confessor raised the abbey at Westminster just west of the capital. Preceding that most famous building in English history by a few years was the abbey church at Waltham in Essex. This was built by

13   *St Andrew's, Greensted-juxta-Ongar*

Harold, who endowed it with lands, valuable ornaments, plate and books, and installed a dean and 12 secular canons to work in the forest communities of southwest Essex. The church was consecrated on Holy Cross Day, 3 May 1060 by Kinsige, the Archbishop of York, in the presence of the king and queen. It became a place of pilgrimage for the Saxon people and was always regarded by Harold with special reverence; and it is believed that after his death at Hastings his body was removed for burial at the high altar of the abbey.

Not far from Waltham, beyond the present forest, there lies at Greensted, close by Chipping Ongar, the little log church of St Andrew, which is a unique survival from the period. When it was first built is not known, but the vertically split logs of the nave wall still bear the marks of the adze as they were worked by their builders. The modern technique of dendrochronology has dated these timbers to between *c.*1060 and 1100 which, although later than had until now been believed, still defines St Andrew's as the oldest timber building in Europe. The results of a Danish team's excavations at Greensted in 1960 established that there was once a chancel similarly constructed. There is none other like it in the whole of England or indeed Europe. Its role in the story of the church in Essex is not as dramatic as that of the earlier Saxon church at Bradwell, but it was associated with the East Anglian king, Edmund, who was martyred by the Danes at Hoxne in A.D. 869. When in 1010 the Danes again threatened the East Anglian homelands the remains of the king were carried to London where they lay in the safety of St Gregory's. After the defeat of the Danish raiders in 1013 the remains were returned to Bury St Edmunds, and on the way rested overnight at Greensted. It is perhaps surprising that this most charming of all Essex churches was not re-dedicated to St Edmund, for not many village churches are honoured by the presence of a saint even in death. The dedication to St Andrew may, however, be very early and indicate an original Celtic foundation. If the church at Bradwell evokes such poignant memories of the Conversion and the abbey at Waltham of 'Harold Infelix', there is none in Essex that more vividly recalls the reality of the forest churches in which our Saxon ancestors worshipped than Greensted.

There are about 25 other churches in Essex that still contain architectural features of the Saxon period, although none are as important historically as Bradwell or Greensted. It will be possible to mention but a few. St Katherine's at Little Bardfield has an impressive late Saxon tower. Hadstock and Inworth, too, have work of the later Saxon period. Holy Trinity at Colchester has a fine triangular-headed archway made from Roman tiles by the Saxon masons. There is early work at St Mary's Prittlewell, and Saxon chancel arches are to be seen at White Notley, Great Hallingbury and Strethall. There is no doubt, too, early work still unrecognised, and the careful and knowledgeable ecclesiologist can still hope to identify minor features in some of the less fashionable churches of the county.

೮೦೧೪

We come now to the last months of
the Anglo-Saxon England of which Essex
had been an authentic part. At the death of
the Confessor in 1066 Harold, amid controversy and in defiance of the claims of William of Normandy, assumed the crown. The
Anglo-Saxon state had arisen in violence
and was to die in violence. It was to end in
blood and glory in Sussex within the year.

In the northern seas was gathering the
last of the great Viking armadas to attack
the English state. Across the channel William and his knights, who also acknowledged Viking ancestry, were preparing to
contest the crown which the Norman duke
regarded as his by right. The Norwegians
were first on the scene when Harald
Hardrada and Tostig entered the Humber
with 300 ships and forced a passage on the
Yorkshire Ouse as far as Ricall. Advanc-

14   *Saxon Doorway, Holy Trinity, Colchester*

ing on York they defeated the northern earls, Edwin and Morcar, on 20 September,
and so began perhaps the most fateful month in our history. Four days later Harold of
England, marching north, reached Tadcaster, and on 25 September, beyond York, he
attacked the invaders at Stamford Bridge on the Derwent. The speed and violence of
the blow shattered the Viking army, and in the rout the elated Saxons pressed home
their victory. Hardrada and Tostig were killed and the remnants of the once ambitious
force that challenged for the English Crown straggled back to Norway in but 25 of their
ships.

Within a few days William, at the head of the most professional fighting force in
Europe, had landed at Pevensey and advanced to Hastings. News of the new and
serious threat reached Harold on 1 October, and he at once marched south to London.
Having prayed at Waltham for the success of his army he left the abbey and continued
south, though the omens were bad, covering the last 60 miles by 11 October. After 300
miles on the march and a great battle with the Vikings his irregular forces could hardly
have been in a condition to challenge successfully the well disciplined and highly
equipped Norman army, and its great military commander. Yet it was a near-run thing.
On 14 October the brave and impetuous Harold and his gallant house-carls died to a
man glorifying the last hours of the old Saxon dynasty. William received the Crown in
Westminster Abbey on Christmas Day, and Saxon Essex, for so long in Danish hands,
once more found itself in the alien grasp of a harsh and powerful ruler.

Chapter 3

ଚ୦୦ଓ

THE NORMANS IN ESSEX

'Not a single hide nor rood of land ... '

It has been said, with much truth, that nowhere in all England did the hand of the Norman conqueror lay more heavily on the land than in Essex. The people of the old Saxon kingdom bore the full severity of the measures taken by William to reward his followers, and to buttress his own position in his newly-won realm. As we shall find when we examine the situation in Essex, revealed 20 years after the Conquest in the Domesday Survey, the Norman usurpers enjoyed the material fruits of their victory to the full.

England was by no means unknown territory to the Normans and it is possible that William himself had been in the country during the reign of his cousin, Edward the Confessor. Furthermore the intercourse between some elements of the Saxon nobility and the Duke's entourage in Normandy had been continuous over a lengthy period. Edward himself was of part-Norman ancestry and valued the cultivated French officials he had appointed to important offices in England. The Bishop of London was one. His sheriff in Essex, Robert FitzWymarc, was another. Some of the political ground had thus been prepared for the invasion of 1066 which was also launched with the Pope's approval and support. After his defeat of the Saxon fyrd in Sussex, and Harold's death, the English crown lay within William's eager grasp. If his title was in doubt his resolution was not. Ever a man of decision, the Duke struck quickly inland from the battle-field at Hastings. By-passing London, where the bishops had gathered to receive him, and leaving Southwark in flames, he crossed the Thames and moved into Hertfordshire, where he accepted the allegiance of Edgar the Atheling at Berkhamsted. At Winchester, Edith, Earl Godwine's daughter and widow of the Confessor, surrendered the town to his forces. In Essex, at Barking, he established his court at the abbey, while the Tower of London was being built and received the homage of the Saxon leadership, including Edwin of Mercia, Morcar, and Thurkil. Further resistance was minimal; there was none in Essex. William, within a few months of receiving the Crown, felt sufficiently secure to return briefly to Normandy, leaving the affairs of England in the hands of his brother, Odo, the Bishop of Bayeux, and his minister, William FitzOsbern.

The great abbey at Barking, enjoying even then the prestige and influence of 400 years of history, was well chosen as the seat of Norman authority while the position in London was consolidated. It was conveniently near the capital and provided ready access to the sea. Furthermore, the goodwill of the abbess Alfgiva, who was treated with the utmost consideration, was important to a King, anxious to establish his credentials with the Anglo-Danish people whom he now ruled. The abbey was left in possession of its properties and continued to enjoy its rights and privileges. The support of the church, then a political force in the land, William could not afford to forfeit. With purpose and much political skill the King, through the administration and social machinery he established, secured his personal position. Opposition he crushed ruthlessly by force of arms and even the rebellious activity of powerful subjects, which included his own brother, Odo, never seriously threatened his authority. The main threat to his throne was perhaps from his continental rivals, but in such a case he could have relied on popular support, for his English subjects would have seen no profit in exchanging one continental adventurer for another.

Despite the maturing political development of the Anglo-Danish state that grew up in England during the later phases, its economic growth had been unspectacular. Considerable areas of the country remained undeveloped to any degree and under-populated. The most densely settled areas were, in fact, in East Anglia and Essex. The advent of the Normans, with their drive and the centralisation of political control, accelerated the economic and social processes. The total population in 1086 at the time of the Domesday Survey has been estimated at about 1,250,000 people. The evidence of the Survey suggests that there were about 80,000 in Essex. But important as were the dynamics of the Norman state, the most profound and permanent result of the Conquest was the diversion of English society from insular and northern attitudes towards the influences of western European political and cultural experience. The echoes of that continue to stimulate our political and corporate life today.

Although the 20 years of William's reign was a period of harsh government and heavy taxation, the immediate impact was felt mainly by the land-owning classes. For the remainder there is little reason to think that their general status was significantly changed. But the severity of Norman rule was felt by all. William, the Anglo-Saxon Chronicle tells us, was of 'great sternness' and the Norman nobility was not notable for gentleness or compassion. Law was strictly enforced, and in the forest areas the Essex villagers were painfully aware of the King's love of the chase. The preservation of game for the royal sport demanded onerous laws and regulations that were rigorously upheld by heavy penalties. William's affections, it was sardonically observed, were reserved for the beasts of chase and venary–'he loved the tall stags', says the Chronicle, 'as if he were their father. He also appointed concerning the hares, that they should go free'. Large tracts of the countryside, including vast areas of Essex, were afforested and thus subjected to the forest laws. Only in the ecclesiastical lands were the changes minimal, for, like Barking, the other monastic foundations were generally immune from confiscation as part of the policy of consolidating church support. Waltham Abbey, because of its association with Harold, was a notable exception and was deprived of much of its landed property, though even this was eventually mainly restored. Harold's many estates in the county–as *terra regis*–were forfeited to William himself. Indeed, almost every other English landowner in Essex was dispossessed in what was by far the most extensive transference of land ownership in our history.

಄ಃ

All over the country, in town and village, there are the remains to this day of the numerous castles built during the Norman era to uphold the King's authority and safeguard the estates of the Norman aristocracy. Again the words of the Chronicle illuminate the situation–'castles he caused to be made, and poor men to be greatly oppressed'. At first the castles were of the motte-and-bailey type surrounded by ditch and rampart, the motte itself being usually defended by a wooden palisade. In Essex there were a number of this type, but there was also the castle at Colchester, built with materials from the decayed Roman city and rivalling the great White Tower that guarded the capital. Others were later reconstructed in stone and brick, there being 12 in the county. Of these four– Colchester, Tilbury, Landguard (geographically in Suffolk, but administratively regarded as an Essex port at the time), and Hadleigh–were owned and garrisoned by the King. The remainder, such as Castle Hedingham, Pleshey and Rayleigh, were built by the greater landowners to dominate the countryside and protect their estates. Collectively, they represent a major achievement of medieval military architecture, and their massive, if crumbling, defences still continue to resist the ravages of time and man.

The finest example of Norman military architecture in Essex is the keep of Colchester Castle, which was at least twice as large as the White Tower in London, and, like that, built very soon after the Conquest. The outer works of this fortress, strategically important while the threat of Scandinavian invasion lasted during William's reign, have now disappeared. They consisted of a deep surrounding ditch with an earthen rampart, constructed over the old Roman walls, and palisade. The keep, reputedly the largest in Europe, was built on the podium of the Roman temple and was over 90 feet high. As they are contemporaneous and of similar conception, it seems likely that the same architect, one Gundulph of Bec, later the Bishop of Rochester, was responsible for their design and construction. Architecturally the castle at Colchester was impressive. In the traditional massive proportions that we associate with Norman building it was built of re-used Roman masonry, septaria from the Essex coast, Barnack from Northamptonshire, ragstone from Kent, and Caen stone from Normandy. The

15   *Colchester Castle, 1832*

widespread provenance of the materials alone illustrates the considerable importance with which the castle was viewed in the defensive arrangements of the Norman state. Although much reduced in scale, the building still contains many interesting architectural features of the period.

The actual date when Colchester castle was built is not known. Its building appears, from later documentary evidence, as having been started in *c.*1075. It was not recorded in Domesday Book, but that is not necessarily significant and the circumstantial evidence suggests an earlier date than 1086. The first reference to the castle occurs in a document of 1101, by which time it was conferred by Henry I in confirmation of the original grant by William II on Eudo the dapifer (steward) of William I and his successors. As a royal castle during Norman times it was tenurially linked with the Hundred of Tendring and thus provided revenue as well as security for the Crown. Eudo was one of the Conqueror's most trusted supporters having campaigned with him at Hastings and received his due reward in a liberal grant of Essex manors of which he was tenant-in-chief and appointed by the Conqueror as Seneschal of Colchester Castle. He died in 1120 and was buried at Colchester in the Abbey of St John the Baptist which he had founded. The castle later came by marriage into the hands of the important de Mandeville family. However, Geoffrey the grandson of Eudo, who received the grant from Queen Maud, never in fact assumed the office of Constable that went with it. This was presumably because the King was reluctant to confer another important role on an already powerful family.

Of all the other castles of Norman Essex the most imposing is that which dominates the attractive little town of Castle Hedingham. It was built in *c.*1135 by Aubrey de Vere,

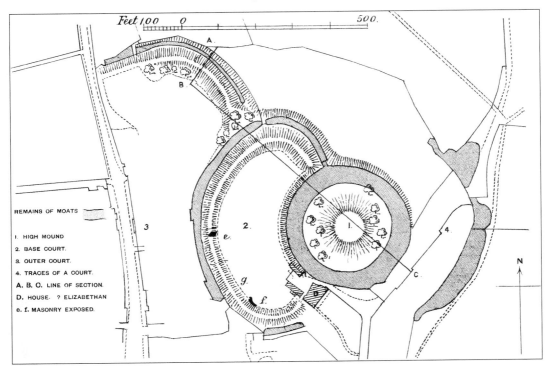

16 *Plan of the earthworks of the Norman castle at Chipping Ongar*

whose father had also received his extensive estates in Essex as part of the spoils of
the Conquest. The de Veres, subsequently
the Earls of Oxford, were one of the foremost families in medieval England and presided over their properties from Castle
Hedingham for over 500 years. The castle
was constructed of flint rubble faced with
Barnack limestone. Its walls were 12 feet
thick at the base and the towering keep
topped 100 feet. This impressive feature of
the de Veres' fortress home still remains,

17 *Hedingham Castle, in the 19th century*

as do the outer defensive earthworks, but the remainder of the castle was dismantled in
the 16th century. Like Castle Hedingham, the Norman castles at Rayleigh and Chipping Ongar brooded over the villages that grew up in the shadow of their walls. The
castle at Rayleigh is referred to in the Domesday Survey of 1086 which records that 'in
this manor Sweyn made his castle'. Sweyn was the son of the Breton, Robert FitzWymarc,
whose vast Essex estate was centred on Rayleigh. Built on the typical motte-and-bailey
model of the Norman baronial castles, little now remains but the impressive mound
and its clearly defined outer defences. It served its purpose of dominating the area for
some three centuries. At Chipping Ongar, where lived Richard de Lucy, the castle is
now but a minor topographical feature, although the ramparts originally enclosed a
sizeable area. It could well be, in fact, that Chipping Ongar was one of those Norman
strongholds which, as recent excavation has indicated in other parts of England, may
have been constructed on the site of an earlier Saxon fort. If this was proved to be so,
that would be a circumstance with new and interesting implications for the history of
the later Saxon period in Essex. Another interesting Norman stronghold in Essex is that
at Pleshey, the defences of which encircle the whole village. This was the home of the
de Mandevilles, the Earls of Essex, who were endowed with vast estates, including an
area of more than 12,000 acres around Pleshey which was their main seat.

This classic motte-and-bailey site is thought to date from *c.*1100 when Geoffrey de

Mandeville was High Constable of England
and one of the most powerful men in Essex.
His extensive manorial estate was concentrated in the adjacent parishes and further
afield. From the de Mandevilles it was con-
veyed by marriage to the de Bohuns and
eventually became a royal property. Apart
from the mound, the most conspicuous of
its remaining features are the inner and outer
baileys that define the boundaries of Pleshey
village and the 'olde arche of bryckworke
in the Inner dyche' as described in a Crown
Commissioner's survey of 1558/9. The latter is said to be unique in Britain and the

18 *Ruins of the Norman castle at Saffron Walden, 1787* oldest such bridge in Europe.

19 *The Norman motte and bailey castle at Pleshey*

The bleak remains of the structure that was once hidden away in the motte and formed the lower parts of the castle at Saffron Walden again remind us of the dominant status of the de Mandevilles in Norman Essex. It was built in the early 12th century and, like Pleshey, was in the hands of the de Bohuns in the 14th century, although by then it is believed to have been in ruins. It was this widespread and still remarkable network of baronial castles that maintained the stability and security of the Norman state.

But it was not in castles alone that the Normans left their imprint on the topography of the county. Theirs was a period in which the parochial system, already established in Saxon England, was further developed and in which many of the larger religious communities were founded. The development of monastic institutions was, indeed, one of the principal features of the age. Most of the religious houses of medieval Essex were founded and endowed by Norman patrons. There were eight Benedictine monasteries in Essex, among them the Abbey of St John the Baptist at Colchester, founded in the 11th century, and the priories of Wix and Castle Hedingham, which dated from the 12th century. But the most important was Barking, which was of Saxon foundation, as we have seen.

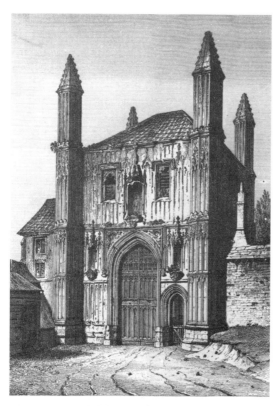

20   *St John's Abbey, Colchester, 1808*

The Cistercians, founded by Stephen Harding, a Dorset man, and the most flourishing order of the time, established abbeys at Stratford Langthorne in 1135, Coggeshall in 1140, and Tilty in 1153. At Waltham was the most important house of the Augustinian order in England and their brethren were at St Osyth from the early years of the 12th century. The Premonstratensians were at Beeleigh. Colne Priory was endowed by Aubrey de Vere as early as *c.*1105 under the aegis of the Benedictines at Abingdon, who shortly afterwards were referred to in a charter issued by the Archbishop of Canterbury as wishing to serve God 'in a certain church in Essex'.

Of the parish churches of Essex it may confidently be said that nearly 200 retain some architectural feature of the Norman period. The rounded arch, the zig-zag dog-tooth and chevron decoration, the massive cylindrical columns and the deep-splayed simple window forms are all present in the ecclesiastical architecture of the county. A complete inventory of the Norman architecture and art of the parish churches of Essex would take us far beyond the bounds of this chapter, and try the endurance of the reader. But the relevance of the Norman contribution to the parochial life of the Essex villages is sufficient to demand at least a brief survey. The best, more or less complete examples, of the smaller Norman parish churches in Essex are, in my view, to be found at Copford, Rainham, and East Ham. All these should be visited by the enthusiastic Essex topographer who will probably find Copford the most satisfying if only for the quite remarkable range of wall-paintings that has survived to glorify this church. Thanks to the unpremeditated, but timely, application of whitewash, which was meant to obliterate them, many of these brilliant and inspiring murals were preserved and eventually restored by the Victorians to their original hues and quality. The centre-piece of these exceptional examples of religious art, which date from about 1150, is a dominant Christ in Glory seated on a throne encircled by a rainbow and supported by angelic figures. In the apse and nave there is also a breathtaking series of biblical figures, saints and soldiers, priests and parishioners,

21   *Gateway of St Osyth's Priory, 1833*

pronouncing the universality of the church. Christ is seen, too, with the centurion and Samson struggling with the lion.

In an enthusiasm for the wall-paintings at Copford I should not like to divert attention from the Norman excellence that is secreted in the urban sprawl of metropolitan Essex at Rainham and East Ham. At both Saint Helen and St Giles, and Saint Mary Magdalen the discerning visitor will enjoy the graceful line, vigour and proportions of the period features of these two lovely Norman churches. The characteristic apsidal ground-plan at East Ham will be noted, too, at Hadleigh, where the parish church of St James-the-Less dates from the same period. Externally the most conspicuous feature of the parish church is often the west tower. While I must not invite comparison with the unrivalled splendour of those of the churches of Somerset or the quality of East Anglian towers there are some few, but interesting, Norman towers in Essex that ought to be mentioned. In particular, I would draw attention to those at Corringham, Felsted, and Finchingfield. For those to whom the enigma of the round tower, almost all of which are in East Anglia, is a challenge there are Norman examples to be seen at Holy Innocents, Lamarsh, St George, Pentlow, and St Mary, Great Leighs. Excellent Norman detail may be seen also in the doorways of St Mary's at High Ongar, St Andrew's at South Shoebury, St Nicholas at South Ockendon, and St Mary the Virgin at Stansted Mountfitchet. There is a superb ornamented chancel at St Mary the Virgin, Great Canfield and a fine and rare wheel-window at Castle Hedingham. Of fonts, good examples of Norman origin will be found in St Nicholas, Fyfield, All Saints, Norton Mandeville and St Peter's at Hockley. I ought not to omit, in this brief and over-generalised survey, to remark upon the beautiful environment that should attract lovers of Norman architecture to Great Braxted.

22 *'Christ in Majesty': 12th-century wall-paintings in the Norman church at Copford*

However, of all the parish churches in the county the supreme example of Norman vintage is Waltham Abbey. Now greatly diminished from its former size, what remains is one of the most distinguished ecclesiastical monuments of Essex. Built at the end of a causeway that traversed the marshlands of the Lea valley, it was one of the great monastic foundations. The nave, transepts and choir of the Norman abbey were later to be demolished at the Dissolution in 1540; the cloisters and chapter house have also been lost. Those remaining parts of the building that constitute the existing church were reprieved by Henry VIII in response to the appeals of the local parishioners who protested their need of a parish church. We are left with a powerful expression of the major idioms of Norman architecture. In the mould of Durham, its only Norman superior in Britain, it exhibits the characteristically massive spirally-grooved columns that support

Drawn by C.H. Campion   WALTHAM ABBEY CHURCH.   *Engraved by J. Rogers*

23   *Waltham Abbey, 1831*

the nave arcade, with their scalloped capitals and the familiar semi-circular arches. The
Norman work dates from the rebuilding of 1177, when it was refounded by the Augustinian canons. Sir Nikolaus Pevsner has compared it with Canterbury before Yevele
rebuilt the nave of England's premier cathedral. His testimony to the quality of its
Norman features suffices to rank this historic Essex church among the most significant
buildings of the age in the whole country.

೫೦೧೩

'Not a single hide nor rood of land … an ox, or a cow, or pig passed by that was not
set down in the accounts'–so wrote the chronicler, in astonishment and indignation, of
the great Domesday Survey of 1086. At midwinter in 1085 the King and his court were
at Gloucester, where there was 'much thought' and 'deep speech' in the Witan. As a
result King William's commissioners were despatched to every part of the land to survey
and record, in extraordinary detail, the tenurial structure and economic wealth of England. The purpose of this unique and gigantic undertaking has been the object of much
learned investigation and controversy. It was at root, argued Maitland, in his 'Domesday
Book and Beyond', a geld book designed to measure and exploit the taxable capacity of
the realm. Sir Frank Stenton has opined that William's object was to learn the essential

facts about his kingdom. It was thus the basic dossier for the political, social and fiscal management of the country. It provided, as we shall see in analysing the results of the Essex survey, a comprehensive range of information in these fields unrivalled in any society until comparatively recent times.

The findings of the survey are recorded in two books. One, the larger volume, covers the greater part of the country; the other, the so-called Little Domesday, in fact contains 900 mostly vellum pages and in much more detail describes the eastern counties of Essex, Norfolk and Suffolk in that order. The Essex historian is fortunate in that the information contained in the Essex entries

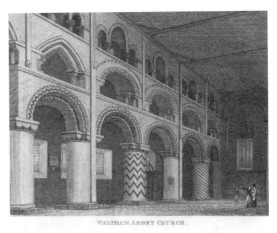

WALTHAM ABBEY CHURCH.

24 *Waltham Abbey: the nave arcade drawn by John Ogborne, 1814*

is generally fuller and more consistent in its range of detail than for any other county. There is naturally a variety of information, but it is generally presented to show the overlordship, occupation, fiscal area, and value of the land in each parish, the related details and personal status of the subordinate classes, the capacity of the land, plough-teams, animals and other economic details. The information given is expressed in such a way as to indicate the comparable data for the reign of Edward the Confessor–'*tempore Regis Edwardi*'–and at the time of the survey. R.W. Finn has pointed out the interesting fact that in the whole survey the compilers faltered only twice in references to King William 'conquering' or Harold 'reigning'. Even after 20 years it would seem the King, in insisting on regarding Edward as his immediate predecessor, was still anxious to sustain the legitimacy of his own claim to his cousin's throne.

Although Essex was surveyed along with East Anglia, the tenurial organisation of the county, which was based on the hide as in the rest of Saxon England, was different. This is further evidence of the resistance to Danish influence which distinguishes the county from much of the former Danelaw. From the survey we derive, in some depth, a remarkable picture of the social and economic aspects of life in the county, which was then largely wooded country apart from the open fields of the west and the marshy fringes of the coastal and river boundaries. Aside from Colchester and Maldon it was generally an area of hamlets and small villages relying on agriculture, animal husbandry, and a little fishing for the essentials of life. We may see, too, the profound and appalling consequences of the Conquest for the English landowners. The dispossession of the major figures in Saxon Essex, Harold himself, Ansgar, Wulfwine, and Withgar is painfully apparent. The lesser men, too, like the freemen Algar at Purleigh and Leftan at Witham, Orgar the thegn at Chingford, Alestan, at Hanningfield, and the priest at Rainham suffered confiscation. The takeover was virtually complete. Except for a few relatively minor forest or manorial officials, every Englishman 'small or great' forfeited the land he freely held. In their place we see the names of William I, the Norman baronage, and the victors at Hastings. King Edward had not directly held any of the largest estates in Essex, though Harold had extensive holdings, acquired by William, at Writtle, Hatfield Broad Oak, Havering, and Witham among other places. Other major landowners in Essex

25   *Geoffrey de Mandeville*

before the Conquest were Earl Aelfgar of Mercia and East Anglia, the Bishopric of London, and various religious houses. The Domesday Survey shows that, after the Conquest, vast domains were granted to Odo, the Bishop of Bayeux and William's half-brother, in his personal capacity, and Count Eustace of Boulogne, whose honorial court was held at Witham. Eustace's great estate, the largest of the baronial fiefdoms in Essex, included lands in some eighty other manors apart from Witham. A number were let to important Norman tenants like Adelolf de Merk, whose name survives in Marks Manor adjacent to Great Dunmow. After Eustace's the largest Domesday fief was that of Geoffrey de Mandeville, who, as well as possessing lands at High Easter, Great Waltham, Pleshey, Leigh, Terling, and the Rodings, enjoyed the ownership of other properties in Essex and considerable estates in several other counties. Other prominent names in the Essex Domesday record were those of Aubrey de Vere of Castle Hedingham, Sweyn of Essex, who possessed the Honor of Rayleigh, Robert Gernon, who has left his name in Theydon Garnon, Eudo, the dapifer, and Peter de Valognes, the Sheriff of Essex, whose land lay largely in the southwestern Hundreds of the county.

There are examples, too, of important Norman nobles whose properties in Essex were relatively modest, though they held great estates elsewhere. One such honorial magnate was Count Alan Rufus of Richmond in Yorkshire, whose barony was one of the greatest in England. He was tenant-in-chief of a number of sub-infeudated estates in Essex at Epping, Finchingfield, and Willingale Spain where the d'Espagne family, whose name survives in more than one instance today including the Ruggles-Brise residence of Spains Hall at Finchingfield, were his tenants. Henry de Ferrers, one of the Domesday commissioners, held five lordships in Essex, though the main concentration of his honor was in the Midlands. Similarly the estates of the Abbey of Ely show that by the time of the survey 18 properties in Essex, at Great Braxted, Hadstock, High Easter, and Leaden Roding among them, had been returned to them by the King. These examples provide a good illustration of the shrewd policies of the Norman monarch in frequently, though not always, dispersing the ownership of land to prevent the consolidation of power by potential rivals and appeasing the church.

In this great re-distribution of properties the church authorities were, in many cases, allowed to retain their lands within the overall control of the Crown. Barking

Abbey held numerous manors as did the Cathedral of Canterbury, as at Southchurch and Bocking. Battle Abbey, among other material benefits, was granted the church and tithes at Great Sampford. William I retained that manor in his own domain although leaving it in the charge of his dapifer, Godric, a Saxon who had in fact sided with the Norman king and was thus presumably locally unpopular.

In the Essex Domesday are entered the economic and social particulars of 440 settlements. They were manifestly small rural communities living in feudal conditions and relying upon agriculture for the means of life. Only two, Colchester and Maldon, were sufficiently developed to be described as boroughs, which were surviving English institutions that proved more resilient and influential than might have been expected by the Norman administration. However in these cases the bulk of the population derived its livelihood from agriculture in some way, whether from the produce of smallholdings or in trading. Heavily taxed, the small urban community of king's burgesses held their properties, some 400 houses and small acreages in the environs of Colchester, by grace of William I. The total population of the town was probably over 2,000. The other royal borough was Maldon, where a community of 1,000 or so people lived in 180 houses, according to the survey.

Typical of most of the settlements of Essex were the manor of Chingford St Paul's in the Waltham Hundred and Great Waltham in the Chelmsford Hundred. The Domesday entries are expressed with remarkable concision in an abbreviated Latin form.

That for the manor of Chingford St Paul's has been translated in *Domesday Book: Essex* (Phillimore, 1983) as follows:

> Hundred of Waltham.
>
> St Paul's held CHINGFORD before 1066 as 1 manor, for 6 hides. Always 2 ploughs in lordship. Then 3 men's ploughs, now 4. Then 7 villagers, now 8; then 3 smallholders, now 6; always 4 slaves.
> Woodland, 500 pigs; meadow, 50 acres; 2 fisheries. 9 cattle, 2 cobs, 27 pigs, 100 sheep.
> Value then £4; now 100s.
> From this manor, Peter of Valognes took away 1 hide and 8 acres of meadow which belonged to the manor before 1066, and woodland for 50 pigs. Value 10s.
> From the same manor, Geoffrey de Mandeville took 10 acres of meadow.

An entry for Great Waltham reads:

> Hundred of Chelmsford.
>
> Geoffrey holds (Great) WALTHAM in Lordship, which Asgar held as a manor, for 8 hides before 1066. Always 72 villagers; 28 smallholders. Then 14 slaves, now 13. Then 6 ploughs in lordship, now 5. Then among the men 42 ploughs, now 36.
> Woodland, 1200 pigs; meadow, 44 acres; always 2 mills; now 10 *arpents* of vines. Then 5 cobs, 12 cows, 50 pigs, 80 goats; now 3 cobs, 11 cows, 60 pigs, 132 sheep, 7 goats, 20 beehives. Value then £50; now [£] 60.
> Of this manor Hubert holds 1 virgate. ½ plough.
> Value 5s in the same assessment.
> Walter (holds) 1 virgate. ½ plough.
> Value 5s in the same assessment.

Thorkell (holds) 1 virgate.
2 smallholders. ½ plough.
Value 5s in the same assessment.
Walter (holds) 30 acres, Thorkell 30 acres and Hubert 30 acres.

It will be seen that both entries, as was standard in the survey, described the tenurial position as it was in the time of Edward the Confessor and the details and values of the resources of the manors at the time of the grant and at the Survey in 1086. Here we have an example, at Chingford, of a manor in ecclesiastical ownership from the time of Edward, and apart from minor alienations to Peter de Valognes and Geoffrey de Mandeville, confirmed by William I. It was to remain in the hands of the Dean and Chapter of St Paul's Cathedral until 1544, when it was acquired by Henry VIII. At Great Waltham Geoffrey de Mandeville, having dispossessed the luckless Asgar after 1066, counted the manor among his vast possessions in central Essex. Three tenants, Hubert, Thorkell, and Walter, held a mere virgate–30 acres–each.

Each of the two manors was occupied by a peasant population of unfree men– villeins, bordars, and serfs and their families, a common pattern throughout the county. Nothing, as the chronicler noted, was passed by. Pigs, sheep, goats, cattle, horses were all logged along with the plough-teams and an assessment of the capacity of the manor lands to support such domestic animals. Thus it was throughout the county. But there are several entries in the two I have selected that are of particular interest. At Chingford it will be noted there were recorded two fisheries. In fact, there were four others along the Lea in Chingford's other manor, that of Robert Gernon, and with six fisheries Chingford exceeded all other places in Essex in this respect including those along the Thames and on the coast. At Great Waltham there were noted 20 hives of bees and a vineyard. The latter crops up elsewhere in Essex in the survey on the manor lands at Castle Hedingham, Rayleigh and Pleshey, where they no doubt provided the wine for the lord and his household who lived in their castle homes on these estates. Bees were more important than perhaps at first sight may be thought. Sugar was scarce and ex- pensive and honey was a good substitute for sweetening and for making mead. The wax, too, was in demand for candles and for other domestic purposes. There were more than 600 hives on the demesne lands of the Essex manors in over 100 apiaries, mainly in the north of the county. The largest was at Shortgrove, but there were others of substantial size at Saffron Walden, Thaxted and Newport, as well as that noted at Great Waltham.

Throughout the other manors of Domesday Essex we read also of the mills, at this time water-driven, for windmills do not appear in Britain until the 13th century. There were at least 150 noted in the Domesday Survey of Essex particularly along the River Lea, and in more remote areas such as the Freshwell Hundred where there were four located in Bardfield and the Sampfords. Also recorded were the saltpans from which was produced that most useful commodity, and the wicks, a name that when it survives invariably denotes a dairy of medieval date. The overall picture of the county is of a largely undiluted agricultural community of peasant labourers and their families prising a precarious living from the lands they enjoyed at the price of their labour and subser- vience. Much of the county was still forest, but throughout the open lands arable farm- ing was the principal economic activity. Down in the marshlands there was pasturage for sheep in large numbers from which was obtained mutton, wool, milk and cheese. At

Southminster there were no less than 1,300 sheep in 1086, and at Fobbing seven hundred. But it was on the ox-plough that most of the population relied for their sustenance. In parish by parish we may see in Little Domesday this authentic and eloquent record of Essex rural life in Norman England. It is the most remarkable document of English history and even now, despite the assiduous attention of our greatest historians, has not yet surrendered all its secrets.

ဆဝလ

Before the Domesday Survey was completed William left England for Normandy. He never returned and within a year died at the age of sixty. He was succeeded by his third and favourite son, William II, who was to die in mysterious circumstances in the New Forest in August 1100. Although he inherited the Conqueror's dynamic energy, William Rufus had none of his father's moral stature or political genius. Profligate and uncouth, he dissipated the royal fortunes. In the absence of his elder brother, Robert, the Crown was seized after Rufus's death by the younger son of William I, who reigned as Henry I until 1135. During the vigorous administration of Henry I and under Stephen we may discern the beginnings of the English revival which was to gather further momentum under the Plantagenets. In Essex, however, Norman power was still paramount, and we find Geoffrey de Mandeville created Earl of Essex in 1140. In the following year he was appointed to the posts of justice, sheriff and escheator of Essex and by his marriage to one of the de Vere daughters he consolidated his great authority in the county. But as so often in medieval England, power was not easily shared between the Crown and the greater nobility. Accused of treason, de Mandeville was forced to yield his strongholds of Pleshey and Saffron Walden and flee with his supporters to the Isle of Ely to meet his death at Burwell in 1144.

In this brief chapter of Essex history we have surveyed the Norman achievement. Theirs was a period of strong and effective administration. Norman military authority and governmental capacity provided the impetus and stability that lifted England out of the doldrums that afflicted the declining years of the old Saxon dynasty. Harold, it is true, might have done much to re-invigorate English society, but he stood in the path of William's ambition. Under Norman rule England witnessed the growth of feudalism, the consolidation of the manorial system, the rising power of the church, and the spread of monasticism. The gulf between the Norman aristocracy and the English people was wide and must have seemed unbridgeable. Yet in the end the de Mandevilles, the de Veres, de Lucys and the other Essex magnates, along with their alien kith and kin in the remainder of the country, opted for English nationhood. All that is left is their massive and vigorous architecture and their names, anglicised and assimilated, as at Virley, Norton Mandeville, Belchamps Otton and Stapleford Tawney.

Chapter Four

꧁꧂

MEDIEVAL ESSEX

'John Ball hath rung your bell'

To attempt, as one must, within the scale of this book in a single chapter to traverse the history of the county between the Normans and the Tudors is a task of Sisyphean character. It is not only a lengthy period, but also complex and difficult. At the county level, only a few studies like those of the former county archivist, Kenneth Newton, who devoted his medieval scholarship in particular to Thaxted and Writtle, are available to lesser historians in groping into the depths of the complicated structure of society in that period and assessing the relationship of national events to the fabric of life in the countryside and minor urban communities. Yet we must look at the growth of institutions, still relevant to life today, to the evolution of society from feudal manorialism to corporate responsibility and the emergence of national as opposed to class and factional allegiances. Civil strife, Magna Carta and the advent of parliamentary life are conspicuous as the highlights of the political panorama of that turbulent age. Their implications were naturally of national significance, but among the villagers of Essex it was the impact of other major episodes such as the Black Death and the Peasants' Revolt that was most acute.

Aside from the few great landed families who still largely enjoyed their share of the inheritance of wealth, power and privilege bestowed on their ancestors after the Conquest and the 'new' county folk, the mass of the common people of Essex constituted the human ballast on which manorial life rested. Life for them, as was the common experience of medieval Europe, was burdened with disease, war and poverty. There had been a general acceptance in Essex of the situation following the Conquest and the peaceful life of the countryside centred on the manors. The focus of authority in these sparse rural communities was the manor house and the court where the lord, or his Steward, accepted the homage and services due to him from the peasantry in return for their enjoyment of the meagre resources and security offered by their servitude. The pattern of services, dues, tolls, heriots and reliefs varied from manor to manor according to local custom and the effectiveness of its administration by the manorial officials. It was not uniform; nor was it static, and it would be unsafe to assume that the manorial arrangements that may be apparent from the Court Rolls in one manor necessarily applied even in adjacent areas. The common thread was that of a relationship, heavily weighted in favour of the lord of the manor, of services and rewards between the servile classes and those in whom property, franchise and jurisdiction were vested. The changes that occurred between the advent of the Plantagenets at the beginning of the period and the demise of the Yorkist dynasty over 400 years later were of manifest significance. But the essential elements, in varying degree, were present throughout and exercised a definitive influence on the course of

26 *Reconstruction of a medieval farmstead at Stebbingford, Essex, by Peter Froste*

the history of the period. We shall now consider how, in the wider context of national events, Essex and its people were involved.

Topographically, the changes in the face of Britain that had been in train from the beginnings of settled community life gathered momentum in the medieval period. Each generation of cultivators made their contribution to the process of harnessing the resources of the forests and wastes to sustain the growing population. In Essex the clearances of the heavy forested claylands, begun by the Anglo Saxons, continued. The daily round of husbandry and the performance of manorial obligations was complemented by the gradual process of levelling, draining and clearing the vegetation of unproductive areas. These early Essex farmers won their lands from the forests and the marsh-ridden coastal fringes to create the fertile and contrived landscape we see today as we travel the county's roads and lanes, modified, it is true, in some places by the effects of later enclosure. Alongside this pioneering activity social and economic changes were modifying the status of man and his relationship to the land on which he toiled. The rise of the copyholder and other minor classes with a lawful tenurial stake in land was a manifestation of the breakdown of servile obligations, the development of a system of leases and the commutation of labour services. The laws of inheritance, which led to the fragmentation of large aristocratic holdings, added their influence to the growth of the classes that in the end were to create the social equilibrium that the

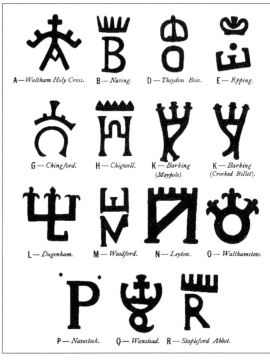

A—*Waltham Holy Cross.* B—*Nazing.* D—*Theydon Bois.* E—*Epping.*

G—*Chingford.* H—*Chigwell.* K—*Barking (Maypole).* K—*Barking (Crooked Billet).*

L—*Dagenham.* M—*Woodford.* N—*Leyton.* O—*Walthamstow.*

P—*Navestock.* Q—*Wanstead.* R—*Stapleford Abbot.*

27 *Epping Forest cattle markings*

peace and progress of the nation as a whole demanded. It was to be a long process, punctuated by events that made a dramatic impact on the minds of the people and were of major importance in the story of the county. But before resuming the historical narrative with which I have to connect the themes of this book I should like first to devote a little space to the subject of the forests which is of much importance to the county history of Essex, especially in the period with which this chapter is concerned.

৪୦C୪

I shall not attempt here to repeat the broad general history of the Forest of Essex to which I devoted much of a chapter in *Discovering Essex in London.* But the significance of the forest terrain and the jurisdictional and social influences of the forest laws to the pattern of life in medieval Essex was such that some reference is required. As I have indicated, forest and fen, marsh and moor were retreating as the efforts of man to enhance the quality of his family life rolled forward the frontiers of human environments. Yet, after several thousand years of endeavour, the sparse population and limited technical resources had left most of the country still in a wild state. In Essex the countryside was, on the whole, still fairly thickly wooded, the claylands in particular offering hospitality to oak, elm and hornbeam, whose roots flourish in the warm, moist earth of a county which, climatically, is one of the low-rainfall areas of the island on which we live. But the encroachment of locally powerful men, anxious to enlarge their estates, the illegal assarts of humbler folk, and the ravages of civil war made marked inroads into the woodlands of the county. It is important to recognise, however, that forest law, which circumscribed much of the freedom to which the common man was beginning to aspire, was not restricted in its application to forest land as that would be commonly understood today. The areas of afforestation to which the jurisdiction of the forest courts extended was a matter of legal and not topographical definition and thus the cause of much litigation, resentment and violent dispute. The destruction of the trees might well be tolerated, even necessary, but the maintenance in law of the afforested areas was another matter and one that engaged the interests of the Crown, the nobility and peasantry alike. It was not until 1543, when Henry VIII's Act for the Preservation of the Woods was enacted, that conservation of the trees for economic purposes, in that case shipbuilding, became a significant feature of forest policy. Prior to that the issue of policy centred on jurisdiction, revenue, and the sporting facilities offered by the presence of game that was jealously safeguarded in the royal interest by the forest officials and the authority of the forest courts.

The whole subject of forest law and jurisdiction in medieval England, vestiges of which still remain, is one of much complexity, but of infinite interest. The nomenclature of the courts of the Chief Justice in Eyre, of Swainmote and Woodmote has an antiquarian flavour and appeal, but they existed for serious and important social purposes. They were concerned not only with the preservation of privileges, but also the control of the common rights, which usually of a customary nature tended to vary from place to place, and were similarly endowed with a terminology that is at once esoteric and engaging. In the records of the forest courts of Essex are the cases relating to the common rights of estovers, turbary

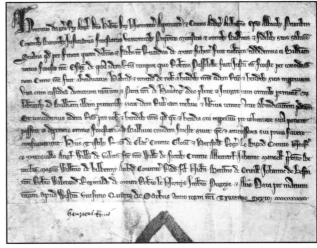

28 *Grant to Richard De Munfichett of the Forest of Essex, in 1252*

and piscary, which allowed those enjoying the privilege to take wood and turf for fuel and building and other domestic purposes, as well as fish for the table. A whole range of special and private franchises also grew up alongside the general pattern of common rights. These resulted from royal indulgences granted from time to time in recognition of services or special duties. An interesting case in point was the right exercised by the monastic community at Wix to maintain a pack of harriers to hunt hares within the Forest of Essex for the benefit of their sick brethren and paupers.

While the minor forest courts confronted the Essex poacher with the full rigour of the law, at a higher level the maintenance of their jurisdiction over forest land and the preservation of 'vert and venison' occupied the forest eyre, the Steward of the Forest and, as occasion demanded, special commissions appointed by the Crown. The delineation of the afforested areas was definitive and therefore the cause of much dispute and manipulation. One Essex case of the 13th century provides a good example. A deer, clearly having escaped from the royal forest and found drowned in the Thames, was taken away by one John Staf of East Tilbury. This led to his arraignment by the Steward of the Forest, Nicholas Sifrewast, before the forest court. But on examining the evidence the justices declared that no offence arose as the animal had been found beyond the limits of the afforested area. Whether a parish was 'within' or 'without' the forest thus had considerable practical significance for the villagers who necessarily relied on the natural produce of the land for their staple needs. This was, therefore, a matter of fundamental importance for the social order of Essex of which vast areas–at one time almost the whole county–were for the purposes of legal jurisdiction 'within forest'. The perambulations of 1225 that followed the Forest Charter of 1217 resulted in most of the county being relieved from forest jurisdiction, but as the fortunes of the Crown fluctuated the pattern changed. By 1228 the position was reversed and the venison inquisitions for the county of 1238-40 show that as far north as Colchester and the marginal lands along the Stour forest law prevailed. By the early 14th century the position had changed again. Such was the interplay of power and privilege in a society still unable to define its values in any more rational terms.

The legal armoury of the medieval forest authorities was not simply confined to the vigilance of their officials and the forest courts, for at one time special forest prisons were provided to reinforce the apparatus of the law, or to confine accused persons pending their appearance before the justices. A number of such special prisons is known to have been built in the 12th century, and one at Writtle in Essex is believed to have been originally provided for that purpose. But such custodial facilities were never universally available and the subject has never been fully researched. Nor is it clear what obligation rested on the county gaols to receive forest offenders, although in 1236 the Constable of Colchester Castle was charged to do so by the forest authorities. Thus we may see that for the people of Essex the forest was a feature not merely of the landscape but of the essential fabric of their daily lives.

℅℃

To the Essex peasantry nothing could have seemed more final than the Norman usurpation. Yet already during the reign of Henry I the first signs of the English revival could be detected. Thereafter followed a period of confused dynastic conflict and by the middle of the 12th century the perspective of history now reveals that the assertion of freedom was inherent in the incipient development of new secular and religious attitudes. The train of events that led to the Peasants' Revolt in Essex and the evolution of the religious basis of our society through Lollardism, the Reformation, Puritanism, and Nonconformity, was already in motion.

At Henry I's death in 1135 he had nominated Matilda, the wife of Geoffrey Plantagenet, Count of Anjou, as his successor, but for the ruling classes in which effective power resided the time had not yet come, as it did thrice in the 16th century, when the Crown could be entrusted to female hands. The Council therefore opted for Henry's nephew, Stephen of Blois, grandson of the Conqueror, and thus precipitated a civil war in which Essex was deeply involved and which ravaged the land for eight terrible and fruitless years. Stephen, though brave, was hardly of a calibre to cope with the anarchy that now settled on the country or the power of the magnates, like the formidable Geoffrey de Mandeville, who from their fortified estates dominated and desolated the land. de Mandeville, who had allied himself, through marriage, with that other great Essex family, the powerful de Veres, was in a strong position. His power based on the Tower of London, of which he was Constable, and the strength of his fortresses at Pleshey and Walden in Essex placed him beyond the control of royal authority. Matilda's invasion was launched in 1139 and de Mandeville was sufficiently independent and unscrupulous to change sides to his personal advantage whenever the tide of events made it propitious to do so. He deserted Stephen, who in 1141 had created him the first of the Earls of Essex, but a few years later he paid for his infidelity and the destruction he had caused. Arrested and charged with treason he forfeited his castles and lands in Essex. He was lucky to avoid execution, and after his escape from custody he took refuge in his old homelands in the Isle of Ely, but was killed in 1144.

It was the moral leadership of the church and the general desire for stability and order that rescued England from the anguish of outrage, perfidy and political squalor to which the struggle between the rival claimants had reduced the kingdom. The accession of the resolute, if restless and sometimes reckless genius, Henry II, held out the promise of an end to disorder and malpractice. The Angevin dominions he inherited ranged from Gascony through England to the frontiers of Ulster and Connaught. Apart from this able and effective monarch, one of the most dramatic personalities of English history, whose features are portrayed in a window-splay in the lovely old Essex church at Hadleigh, appeared on the political scene with fatal consequences—Thomas Becket 'the woodchopper'. This man, of humble birth, became Henry's friend and counsellor. The retirement of the aged and ailing Archbishop Theobald led to Becket's appointment, first as Chancellor of the Realm, and then, at Theobald's death, to the Primacy of England. But Becket at court was one thing; the pre-destined martyr at Canterbury was another. From the outset his bid for supremacy brought him into direct conflict with the King to whose will he was no longer amenable. His enforced exile in France ended in reconciliation with Henry in 1170, but the final drama was not long deferred.

In the Harleian manuscripts and in a painting by Matthew Paris there are vivid portrayals of the act that horrified Christendom when the Archbishop was struck down by the swords of Reginald Fitzurse and his accomplices before the altar at Canterbury. The home of one of the malefactors, Richard Brito, was Barton Hall, which lay on the broad estuarine lands by the Roach at Great Stambridge, where the enormity of the evil deed must have shocked even that remote area of the county. Henry's penance averted the worst consequences for his personal position, though his life was to end in the bitter circumstances of revolt and the intrigue of his own son, Richard of Aquitaine. But we should remember his achievements in the fields of government and legal reform. From the chaos of Stephen's reign Henry's genius for administration was to create new standards of efficiency and enhance the supremacy of the Crown. He was energetic, too, in ruling his kingdom. In those times the government, to the personal cost of the governed, was itinerant, and it is known that in May 1157 Henry II, with all the apparatus of his court and administration, was at Colchester. There the loyal, if reluctant, citizens would have been required to offer lodging and hospitality to the considerable retinue that the royal itinerary demanded. Contemporary records refer to the response of the burghers and the encampment the royal troops set up in the fields beyond the walls of the old Roman city.

It is ironical that Richard, Henry's dashing, but unscrupulous son, should have secured such a glamorous image in the folklore of our history. Perhaps that was inevitable. The father carried the burden of an Archbishop's martyrdom; the son challenged the infidels whose minatory banners fluttered in the tornado of religious fanaticism that erupted in the Middle East. But his subjects in Essex can hardly have been whole-hearted supporters of a policy that deprived them of their king as well as their wealth, for, until Richard's accession, England had played no part in that remote conflict for the souls of mankind. The crusades, however, have, as elsewhere, left minor marks on the topography of the county and the tombs of these adventurers are still exhibited with pride in some parish churches. It was expedient, too, for the knights of the Crusades to be endowed by the Crown and the nobility. Thus William de Ferrers, lord of the manor of Stebbing, granted the advowson and the great tithes of the church to the Knights Hospitaller. His grandson, Robert, was among those killed crusading with Richard in the Holy Land. Further misfortune was to befall the family when they cast their lot against the king in the Barons' War to which we shall come later in this chapter. We may also note the Knights Templar and Hospitaller of the Order of St John ensconced on their estates in Essex.

29 *Medieval barn at Cressing Temple*

The Hospitallers are first noted in Essex at Chrishall in *c.*1125 and more land grants were made to the Order in Essex than in any other county; almost 600 in all. Before the end of the 12th century they had received large grants in the area of Bumpstead and the Sampfords. When the Knights Templar, who had held the Cressing estate since its bestowal by Queen Matilda in 1137, were dissolved in 1312, their properties were transferred to the Hospitallers and included the Templars' important preceptory at Cressing.

The magnificent medieval barns at Cressing Temple and the little round church at Little Maplestead in which the Hospitallers offered their prayers for the success of the Crusades for two centuries are symbols of that noble but ill-managed episode of western civilisation. Its practical impact in England was fiscal and constitutional, for Richard's disinterest in the fortunes of his English domains strengthened the institutions of representative government; and signalled the ultimate withdrawal from continental entanglements. But all this had little contemporary significance for the ordinary people of Essex—except that they were poorer for it, and worse was to come.

ঙ০ঙ

Richard, Coeur de Lion, was followed, in 1199, by John, the sixth and youngest son of Henry Plantagenet. The verdict of historians and his contemporaries on this virile, able, but dishonourable and insolent sovereign, although tending now to be modified, has generally been harsh and largely unmitigated. The memory of his reign is of desperate civil strife, disaffection and despoliation—its monument, Magna Carta, has assumed, as our constitutional history has evolved, its central role as the symbol of English political liberties.

The nobility of Essex were closely concerned in the events surrounding that historic landmark in our national story. Following a secret gathering of the barons, including several from their great Essex estates, at Bury St Edmunds in 1215, they offered violence to the King. London and the church under Stephen Langton threw their decisive weight into the issue on the side of the barons. Led by Robert FitzWalter, lord of Dunmow in Essex, and styled by his now invincible followers 'Marshal of the Army of God and Holy Church', the demands laid before the King by the

30   *The Round Church, Little Maplestead*

barons at Runnymede in June were irresistible. Under duress and in ill-faith the King sealed the Great Charter that was published and formally sworn in the hundred and town-motes in Essex and throughout the land by royal proclamation. But John, outraged and deserted, had by no means conceded defeat, and as he signed his cynical and defiant mind was already contemplating the further trial of strength upon which he had determined to embark.

The Charter itself contained over 60 clauses, a pragmatic recital of past injustices and fundamental human rights as befitted the most celebrated document in English constitutional history. Among the 24 elected executors charged with upholding the Charter were the third Earl of Oxford, Robert de Vere of Castle Hedingham, John FitzRobert of Clavering Castle, Richard de Mountfitchet of Stansted, William de Lanvallei of Colchester, Gilbert de Clare, and, of course, FitzWalter. The prominence of these Essex men obviously put the county in the forefront of the struggle. Before the year was out John had rallied his forces and other foreign mercenaries to his cause and marched against the rebellious barons. At first his undoubted military talents brought some success. Philip, King of France, in support of the barons had landed some 7,000 troops at Orwell on the Stour in November 1215, some of whom garrisoned Colchester Castle. Meanwhile, John was besieging Rochester, and it was not until January 1216 that Colchester was invested and eventually forced to surrender to the King in person. At Pleshey, Geoffrey de Mandeville was also under siege by a detachment of the King's forces led by Savaric de Mauléon and the Earl of Salisbury. Castle Hedingham was captured, and Tilty Abbey desecrated by John's foreign

31   *The Fitzwalter seal*

mercenaries, who laid waste the county, exacting tribute where they could as the bitter fighting continued. At the end of May Prince Louis of France himself landed in England to grapple with the excommunicated king. The destruction of homes, churches, crops and forests in Essex and East Anglia continued, and the county for long bore the terrible marks of this wanton strife.

Final disaster, when the fortunes of war had already turned against him, struck the King when making a forced crossing of the Welland on the flood tide, and his train was lost in the waters of the Wash. John, harassed and sick with dysentery, was borne to Newark by his remaining supporters to die on the night of 18/19 October 1216. So ended the personal tragedy of his reign. He had begun by losing the Angevin Empire he had inherited, and through perfidy and rapacity he brought himself into fatal conflict with the nobility of England and the Papacy. His dynamic energy and cunning ability were not enough to sustain him on such a disastrous course. After his death the rebel magnates, including Robert de Vere, who recovered his estate at Hedingham, were restored to their former power. A year later the de Veres would be found campaigning with Edward III in Scotland and among the ranks of the English at Crécy and Calais. Such were the fluctuating fortunes and loyalties of this confused and violent era of English history. Life for the peasant population of the county was hard and insecure. The time, politically, to exert themselves had still to come. The interfaces of political and dynastic rivalry did not yet extend to the affairs and interests of the people at large. In Essex, the clay on which they lived was still the most important ingredient in their daily lives. The epitaph on this chapter of the nation's story may be taken from the writings of Robert Davenport. FitzWalter, the leader of the barons, whose name is now inscribed indelibly in the annals of England and Essex, is believed to have been buried at Little Dunmow. In a reference to that Essex priory and King John, FitzWalter, in Davenport's words, proclaims, 'weep, weep there pay your sacrifice'.

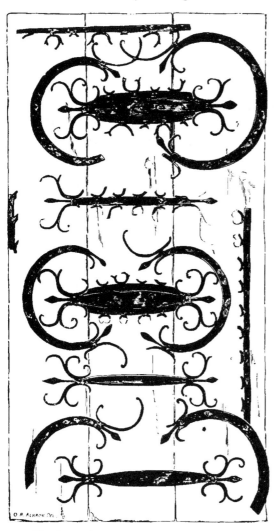

32 *Ironwork at Eastwood Church, near Rochford.*

രാൽ

One of the main features of the medieval period was the growth of church life

33   *The Bell Tower at Barking Abbey*

and monasticism. Important, too, were the changes in the balance of power between the baronage and the Crown. Throughout the country the tangible symbols of these developments are visible in the parish churches and the extensive remains of the religious houses and the baronial strongholds. It was an age when churches, monasteries, priories, and abbeys, castles and estates were built and created as the wealth and influence of these major elements of English society prospered. Barking Abbey, with its royal patronage, continued to exercise considerable authority throughout Essex. The Abbess enjoyed precedence among all others of that rank in England and in consequence exercised powers and rights comparable with those of a feudal magnate. It was a high profile post; even Henry I's Queen, Maud, was Abbess for a time. Premier families in the county like the Tyrells of Little Warley, the Fitzlewes of West Horndon and the Suttons of Wivenhoe placed their daughters at the Abbey. With its considerable resources, landed property and social connections it was a centre of power and influence in medieval Essex.

The splendour of such Benedictine houses and their glorious ritual was succeeded by the simple pious regimes of the Cistercians, who established their first house at Waverley in 1128. The interplay of interest between the nobility and the church was evidenced by the endowment, from varying motives, of further houses. Tilty was created about 1153 by Maurice FitzGeoffrey, who endowed his foundation with land for its support. Stephen and Maud established the Cistercians at Coggeshall in *c.*1140, and

34   *Thaxted Church, c.1760*

the great Thames-side abbey at Stratford Langthorne was endowed in 1135 by William de Monfichet. The Austin Canons, too, enjoyed the patronage of the great lay families and the Black Canons were endowed at Bicknacre in 1147. The Knights Templar and Hospitaller, described by Dr. Reaney as 'half-soldiers, half-priests', I have already mentioned. Founded to sustain the pilgrims and the Holy Places and pledged to chastity, poverty and obedience, they possessed considerable properties in Essex. The Templars went to Cressing in 1136 and the Hospitallers were at Little Maplestead 50 years later. At Beeleigh, Prittlewell, Wix, Waltham, and St Osyth is still the evidence of this massive religious effort.

The medieval heritage of the parish churches of Essex glorifies the towns and villages of the whole county. Nowhere is one far from some priceless vestige of that most prolific and inspired age of architectural achievement. Apart from isolated examples, as at Berden and Good Easter, there is little significant structural work of the 13th century in the churches of the county. But with the development from the 14th century of the Decorated and Perpendicular phases of the Gothic style the churches of Essex enjoy their full share of the most outstanding period of English ecclesiastical architecture. Of the Decorated style Lawford is the supreme and consummate example of artistry and conception. The great and exhilarating Perpendicular edifices at Thaxted and Saffron Walden need no further recommendation from me. They have been amply described by more competent observers than I. Essex is the county of timber building, and I must mention in passing the fine and important originality of the hammerbeam roof at Tendring and the matchless framed tower-belfries of Blackmore and Navestock.

Of significance in the inventory of medieval church ornaments are the oaken effigies (*c.*1400) of Knights at Danbury, the FitzRalph brass (*c.*1323) at Pebmarsh and the rare and wonderfully decorated 13th-

35   *Virgin and Child at St Mary's, Great Canfield*

36 *The 13th-century chest in Newport Church*

century altar chest at Newport. Nor can I
omit to re-assert what I have written elsewhere, that in my view the exquisite 13th-
century mural of the Virgin and Child
above the altar of St Mary's at Great
Canfield is the most beautiful example of
the visual arts of any period to be found
anywhere in the county. I would rank it
with the Armada Jewel and Constable's
view of Dedham Vale, both of which have
special significance for Essex.

The castles of Essex bear witness to
the growth of the power of the baronial
families. Their role in the struggle with John
has already been described. Colchester, after his death, remained in the gift of the
Crown until it was finally alienated in 1629.
The baronial castles like those at
Hedingham, Walden, Pleshey, Rayleigh
and Clavering continued as centres of
political manorial power until they eventually passed into royal ownership, decayed,
or were pillaged, like Hadleigh, for building materials in a later age. When John
died, his nine-year-old son, Henry III, inherited a kingdom in which castles and the
great and simple parish churches symbolised the major social forces of his long and
eventful reign. We may still see this tangible reminder of the 13th and subsequent
medieval centuries on the face of Essex

37 *Brass of Sir William FitzRalph in Pebmarsh Church*

today. Collectively they represent, apart from the geography of the land itself, one of the most emphatic aspects of topographical evidence for the history of the county. In this aspect they may be compared with the town and country houses of the 16th to 18th centuries and the urban conglomerations and communications of the modern period.

৪০০৪

During his minority the affairs of Henry's realm rested, after the death of the Earl Marshal, in the hands of Hubert de Burgh. Henry, though often prone to foreign influence, nevertheless achieved during his long kingship of 56 years, and despite the tribulations of the Barons' War, a significant measure of consolidation and stability after the political and economic legacy of his father's ruin. He lived in a time when the builders of the great cathedrals defied the limited technical resources at their disposal with an inspired courage that still thrills us today. But as with his father, the light of Henry's outstanding monarchy was to be extinguished in conflict. In the struggle with Simon de Montfort, despite Henry's triumph at Evesham in 1265, his hour had passed and it was with Edward I that the fortunes of England rested. The people of Essex, when Henry mounted his successful threat to the rebels in London from his headquarters at Stratford Langthorne, had glimpsed the posturing of a conflict with which they were hardly concerned. Much the same was true of the political and military aspects of the reign of the three Edwards who succeeded him. The implications of the conquests of Wales and Scotland were beyond the horizons of Essex folk, although they would ultimately benefit from the judicial and administrative reforms of the period. In the hamlets and villages of the county life was still determined by the constraints and requirements of manorial privilege and custom. The proud pennants of English chivalry as the King's forces harassed their Welsh and Scottish victims symbolised nothing for the majority of the people of Essex. The pursuit of dynastic ambition had less relevance to their lives than the pervading presence of the church and such archaic manorial rights as they enjoyed. As, for example at Borley, where the village labourer received from the lord of the manor, in return for loading his hay, a measure of wheat, small portions of butter, milk, cheese and other basic edibles and 'as much hay as each man could lift on the point of his scythe'. Such was the nature of village society in an age that we still more readily associate with the heraldic devices and genealogy of the great, the miracles of Gothic architecture, and the futile campaigning of feudal armies. There were, however, two major episodes in this age, both of considerable national consequence, in which the county, too, was greatly concerned, and from which perhaps no family in Essex was immune: the Black Death and the Peasants' Revolt.

At the time of the Black Death England was still under-populated despite the growth of numerous small urban communities and the clearance of previously wooded terrain. Research suggests that mortality during the Black Death, though of serious proportions, was not as catastrophic nationally as has for long been believed. Estimates of the loss of a third of the population of about four million are now thought to be grossly inflated. A proportion of between five and 10 per cent might be more realistic. That, in all conscience, was a national disaster, and there is evidence of the uneven incidence of the pestilence that raged during 1348/9 with appalling results in certain localities. The plague was first reported in London at the end of September 1348 and flared unabated throughout the winter to the late spring of the following year. It appears to have spread to London from the southern counties and soon extended its fatal grip to Essex and East Anglia and beyond to the Midlands and Wales. It was more than three years before it receded from the lives of the afflicted and by then had decimated the population of England. The subsequent outbreaks during the period 1356-69 were intermittent and of less intensity.

Much of the evidence for the effects of the Black Death in Essex still remains to be retrieved from the county archives and evaluated in the context of the mass of ecclesiastical and manorial records that may throw light on the various aspects of the social conditions that prevailed at the time. We have but a partial picture and some of the vital knowledge will never be recovered. If, as we might assume, the current assessments of the national situation are valid, the local evidence for Essex suggests that the people of the county, as did those in London, suffered more severely than others in more distant parts of the country. This would be a reasonable inference from the geographical considerations alone, but the disparity may have been much greater than I certainly would previously have supposed. The diocesan registers, which record the vacancies in benefices throughout the county, and the measures taken to remedy the situation that resulted from the loss of many clergy, victims of the plague in that ghastly winter, illustrate the severity of the outbreak. The clergy, it is true, might well, since their pastoral duties would have made them more vulnerable than most as they exposed themselves to infection in ministering to their parishioners, have suffered unduly. But the manorial records, too, provide further evidence for the view that Essex was, in general, sorely stricken by the rat-borne plague that had originated in continental Europe.

K.C. Newton has stated that in the first outbreak in the manor of Fingrith Hall, Blackmore, almost 90 per cent of the landholders were affected. It is recorded in Moulsham no rents were received from 31 tenements because the tenants were dead and that local works had been abandoned for lack of labour. Whereas there were 240 tithing men in Great Waltham in 1328 there were only 131 in 1400, a manifestation of the loss of population caused by the Black Death in a parish in central Essex. The court rolls at Great Canfield, Birdbrook, the Rodings, and at Wickham Bishops also reveal the same grim picture of high mortality. The prevalence of heirs in their infancy illustrates vividly the impact on family and community life that must have resulted from the death of young parents and elder children. The disruption that must have occurred when, as clearly happened, whole families were lost with consequent fragmentation of their inheritance can be imagined, although we have no precise picture on which to base a considered historical evaluation.

What general conclusions then should be drawn, albeit with some reservations, from the patchwork of documentary and circumstantial evidence that has so far been recovered? The county bore, with other hard-hit areas in the south-east, the brunt of the tragedy and although there is, on the barest evidence, some reason to think that the economic recovery was comparatively swift, its social effects were of a far-reaching and permanent character. But it is of its human aspects that we can speak more confidently and with a more sympathetic understanding about the effects of the deadly disease from which so many people of the county perished. It brought grief, fear or despair into every home in every village of Essex. We must see the years of the Black Death as among the darkest episodes in the county's story. Not since the Norman Conquest had fate laid its remorseless hands so heavily on the whole population or so profoundly disturbed the tenor and pattern of private life. Of that we may be quite sure; and history is as much concerned with such as with anything else.

৪০৫৪

If the role of Essex during the Black Death was necessarily passive, the reverse was the case in the next major event I shall describe in the county's history during its medieval period. In 1381 the protesting villagers from the Thames-side communities of the county ignited a revolt, the embers of which still glow, faintly, but unmistakably, across the intervening gulf of 600 years of political and social evolution. Not since the Boudiccan rising of A.D. 60-61 had there been a general insurrection in which the common people had been so closely involved. Then, as in 1381, the causes were, as Rudyard Kipling so perceptively identified them with the national character in his evocative verse, rooted in a sense of injustice. It was not principally economic factors that lay behind this ugly episode, as would appear from the immediate issue that sparked off the rebellion. Indeed, in Kent and Essex, which were the main centres of the trouble, there is good evidence to show that in economic terms the peasantry were better placed than elsewhere. The cry 'John Ball hath rung your bell . . .' was more basic than that. It was concerned with the dignity of human personality and the respect for fundamental freedoms; not taxation.

The attack on the Tax Commissioner and John Bampton, an Essex J.P. by the peasants and fisherfolk of the south Essex villages of Fobbing, Corringham and Stanford-le-Hope at Brentwood on 30 May 1381 was the focus of the discontent that was prevalent in the county. In the previous November Parliament had imposed a new poll tax of three groats on everyone over 15, apart from paupers, which not surprisingly, resulted in much evasion in which local officials were themselves implicated. The false returns received in London resulted in a new tax census which occasioned the unfortunate Commissioner's visit to Brentwood, where he was to reassess the return for the Barstable Hundred. The blunt and insolent refusal of the men of Fobbing to co-operate led to an outbreak of premeditated violence when Bampton rashly ordered the King's sergeants-at-arms to arrest the spokesman. The Commissioner and his men, lucky to escape from the incensed mob with their lives, fled to report the incident to the Council in London. Undeterred and still ignorant of the true situation, the authorities made further attempts to enforce the tax and apprehend those involved in the riot. Sir Robert Belknap, the Chief Justice of the Common Pleas himself was commissioned to bring them to justice. But at Brentwood on 2 June he and his retinue were also molested by the still recalcitrant villagers. The court was wrecked and its papers seized and destroyed. The fracas developed to the point of murderous violence. Three local jurors were taken and beheaded by the rioters, after which the situation deteriorated still further and serious disorder spread throughout the county.

Meanwhile, rioting had occurred in Kent and the rebellious groups in the two counties, by now in coalition, rallied the countryside to their support. After releasing John Ball, the Colchester priest, who was one of the principal leaders of the rebellion, from the Bishop's gaol at Maidstone, they marched on London. There the well-known events leading up to the pillage and arson that ended with the death of Wat Tyler at the hands of the Lord Mayor and King Richard's brave but perfidious intervention took place.

In Essex manor houses were attacked and the court rolls burned as they were also at Chelmsford and Braintree and other towns in Essex. The disaffected agricultural workers plundered the sheriff's house at Coggeshall. John Ewell, Escheator of Essex, was murdered. The houses of the justices and unpopular lords of the manor were pillaged. Colchester was taken over by the rampaging peasant mob. There was a concerted attack, joined by the rebels from Fobbing, on the house of Sir Robert Hales, the King's treasurer and a prior of the order of St John of Jerusalem at Cressing Temple. Even the religious houses were defiled and did not escape the wrath of the marauders. In many cases landlords, lay and ecclesiastical, were forced to concede leases and charters favourable to the landless rebels and to deliver estate records to the insurgents for destruction. There is even some evidence that local clergy, sympathetic to the rebellious villagers, were implicated. But apart from John Ball, who was in London with the main rebel forces, the most prominent persons in Essex appear to have been Henry Baker of Manningtree, Thomas Baker of Fobbing, who instigated the first riots, and Thomas Faringdon.

The situation was brought under control when the initiative passed to the government after the dramatic events at Smithfield and Mile End. Peace was restored in London, and for Essex severe retribution was to follow. The leaders of the revolt, including John Starlyng, an Essex labourer, who was said to have murdered Archbishop Sudbury, were beheaded. Faringdon was lucky to suffer imprisonment and eventual release. John Ball was executed at St Albans. But the countryside remained to be subdued. Richard, the young King, rode into Essex at the head of a large force and at Waltham he retracted the promises of guaranteed freedoms he had made to the rebellious gathering at Mile End on 14 June. The force of the insurrection in the county, however, was not yet spent, and after dispersing, in anger and disappointment, from Waltham, the Essex rebels reassembled at Billericay, Rettenden and Great Baddow, where they prepared to continue their resistance. The King's forces, under the command of his uncle, Thomas of Woodstock, and Sir Thomas Percy, had little difficulty in overthrowing the rudimentary defences of the rebel groups. In one engagement many hundreds were killed and captured. The remnants fled to continue the struggle from Colchester. But, receiving little support from the townspeople, they retreated to be routed over the county border at Sudbury by FitzWalter and Sir John Harlestone, loyal supporters of the Crown.

Richard entered Chelmsford on 2 July when he issued a proclamation formally revoking all the pledges he had made. Many of the Essex rebels went to the King and his court at Havering to seek mercy and pardon, but the leaders were tried and executed. Others forfeited their personal belongings. Thereafter, judicial inquiries, led by the Chief Justice, Sir Robert Tresilian, were held throughout the county to complete the process of retribution. Relevant records, post-dating the revolt, show that, as was to be expected, it was accompanied by localised lawlessness of a more general character. An order to the Sheriff of Essex, made at Westminster on 18 October 1381 to investigate and, if appropriate, rectify the unlawful possession of three cottages owned by a John Lependen of Dunmow, referred to 'enemies who rose in the late insurrection'. It went on to assert 'that things so done in time of that disturbance are of none effect'.

Another painful and significant episode in county history came to an end, although local agitation, with some success, continued from time to time into the 15th century against manorial servitudes, especially in the area of the forest parishes around Epping. Indeed, despite the vigour with which Richard's officials reasserted the authority of government, it was never possible wholly to restore the manorial arrangements to their former state, although the customary powers remained strong. The process that was to end in the emancipation of the depressed peasant classes, although not then rewarded with conspicuous success, had become irreversible. Essex had been in the forefront of the issue.

೮೮೮

Throughout the several centuries of the Middle Ages we have been considering in an Essex setting, England was slowly evolving to the point where, soon, the historian can now see the beginnings of a new era that ended only with the development of modern technology in the19th century. I have described the impact on Essex of the Conquest and the cohesion that the unified and authoritarian administration of the Norman period produced. Such are the nodal points of history; they may be military, political, or economic. In this all too brief appraisal of Medieval Essex we have touched but lightly on the changes that were taking place and the major events, such as the Black Death and the Peasants' Revolt, that gave added impetus to the process, or, like the insurrection, were also symptomatic of it. The age was to experience at least two other such examples of historically important factors, the continental campaigns of the English kings and the Wars of the Roses that we have yet to note.

But it is convenient at this point to consider briefly the picture presented by the changing face of Essex, in town and countryside, in its social and economic aspects. In the previous chapter I have remarked that in the Domesday Survey only two places in Essex, Colchester and Maldon, enjoyed the description of borough status. During the medieval period economic factors led to the growth of many small rural or coastal villages which today are familiar as the towns of Essex. The stability created by the Conquest was favourable to trade, and flourishing markets grew up in a number of places. By the mid-14th century there were more than 70 licensed in Essex. Economic life was also stimulated by the wealth and power of the monastic communities we have already noted. Until towards the end of the 12th century town charters were rarely obtained but, later, boroughs like Harwich in 1319 were accorded by royal warrant special trading rights, and a limited measure of local self-government. Maldon was chartered in 1171 during the reign of Henry II. The Empress Matilda granted Geoffrey II de Mandeville a charter in 1141 which resulted in the transfer of the market in the royal manor of Newport to Walden (later Saffron Walden) and local roads were diverted to serve the new market which had been established in the grounds of the castle. The town charter, which among other privileges confirmed the free status of Walden burgesses and the market rights, was obtained some time between 1299 and 1322. Special rights in the river Colne, which led to the development of the oyster cultivation industry, were secured by Colchester from Richard I. With the parallel development of market rights and parliamentary representation the growth of small and locally powerful towns became a feature of the age. Privileged townspeople called burgesses appeared in towns throughout Essex such as Thaxted, Harwich, Manningtree and Writtle. Witham had become a market centre by 1147. Maldon, already a minor port handling coal, lime and building materials, developed a market function also. Chelmsford, too, was a market town by 1200.

By the 13th century Essex farmers and the monastic houses had been exporting wool to the continent, mainly Flanders and Italy. But following the measures taken by

Edward III in 1336 in prohibiting such exports in order to foster the cloth trade at home, towns such as Colchester, Coggeshall, Dedham and Braintree began to assume a wider economic role in the life of the county. The restored market-house at Horndon-on-the-Hill symbolises the wealth that the wool and agricultural markets generated in hitherto small and insignificant rural settlements. The splendid timbered house of *c.*1500, that a wealthy clothier gave to his son, Thomas Paycocke, at Coggeshall as a wedding present, graces not merely that now over-used western entry into the town, but epitomises the wealth, and taste, that the new merchant classes

38   *Paycockes, Coggeshall*

enjoyed. The most famous of all timber-framed civic buildings of Essex, the Guildhall at Thaxted, where an important local cutlery industry of which we know all too little flourished, is similarly symbolic of the changing economic and social scene. The cutlery industry almost certainly established the claim of that charming Essex town to borough status. Chelmsford, with the advantage of its geographical position in the centre of the county on the Chelmer and astride the axial land communications of Essex, was also developing its administrative role. The decline which checked economic growth later in

39   *Guildhall and town scene at Thaxted, 19th century*

the 16th century, due largely to political factors, did not materially alter the balance of power between town and country that the rise of these towns had created.

The political significance of these developments was that previously local author-ity–political and economic–had normally resided in personal franchises conferred by the Crown. By the 13th century there began to emerge a pattern of local powers, granted in corporate terms not only by the King but by the landed nobility who entered into such arrangements with the burghers of the influential commercial classes in the smaller towns on their estates which gained a consequential degree of independence from the manor. The social significance of this liberation from personal authority, together with the move-ment towards agrarian freedom in the countryside, will be readily apparent. Readers interested in the practical causes and effects of this development in local relationships in Essex should turn to K.C. Newton's erudite and important analysis of the situation in his book on medieval Thaxted which I have listed in the reference note.

In the countryside there was no marked change in the techniques of husbandry and the general pattern of agricultural practice. But underlying developments of social and economic importance were eroding the fundamental characteristics of manorial life. The commutation of labour services, one of the essential elements of the system, gathered force and the surviving manorial records show how economic and social pressures slowly forced the lords of the manor and estate holders to hire the men that farmed the demesne lands formerly worked by villein labour. The stewards' accounts contain the minutiae–payments for reaping, weeding and ploughing for a few pence an acre at rising rates as free labourers asserted the power that scarcity conferred on them–of basic social change of historic importance. Of course, as the court rolls will reveal, much of the apparatus of the feudal system remained, and in the 15th century there was even some revival of the powers of the manorial courts in some places, but by the end of the period villeinage was at an end. Labour shortage, rising wages, the Black Death, and the Revolt had all combined with the natural aspirations of the peasantry to accel-erate the process of emancipation. Essex, along with the rest of the kingdom, was moving from its feudal condition towards a more open and mobile society.

In some instances it can be shown that the continuity of power and ownership of major estates was a real and potent factor in the social structure of the countryside. Generally speaking, however, few of the descendants of the Norman magnates were still enjoying positions of leadership as the medieval period drew to its close. Marriage and wardship played a great and complicated part in this process. One Essex example, which is self-evident in its likely results on family inheritance, must suffice. A wealthy heiress, Galiena de Damartin, 'married' her first husband when only seven years old. She was to espouse a second and third in due course. But an impressive exception to this state of affairs in the family traditions of Essex was that of the de Veres, who maintained their status and authority in unbroken descent through the generations of over four centuries since the first of their forebears landed with William at Hastings in 1066. Similarly the FitzWalters, descendants of Ralph Baynard, enjoyed their inheritance through 10 gen-erations before the family estates were fragmented in 1464. The general picture is of the newly rich, like the Paycockes and the Celys, who, having made their fortune in Cots-wold wool and secured by purchase and prudent marriages large estates in Essex, contin-ued to wield much power in the countryside well into the 19th century before the final demise of a social structure that had its beginnings 1,000 years or more before.

ಬಂಡಿ

During the period in which the great pandemic and the insurrection occurred the kings of England waged, in pursuit of their political and dynastic ambitions, what historians have called the 100 Years War. It may be said to have lasted from 1336 to 1431, and was marked by such famous victories as Crécy in 1346 and Poitiers in 1356. Agincourt was won on that legendary day in October 1415. The royal heroes, the Black Prince, Edward III, and Henry V have secure places in English military history and literature. These great events were but flashes of lightning that illuminated the canvas of an evolving national picture in which the muted thunder was represented by the gradual breakdown of feudal institutions, the economic drain of the wars, and the growth, an important by-product of all these factors, of a new concept of national unity. By the mid-14th century French, previously the language of the upper classes and still lingering in official papers, was 'much unknown'. Yet, as I have remarked before, little it would seem totally disappears from English history, and such is the English character that change is accepted rather than embraced. Well on into the 18th century the practice of printing certain official papers in English and French in parallel persisted, and even today there are traces of the same anachronism in our public affairs. A more subtle example of this lies in the common use of a London dialect–in Essex as well as the capital–that continues to ignore the initial 'h', a relic, it is said of lower class imitation of their French-speaking superiors in the immediate post-Conquest period. But the enduring influence of national events is not easily followed in a few paragraphs so we must turn briefly to the part played by Essex in the general picture in a long and what must at the time have seemed endless drama. Not untypical of the treachery in public affairs in medieval England was the abduction from Pleshey and murder of Thomas of Woodstock, Duke of Gloucester, in 1397. The chronicler Froissart describes how in weather 'fayre and hote' Richard II rode out from Havering-atte-Bower to his uncle's stronghold at Pleshey in mid-Essex. Ostensibly a social visit, the unsuspecting Duke was invited to return thereafter with the King to London. Gloucester, son of Edward III and John of Gaunt's younger brother, had acquired much wealth and influence in the county after the Revolt of 1381 and Richard had good reason to suspect him of conspiracy. But the manner of his confrontation with the duke and the squalid murder was dishonourable on any count. After supping and staying with the duke overnight the King and his retinue, accompanied by their intended victim, set forth for London. At Stratford the King left the party, and Gloucester, seized by the Earl Marshal's men, was hustled to the Thames and Calais where he was strangled with knotted towels on the King's authority. Pleshey and all his other estates were confiscated. In his interesting book about the Tufnells of Great Waltham, F.W. Steer has noted the prosaic entries in the court rolls of the manor of Walthambury that mark this foul deed. The court on 16 May 1397 was held 'at the will of the lord'. Francis Steer has recorded that the next, on 8 October 1398, was inscribed in the rolls as 'at the will of the lady'–a poignant reference from the vast corpus of information in the Essex archives.

Essex naturally shared with all England the broad effects that flowed from war, pestilence and change. The records tell also of the particular involvement of the county in the foreign wars. At Crécy Essex men-at-arms, including a contingent of 200 archers, were among the soldiers who so decisively demolished the flower of the French cavalry.

Throughout the campaigns the Essex ports of Colchester, Brightlingsea, Harwich and Maldon made their maritime contribution of ships and seamen and their adventures were no doubt recounted, with pardonable pride and embellishment, in the village alehouses and manorial seats for many a day. But, as with the Wars of the Roses, which would follow, the issues at stake were not those that were directly relevant to life as it had to be lived by villagers struggling with their meagre resources who, with the artisans of the small towns, comprised the vast majority of the population. War, like politics and the pursuit of affluence, was not yet a national activity.

In the Wars of the Roses Essex was not the scene of armed conflict, though the nobility of the county and their personal followers were involved on both sides. The 100 Years War had ended with the final loss, despite the famous but indecisive victories of English arms, of France, and it was almost as if the contending parties turned to dynastic civil war as a consequence. Not since Hastings in 1066 had the English witnessed such an encounter on their own soil as that fought by nigh 100,000 men at Towton Field near Tadcaster in 1461. It ended in a Lancastrian defeat, Henry VI's flight to Scotland and the accession of Edward IV, the young, brave and able champion of the White Rose. This confused period saw much bloodshed, treachery, ruthless murder and a continuous struggle for political supremacy by the rival factions in which no less than the Crown of England was at stake. Generally speaking Lancastrian support was centred on the North, the South-west and Wales. London was for York, and Essex, too, though, as I shall explain, there were divisions among the great families in the internecine strife of this deplorable episode of English history. Yet the peasant was not greatly affected, and the middle classes prospered as the demands of war offered commercial prosperity.

Among the Essex nobility the de Vere family, Earls of Oxford, were staunchly Lancastrian. Henry Bourchier, Earl of Essex, Treasurer of England, and married to Isabel of York, was on the opposing side, but on the whole was a moderating influence, no mean achievement in such brittle and extreme circumstances. The FitzWalters, too, whom we note at several points in this narrative, were Yorkists. Oxford was executed and his descendants driven abroad for sanctuary, though they eventually returned with Henry Tudor and were thus present at the final climax to which we shall shortly come. Among the lesser gentry of Essex we find the same divided loyalties. Sir Thomas Urswick of Romford, Recorder of London, deserted the Lancastrian Henry VI for Edward IV and was rewarded for his subsequent exertions in the Yorkist cause by a knighthood in 1471. The Cookes of Romford, who had their seat at Gidea Hall, were at one time associated with the Yorkist faction, but Sir Thomas, falsely accused of dubious transactions with the Lancastrian, Margaret of Anjou, wife of the deposed Henry VI, suffered trial for treason, imprisonment and loss of office, though the family property was in the end recovered. The Earl of Ormond, lord of the manor of Foulness and a staunch Lancastrian, fell into the hands of the Yorkist army at the great battle at Towton Field and was shortly afterwards executed at Newcastle. His brothers were attainted and the family estates forfeited to the Crown. Such were the mixed fortunes of this grim and remorseless struggle. It could only be ended by the emergence of a new and dynamic force with the purpose and panache to seize the power that lay within the grasp of a king of England who could unite the warring factions and capitalise on the changes that were inherent in the transition from a feudal kingdom to the nation-state. Such a man was at hand. When Henry Tudor, Earl of Richmond, landed at Milford

Haven in 1485 the flickering flame of feudal England was about to be extinguished. Advancing through Wales and gathering support he routed the royal forces at Bosworth, leaving Richard III dead, and unmourned, upon the battlefield. And so the curtain fell on a period that had seen war, civil strife, pestilence, revolution, economic and social change of a definitive nature, and, above all, the growth of national feeling that, with all their personal talents, was to sustain the Tudors through one of the most exciting and creative ages in our story. John de Vere, the 13th Earl of Oxford and Castle Hedingham, was among the foremost leaders of Henry Tudor's victorious army. Through him, Essex history has a direct link with one of the most decisive moments of English history.

Chapter Five

ᛈᚣᚳᛃ

ESSEX UNDER THE TUDORS

'Let tyrants fear . . .'

The finale of Henry Tudor's decisive victory at Bosworth was marked by his coronation as Henry VII amidst the acclamation of his troops. Richard, whose crown, recovered from the debris of the battlefield, now rested on Henry's proud defiant head, was quietly interred at the Grey Friars in Leicester. The accession of the House of Tudor signalled the end of the bloodshed and debilitation of generations of civil war. The people of Essex, and indeed in all England, must have been concerned less with the weakness of Henry's title to the royal inheritance than with the prospect of peace and good government. They stood on the threshold, though they could not have known, of one of the great and definitive periods of English history. It was to be an age in which Essex would claim a significant share in the political, intellectual and martial triumphs of a people destined to achieve the greatness that their native qualities and exceptional leadership could command. After Bosworth, England would never be the same again. The usurpation heralded the most exciting century in our history. Not since the last of the Saxon kings had the people of Essex been so closely identified with their monarchs. The Tudors were familiar and significant figures in the county. Essex enjoyed the basic stability and economic growth that Henry VII's competent and purposeful administration bequeathed to his successor. It shared, too, in the trauma of the Henrician Reformation and the abortive efforts of the strong-willed Mary Tudor to reverse the irreversible. As the crescendo of the peerless Elizabeth's long and thrilling reign mounted, her charisma pervaded the county in which she spent part of her life, and to which she was drawn by destiny in a number of poignant and exhilarating episodes. The boy King, Edward VI, Mary and Elizabeth, all lived in Essex as children. Mary and Elizabeth were lodged in the county, from political motives, during their early womanhood. Henry VIII and Elizabeth often hunted in the royal forest in Essex, and were much attracted to their royal residences. Elizabeth's regal progresses in the county are legendary. The themes of this chapter, as we trace the course of the Tudor era in an Essex focus, will be those of change, triumph and tribulation and the involvement of the mass of the people in the county's towns and villages in national events as never before.

ᛈᚣᚳᛃ

Henry Tudor, the posthumous son of Edmund Tudor, Earl of Richmond who died two months before Henry's birth in 1457 and Margaret Beaufort, was descended from John of Gaunt and Owen Tudor. He had spent his early years in Wales, and although the feudal power of the baronage was much weakened there were still powerful men in England with whom he had to contend. But the loyalty of his supporters, duly rewarded after Bosworth in the time-honoured tradition of military conquerors, was sufficient to sustain this talented leader through the difficult early stages of his reign. He was thus able to contain the pressure of rival factions and survive domestic crisis when it arose. Among the deserving followers who had triumphed with him on the field of battle was Henry de Vere, the Earl of Oxford, whose family's name is indelibly linked with Essex and Castle Hedingham. He was rewarded with high office and lesser appointments which nonetheless carried influence and profit. High Admiral of England, Constable of the Tower, and 'keeper of the lions, lionesses and leopards' in the capital's fortress were among the grandiloquent titles conferred on the noble lord. The state papers, which record the offices of profit under the Crown, are replete with the names of Henry Tudor's comrades in arms and political supporters. Like the Conqueror before him Henry was, however, careful to prevent the concentration of excessive power in potentially rival hands. Even the faithful earl at Castle Hedingham was curbed by a £10,000 fine–a colossal sum in those days–when on the occasion of a visit by the King to his Essex seat he paraded a vast retinue of personal retainers, ostensibly in honour of his sovereign, but in contravention of the law. Unlike the Stuarts, the Tudors knew how to govern. Henry's great contribution was that he created order from disorder, prosperity and a renewed respect and prestige for the throne. A man of intellectual and artistic taste, he nevertheless made his major impact in government. Under his direction England was set on the paths of modern government in the process of which the status of Parliament was enhanced and the scene set for the flowering of English genius in the Tudor century. The sowing of the seeds of despotism and the continued and unprofitable involvement in European affairs must be set in the balance in assessing the results of his sojourn on the throne of England. All these trends were to manifest themselves in the eventful reign of his only surviving son, Henry VIII, and the history of the county provides an insight into the whole range of affairs that surrounds these cardinal features of the period. It was Henry and his royal children who promoted and presided over the events that constituted the watershed between medieval and modern England.

Still a month or two short of his 18th birthday, Prince Henry succeeded his famous father in April 1509. In the county there were high expectations of the handsome, vigorous and able youth who, as Henry VIII, was to achieve historical notoriety for the breach with Rome, and his six marriages. This 'young Alexander' was, as might have been expected of a Tudor, a man of action and by no means unversed in the arts and classical learning. Even before the crown was placed upon his head he had married his brother's widow, Catherine of Aragon, at Greenwich. The early years of his reign saw England again favoured with military successes that brought no political advantage. Henry's adventures in France, where he was himself present at the Battle of the Spurs, dissipated his thrifty father's treasure. Apart from the French, the Scots, too, were routed at Flodden, all to little purpose. At home the political scene in England was dominated for more than a decade by the East Anglian-born Cardinal Wolsey. English history, until the advent of modern constitutional monarchy, has few parallel examples of the exercise of such personal power other than that wielded by the monarch himself. As Chancellor and first minister, Wolsey administered the home government and also played the major role in foreign affairs. The inevitable unpopularity that resulted and the failure of his foreign policies led to his downfall and the emergence of Henry as a king enjoying absolute powers and a royal supremacy to which his temperament was already strongly inclined.

But, as history has shown, what was intolerable in a subject was acceptable in a king. When Henry faced his greatest decisions–the break with the Pope and Rome–he could rely on the general support of the people, not least in the strongly Protestant county of Essex.

Catherine's failure to provide an heir, after no less than six pregnancies, Henry's desire for Anne Boleyn, and the consequent proposals for divorce that were referred, without success, to the Papal throne fanned the flames of the Protestant Reformation in England. It was while he was at Waltham in Essex that Thomas Cranmer, a young and brilliant Cambridge scholar, proposed that Henry, who was more than grateful for the suggestion, should seek the combined wisdom of the major European universities on the philosophical and legal issues of divorce. By then the hand of Thomas Cromwell who, after Wolsey, was Henry's chief political adviser, was also at work and he enjoyed much influence until his execution in 1540. Cranmer's reward came with his enthrone-ment as Archbishop of Canterbury in which he crowned Anne Boleyn and supported Henry when, after the Pope's decision in favour of Catherine, the first steps to the personal supremacy of church as well as state were taken.

ᛞᚳᚷ

The Boleyn family were well connected with Essex and the comely Anne was at the centre of the great politico-religious issue that arose from Henry's disenchantment with Catherine of Aragon. Anne's father held the manor of New Hall at Boreham, and was later created Viscount Rochford by the King, who often visited New Hall, which became a royal residence to which he was much attached. The Protestant cause in Essex where 'Lollardy was rife' was already strongly entrenched when Henry took the first steps towards elevating Anne to queenly status. Enquiries by church officials in 1527 had revealed widespread heresy in the county and acts of desecration were not uncommon. Many Lollards were under arrest in a situation that had developed in the county well before Henry contemplated the break from Rome. The Essex Lollards were in the forefront of the Protestant movement and wholly committed to the philosophy and purpose of Martin Luther's dramatic gesture of protest at Wittemburg. On 1 September 1532 Henry made a critical move when he created Anne the Marquess of Pembroke and thereafter treated her overtly as if she was the Queen. His secret marriage to his new bride was solemnised at the end of the following January. The marriage to Catherine was declared null and void, a number of Essex clergy being associated with the Convocation that rejected the Papal claim to jurisdiction in the matter. England's future Queen and heroine, Elizabeth, was born to Anne Boleyn on 7 September 1533. From Essex the Abbot of Stratford Langthorne symbolised the county's later associations with Henry's third child by his presence at her christening at Greenwich Palace. Henry and England were by then fully committed to their course. Opinion in Essex was generally in har-mony with events, but a complicated and profound experience was to come.

In Tudor times Essex fell within the Diocese of London, and one of the factors working in Henry's favour was maladministration of the church and the monastic foun-dations in particular. The ever-refractory issue of tithes stood between church and peo-ple. Plurality, dereliction of duty and immorality figured among the causes of friction with the laity and the general lack of respect for ecclesiastical institutions that fostered the growth, first of Lollardy, then of the Protestant movement generally and enabled Henry to defy the Holy See. As early as 1524 Wolsey had little difficulty in suppressing various religious communities including Blackmore, Wix and Tiptree in Essex, among others, for the benefit of the newly founded colleges at Oxford and Cambridge. Others, such as Bicknacre Priory, had been previously abandoned as the prestige and revenues of the smaller priories ebbed in the tide of dissent and disillusion. But, in painting the picture of decay it must be recognised that much wealth and power nevertheless remained in ecclesiastical hands and would shortly be plundered and usurped by the Crown.

A significant legislative step was taken when in 1534 the Act of Supremacy was passed. Under this Henry 'justly and rightfully' assumed the position of Supreme Head of the Church of England. That marked the end of the ancient religion's power in England, despite Mary's later attempts to revive it, and was a constitutional landmark in our history. One of the first dignitaries of the church to subscribe to this Act when it was presented to the Lower House of Convocation was the Abbot of Waltham. His example was followed by numerous priests throughout the Essex deaneries, who shared a growing sympathy for the Protestant cause with their parishioners. In January 1535 Henry launched the inquiry, the Valor Ecclesiasticus, into the general and financial state of the monasteries. In Essex the Commissioner despatched by the Chancellor, Sir Thomas Audley, to carry out this essential preliminary to the Dissolution was Thomas Legh. He was assisted by John Ap Rice. The folios of the Valor Ecclesiasticus–the King's Book– reveal that nationally the monasteries and other religious institutions–more than 850– commanded an annual revenue of more than £200,000, which Thomas Cromwell determined to secure for the Crown. They found that the annual revenue of all the communities in Essex was in excess of £6,000. Waltham headed the list with a return of £900 4s. 3d.; Barking, the other great house in Essex, was valued at £862 12s. 5½d.; St Osyth and Stratford Langthorne were both found to enjoy revenues over £500. At the other end of the scale were the Carmelites at Maldon, whose yearly income was estimated at no more than £1 16s. 8d. Unfortunately the reports of the Commissioners on the general state of the religious houses in Essex have not survived, but sufficient is known to vindicate the general public disapproval of much in the conduct of their affairs and to provide the justification that Henry and Cromwell sought for the next move.

As a result there was no serious opposition, when the Bill was presented in February 1536, to the proposals for suppressing those monasteries whose revenue was less than £200 per year. It was a politic and modest beginning for what was to be a major and devastating act within a few years. In Essex there was 'not a finger lifted and hardly a voice raised' in protest. Only Thomas Beche, the Abbot of St John's at Colchester, of which the fine Gothic gateway still stands, resisted. Tried for treason he was hanged on 1 December 1539. A dramatic picture in the Egerton manuscripts depicts the judge riding out of Colchester surrounded by pikemen and trumpeters and the citizens kneeling before the entourage. Beche is seen being executed on a hill in the background. The event excited no public sympathy, for he was unpopular, and the King's action was not resented by the common folk, who had little at stake in the great issue between Crown and Church. In this first phase of the Dissolution Beeleigh, Dunmow, Prittlewell, Tilty and the other small houses were suppressed. Only the seven greater abbeys of Essex were temporarily reprieved.

Within a few years, in 1539, the Act for the Dissolution of the Greater Monasteries ratified all the earlier seizures and provided for the suppression of the remaining monasteries and abbeys. Stratford Langthorne fell to the King's Visitors on 18 March 1539. St Osyth surrendered in July, the abbot announcing to his solemn community 'I am the king's subject, and I and my house and all is the king's'. William Petre, in a poignant episode, received the riches of Barking on behalf of the Crown from his close family friend, the abbess Dorothy Barley, on 14 November in the same year. An annual income of over £1,000 fell into the hands of the Crown. The nuns were dismissed to their homes with pensions rather better than those received by the nuns in other religious houses. Dorothy Barley, with a pension of £133 6s. 8d., also received generous treatment. Demolition of the abbey began in 1540, the materials being used in building or repairing royal properties in and around the capital. Waltham, under its abbot, Robert Fuller, hung on to the end, the last abbey in all England to succumb, till 23 March 1540. Within a few years 50 more Essex chantries and religious guilds were dissolved and sold off for the benefit of the royal purse, together with the contents of the major houses.

Among the senior officials of the court who were involved in the operation were a number of prominent Essex noblemen as well as lesser, but rising gentry, such as William Petre and Thomas D'Arcy. The egregious Sir Richard Rich was Chancellor of the Court of Augmentations, Sir Thomas Mildmay was the Court Auditor. These men, and Sir Thomas Audley, the most powerful, received their due share of the spoils, St Botolph's and the Crouched Friary at Colchester, though he soon parted with the latter. Petre purchased his estate at Ingatestone where his descendants still live in the lovely house that was built on the former lands of Barking Abbey. Thomas Cromwell, the leading figure in the acts of suppression, was rewarded with the earldom of Essex and lands including St Osyth's, which after his execution for treason passed from him to Thomas D'Arcy. Thus were the lands and buildings of these once powerful foundations pillaged and despoiled. Curiously enough the King himself does not seem to have benefited as much as one would expect, for he was soon in financial difficulties again, and it was this that led to the attack on the chantries after he had to face Parliament in 1544 with a request to release him from his debts. Furthermore, the acts of desecration committed by village folk, largely unaffected by the major consequences of the Dissolution, caused the King much distress and political anxiety. The Protestant tide rose higher and faster than he had either wished or expected. In asserting themselves in the general atmosphere of crisis the Protestants in Essex turned to the destruction of the beautiful medieval ornaments and treasures in the parish churches, the records bearing witness to the zeal for dissent and reform as the Puritan elements grew in strength and determination. Among the gentry, who had profited greatly from the whole transaction, the exchange of former monastic property created a new and lucrative market in real estate. Politically, the significance of that was that in Essex, and the country generally, a large and influential body of people had a considerable vested interest in the preservation of the situation that had resulted from the eventful decade during which the monasteries had been systematically plundered and their communities dispersed.

One marvels at the will and nerve with which Henry VIII stuck to his purpose. He had grappled with the might of Rome and there had been the trauma of Anne Boleyn's trial and execution for treason. His reign had begun with high hopes. He lived through a period of intense political activity and had to contend with the powerful and self-seeking men at his court. His private life could hardly have been happy, much less uplifting. Yet this arrogant, selfish and ruthless man was at the same time brave, intelligent, and a great ruler. He never aroused any serious popular opposition, and though sick and overborne with the pressure of state affairs he died, defiant and courageous to the end, on 28 January 1547, to be succeeded by Jane Seymour's young son, Edward VI.

ಬಂಡ

Perhaps above all others the Tudor period in England was that in which the people distinguished themselves in every sphere of human endeavour. In conflict, in exploration, in the fields of learning, and in the arts, they crossed the frontiers of achievement and knowledge with a confidence, purpose and spirit that released all their latent energies and talents. The material resources of the nation were modest. But the moral and intellectual capital of the nation erupted in a cascade of triumph and achievement, the inspiration of which still invigorates our national life today. The great Tudors spanned the age of Drake, Raleigh, Shakespeare, Hooker, Bacon, Byrd and Spenser, whose *Faerie Queene* imparted the final touch of magic to the aura of the century wherein her great reign was the apogee. During this era the new learning of the Renaissance was broadcast throughout literate society by the development of printing, a powerful factor in the upsurge of intellectual endeavour. In England the old aristocracy had been severely diluted by the waste of civil war. The church, under political attack, and racked by dissension, could no longer patronise the arts as it had done during its medieval supremacy. In the age, therefore, when Shakespeare wrote his supreme literary masterpieces and when such as Longleat, Montacute, and Hardwick were built by the rich and influential laity it was to the new leaders and rising middle class that the responsibility of patronage passed. Although, following the Order for the Removal of Images in February 1548, much English medieval art was lost forever, more, in greater diversity, took its place. The historical events of the period could easily have created a political and intellectual vacuum. In fact there was an efflorescence of remarkable intensity and quality over the whole range of human activity. It will be my task in this chapter to adumbrate the impact of this on Essex and the contribution of Essex people to the achievement.

In this national adventure it will be seen, as we follow the path of history, that Essex was frequently associated with the great events of the age. Whether the struggle with the Armada or the seafaring sagas such as the circumnavigation by Thomas Cavendish in 1586-8, Essex men were present. But I shall dwell here on the links of Essex with the artistic and scientific accomplishments of the 16th century. Today this is most evident in the wealth of Tudor architecture that still enriches the landscape of the county. In that most comprehensive field of the plastic arts each age has left the imprint of its principal features on the topographical scene. We think of Norman mass, the spatial qualities of Gothic architecture and its intense spirituality, the taste and ornament of Georgian buildings, and the confident and pompous conceptions of the Victorian architects. To me the hallmarks of Tudor building are serenity, grace and texture. In Essex we may savour these and other qualities of the architectural age of red brick and timber, plentiful in the county, and the principal media favoured by wealthy patrons. Stone, which is scarce in the county, was largely forsaken, though the Georgians later exploited its potential with brilliant success in the pursuit of classical perfection and discipline.

The early 16th century witnessed a wave of building and rebuilding by the country squires and yeoman farmers as well of the greater homes of the rich. As their social and

40 *The 'Great Standinge' at Chingford: Queen Elizabeth's hunting lodge*

economic position improved so they enlarged and modernised their homes and introduced such luxuries as integral chimneys and glazed windows. Essex is particularly rich in the timber-framed houses that were constructed or modified in the period. Behind the later face of many a house in the Essex countryside will be found the structural evidence, in Tudor and earlier timber, of this age of improvement. In the towns, too, like Chelmsford which was then growing in importance, are still extant the timbered and tiled houses of the merchants and professional men of the time. Of particular merit is the fine timber-framed house at Coggeshall, Paycocke's, now in the safe hands of the National Trust, that was built by a wealthy clothier for his son on his marriage. The front elevation of this typical Tudor house is a near-perfect example of its type, with significant timbering, carved decoration and handsome oriel windows. Of special interest, as a unique survival, is Queen Elizabeth's hunting lodge at Chingford. This fine old timber-framed building, despite its eponymous association with Elizabeth, dates from Henry VIII's reign when he was engaged in creating a park at Fairmead and was constructed to serve as a 'standing' from

41 *Horham Hall, near Thaxted, 1831*

which to view the hunting. It has some architectural features of note and should not be
overlooked by visitors to Epping Forest.

The county is so rich in the quality of
its brick-built Tudor houses that it is difficult to know which to exclude from a necessarily brief resumé of extant buildings.
William Petre's house at Ingatestone is one
outstanding example in rose-coloured brick,
its facades graced by typical Tudor fenes-
tration and crow-stepped gables. Horham
Hall, Thaxted, described by Leland as 'a
very sumptuous house in Est-Sax', is
moated and notable for the fine oriel window of early 16th-century glass in the great

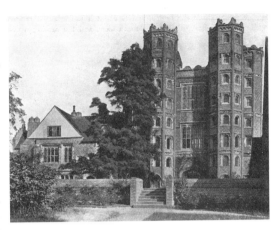

42   *Layer Marney Towers*

hall. The antiquary's use of the expression 'Est-Sax' in his reference to this historic
house is interesting at that late date in the county's history unless it is a purely
orthographical form, which seems unlikely. It was possibly just an antiquarian whim of
an agreeable flavour. Lord Rich's rebuilt Leez Priory must be mentioned, and the
courtyard house of New Hall at Boreham, which is somewhat later. Gosfield in red
brick with blue diaper work is noteworthy as is the extraordinary gatehouse of about
1520 at Layer Marney Towers which represents but the first stage of a vast mansion

43   *Hill Hall, near Epping, 1831*

never built. Secreted in the grimy urban acres of metropolitan Essex is Clement Sysley's splendid Tudor-brick house of 1560. Eastbury House at Barking is a surprising survival and like Paycocke's also protected by the National Trust. Most outstanding in Tudor architecture in Essex is, on Professor Pevsner's authority, Sir Thomas Smith's home at Theydon Mount. Hill Hall, now tragically burned out, but still retaining its handsome facades, has aesthetic distinction. What is more important is that Professor Pevsner has perceived it as an authentic link between Tudor and Renaissance architecture of the earliest provenance since it was commenced in 1567/8. It thus has an importance in the development of English domestic architecture that makes it the most significant building of the period in Essex.

The parish churches of the county make their own contribution to the inventory of Essex brickwork. Notable is the parish church at Ingatestone where vitrified blue headers in diamond patterns embellish the red brick textures of the main elevations. Other fine examples of early 16th-century brick-work include the porch of All Saints at Feering and the English bonded brickwork at St Andrew's, Sandon, where two Latin crosses have been worked into the facing of the west tower. Good early examples of the bricklayer's craft in Essex churches will be seen also at Pebmarsh, St Osyth and East Horndon.

In the learned arts Tudor Essex was well represented. Outstanding among the intellectuals of Elizabethan England was Sir Thomas Smith. Born in 1513 to a small sheep farmer of Chipping Walden, as Saffron Walden was then called, and his Lancashire wife, Agnes Charnock, the young and gifted Thomas's intellectual talents were soon apparent. His scholarship brought him the Vice-Chancellorship of Cambridge University when

44 *Sir Thomas Smith, 1513-1577*

only 30 years of age, and a plethora of academic honours. His most celebrated work 'De Republica Anglorum' is the basis of our knowledge of the constitutional framework of Elizabethan England and it is probable that a comparable work in the field of socio-economics, of doubtful attribution, was the product of his mind also. His part in the political issues of his day and his service in the Queen's councils was less successful, but he was undoubtedly one of the foremost figures of Elizabeth's England. Always devoted to his native county, he created Hill Hall and there spent his last sad and painful days in ill health after a life of creative industry and adversity. He lies, as was his wish, in the chancel of St Michael's at Theydon Mount in a tomb bearing the flame-girt salamander, that his descendants so proudly cherished as a symbol of Sir Thomas Smith's great and resilient personality and the vicissitudes of his life.

William Harrison, who held the living at Radwinter for 34 years and the adjacent parish of Wimbish for 10 of those, was another outstanding scholar in the Essex coterie. His great work was the *Description of England,* printed in 1577 as part of *Holinshed's Chronicles.* It is a brilliant and authoritative commentary on Tudor society and other aspects of the period based on much original research. The value of this work to scholars is now widely acknowledged.

In an age of poetic giants Essex is represented by the relatively unimportant but authentic minor poets, George Gascoigne of Walthamstow, his stepson, Nicholas Breton, and Thomas Lodge of Leyton, though born at West Ham. All three composed verse of characteristic delicacy which is not without charm and still thought worthy of attention by scholars of the period. Essex men, too, served the royal family in tutorial positions. Sir Anthony Cooke of Gidea Hall, Romford, the family fortunes rising again after their disasters in the Wars of the Roses, was tutor to young Edward VI. The Yorkshire-born Roger Ascham, who leased his farmlands at Walthamstow from the Petres of Ingatestone, was Latin Secretary to Mary Tudor and taught the classics to the Princess Elizabeth at Cheshunt. The Cooke family enjoyed a tradition of scholarship and Sir Anthony fathered four daughters of unusual intellectual talents, one of whom, Ann, through her marriage to Sir Nicholas Bacon, became the mother of the celebrated scholar, Francis Bacon, whose intellectual stature has led some, with scant authority, to attribute the works of William Shakespeare to his erudite pen. Another attribution is attached to Edward de Vere, the 17th Earl of Oxford whose family seat was at Hedingham Castle.

The 'father of our music', William Byrd, the greatest composer of his time, was the Queen's organist, like Thomas Tallis, the organist at Waltham Abbey before the Dissolution. Byrd, around whom there is some political mystery in view of his Catholic connections, spent the last 28 years of his life at Stondon Place and the circumstantial evidence, though it has not been substantiated, suggests that he was buried, at his own wish, at Stondon Massey, where he had enjoyed peace and seclusion. In science, the outstanding contribution from Essex was that of William Gilberd, who was born about 1540 at Colchester and died within a few months of the Queen's death in 1603, and thus lived and worked not only in the spirit of the times, but almost precisely within the compass of Elizabeth's own life and reign. He was highly regarded in his profession as a doctor of medicine and was physician to the Queen, but it is his scientific work on magnetism and electricity for which he is justly renowned. It was Gilberd who coined the word electricity from the Greek derivative for amber, and his famous book, *de Magnete,* was of major scientific stature. Respected throughout Europe, his work was based on a new scientific methodology which rejected speculation for empirical experiment and observation. His most important original work was in relation to the magnetic properties of the earth, magnetic fields of force, and what we should now call electrostatics. His inquiring and perceptive mind probed fields which in the sphere of physics modern scientists are still exploring. Along with Sir Thomas Smith he may be regarded as in the highest flight among the academic figures of Elizabethan England.

ఇం

The accession of Edward VI, still in his minority, opened the way for the politically ambitious and popular Edward Seymour, Earl of Hertford, and the young King's uncle, who as Lord Protector of the Realm and Duke of Somerset took charge of affairs. Of interest to Essex history was Sir Thomas Smith's appointment to the lucrative post of

Clerk of the Privy Council and the Mastership of the Court of Requests. Unfortunately for him, his political judgement, always fallible, had put him in the wrong camp, and when Somerset's regime was overthrown and the arrogant and by then unpopular Protector usurped and eventually executed, Smith was isolated and in a precarious position. He was also involved in the marriage negotiations for the proposed betrothal of King Edward and the Princess Elizabeth of France, but otherwise he remained in academic obscurity at Eton until after the King's death, when he re-entered political life. During Edward's brief reign the Reformation movement was consolidated. His first parliament enacted the Act of Uniformity that established Cranmer's Prayer Book and proscribed any other manner of worship. Although in essence not a direct challenge to the Roman church or fundamentally deviant from the old liturgy, this was the point of no return. The churches were stripped of Roman symbols and contemporary Essex church accounts record the defacement of images, the removal of glass, and the lime-washing of walls to cover up the mural representations of scriptural dogma. Much of the plate and precious vestments and holy books found their way into private hands, and even the clergy were not above the suspicion of having indulged themselves in this lucrative trade.

In Great Dunmow 'Yngram and Parker' were paid 3s. for 'takyng downe the altars and carrying aweye the rubbysh' in 1549/50; in the next year the churchwardens paid 4d. for the removal of the rood; the 'tabyrnakyll of Our Lady of Petye' was sold for 5s. The rector of Radwinter, William Harrison, wrote 'All images, shrines, tabernacles, rood-lofts and monuments of idolatry are removed ... only the stories in glass excepted'. It was a tragedy repeated all over the county. The desecration of beautiful medieval works of devotional art in the Catholic tradition deprived the ordinary people, mostly illiterate, of the visual symbols of their Christian faith. Fortunately, however, some of the artistic heritage in the church survived the iconoclasm of the Protestant reformers. At the end of the process the medieval legacy of church furniture and ornament had been largely consumed in the passion to efface the old religion. Unhappily, it was to take several centuries and more conflict before the unjust repression of Catholics was relieved and an appropriate perspective of tolerance to prevail.

After the premature death of Edward on 6 July 1553 a desperate attempt was made to exclude the dedicated Catholic Mary Tudor from the throne. The plot, launched by the Duke of Northumberland, to whose son, Guildford Dudley, Lady Jane Grey, a girl of 17, was married, misfired primarily because the people as a whole would not countenance the blatant and illegal attempt to displace the rightful Queen. Jane, 'with weeping tears', was hustled to London and proclaimed as Queen the day after Edward's death. There was some minor support for her in the eastern counties, but Northumberland's nerve failed him as general opposition mounted. The fleet and the county levies declared in Mary's favour and she entered London, accompanied by her half-sister, Elizabeth, who had joined her at Wanstead, on 3 August, to be proclaimed Queen of England in right of her Tudor ancestry. The sad and tragic Jane was destined for the block, the victim of political circumstances over which she had no control. Among those imprisoned in the Tower on suspicion of complicity in the affair was Sir Anthony Cooke of Romford, to whose scholarship I have referred, but he seems to have contrived his release, for he is known to have been in exile in France in 1554 and returned to England after the accession of Elizabeth, whom he served and entertained at Gidea Hall. Sir John Gates, who had received large estates in Essex from Henry VIII was less fortunate and was executed on Tower Hill for his treasonable support for the Northumberland faction. The inevitable apostate, Lord Rich of Leez Priory, having signed the proclamation for Jane Grey, hastened back to subscribe to the proclamation of Mary.

৪০০৪

After Mary's proclamation those who had held their hands hastened with alacrity to present themselves to the new Queen. The sagacious Sir William Cecil, later Lord Burghley, and one of the greatest figures of Elizabeth's time, kissed hands at Ingatestone Hall. Already rich and influential, he entered Mary's service taking good care to maintain his standing with the younger princess. Mary's accession caused much confusion and some despair in Protestant Essex where there were good grounds for concern about the probable consequences of her devotion to the Catholic faith. Her tenacity had been proven at Copt Hall, Epping, where she was lodged during Edward's reign. Forbidden by royal command to practise the Roman rites, she defied the King's emissaries, among them Lord Rich and William Petre, who were told that she would readily die for her faith and having 'learned how many loaves of bread be made of a bushel of wheat' would fend for herself. Mary's declared intention to return the country to Rome was soon put into effect. The Protestant bishops were deposed. Cranmer and Latimer went to the Tower. The Queen espoused Philip of Spain at Winchester Castle in July 1554 and aroused political opposition by her proposal to exclude the Princess Elizabeth from the succession without the approval of Parliament. In the churches the rood, the mass and the images returned. Protestants faced the fires or exile. The persecution of Protestants in Essex was foreshadowed by the deprivation and arrest of parish clergy who resisted the revival of the Catholic liturgy.

The first of the Marian martyrs were taken from the ranks of the bishops. London and the south-eastern counties of Essex, Kent and Sussex suffered most severely. Bishop

45   *Ingatestone Hall, 1829*

Bonner of London led the attack. Latimer and Bishop Ridley were taken from prison at Oxford and burned at the stake in 1555. Cranmer died in the same way, Latimer having prophetically declared, 'We shall this day light such a candle by God's Grace in England as I trust shall never be put out'. Mary was in a grim and literal sense playing with fire. Although she pursued her fanatical course with brutal and obstinate tenacity she was, in fact, ensuring that Catholicism would never recover its former position in England. It was in the fires of the Marian persecution that the success of the Reformation in this country was finally assured. In three years more than 300 Protestants died in the fires of her religious fervour. At Colchester where Mary had been presented with a silver cup and £20 in gold at her accession, the cup of bitter disillusion overflowed. On 2 August 1557 10 Colchester men were executed in the flames under the castle walls and by the Balkerne Gate. Ten other citizens of the town, including a woman, suffered the same fate before the end of this awful episode. Scores of dissenters from Essex were tied together and dragged along the streets of London on a single rope. A memorial at Stratford recalls the ghastly event of June in the previous year when 11 men and two women perished together in a holocaust that has never been forgotten. Bound and drawn in carts from the city after being delivered to the High Sheriff of Essex, the people whose names are enshrined on the memorial of St John the Evangelist in the Broadway were consigned to the fires. The execution is said to have been witnessed by a vast multitude and the nervous sheriff, sensing support for the victims and fearing that the situation might get out of hand, hurriedly ordered the fires to be lit, ruefully remarking, 'God knowest best when his corn is ripe'. Altogether more than 70 people in the county perished in the persecution. The records testify to the widespread nature of dissent and the retribution that Mary exacted. Rowland Taylor, a doctor of Hadleigh, Hugh Laverstock, a brave old cripple of Barking, William Hunter, a youth of Brentwood, Thomas Higbed, a Horndon farmer, Thomas Bowyer, a weaver from Great Dunmow and John Rogers, the rector at Chigwell, with others from Braintree, Manningtree, Rochford and Saffron Walden were also among those in Essex who were fed to the fires of the counter-Reformation. Abroad Mary was committed to war in Europe in support of Philip of Spain, and Calais 'the jewel of the English crown' was lost. She had been confronted not only with mounting Protestantism but an endemic and virulent English nationalism that could not be denied expression. At the end of her reign England could but await deliverance.

It was in the age of the Tudors that the Essex landscape began to assume the aspect with which we are familiar today. The pattern of fields and hedges, forest and heathland that we now enjoy is, in its general character, that which resulted from the social and agrarian changes set in train by the acceleration of the processes we noted as already developing in medieval England. The county in the 16th century was almost entirely agricultural; the climate and lack of the natural resources necessary for the development of industry before the machine age dictated reliance on the products of the land. Essex was, and still is to a very large extent today, a farming county primarily engaged in growing cereals and vegetables. On the marshlands of the coast and along Thames-side the pasturage was sufficiently good to support sheep. In south-west Essex the demands of the expanding capital promoted a small but noteworthy market for dairy produce. We shall note also the embryo industrial development in the county, but the industrial diversification of the economy was marginal. Essex was in the cartographer's words 'the englishe Goschen'. John Norden, in 1594, so described the county, adding that it was:

> most fatt, frutefull, and full of profitable thinges exceding (as farr as I can
> finde) anie other shire, for the general comodeties, and … this shire seemeth
> to me to deserve the title of the englishe Goschen, the fattest of the Lande;
> comparable to Palestina, that flowed with milke and hunnye

Much of the success of Essex farming in the Tudor and subsequent centuries has been attributed to the beneficial results of enclosure which, though generally regarded as an 18th- and 19th-century movement, in south-east England was carried a long way by the reign of Henry VIII. Generally there was little left in Essex of the common-field system that persisted until much later in the Midlands except in the north and north-west of Essex. But there were still considerable tracts of unenclosed areas of heath, especially in the north-east of the county, of which Tiptree Heath and many other heaths and large village greens around Colchester were conspicuous.

The rising population and the inflation brought about by demand and the debasement of the currency generally stimulated the process of enclosure, which was accomplished with or without consent or agreement according to local circumstances. The economic benefits were quickly felt; the social consequences came later. Thomas Tusser, born of Essex lineage—'In Essex laier, in village faier'—at Rivenhall and author of the celebrated *Five Hundred Points of Good Husbandry*, the farmers' text book for several generations, was adamant about the value of enclosure to productivity and good farming practice. But he was not a successful farmer himself as Fuller's sardonic observation that there were 'none better in theory or worse in practice' asserts. Furthermore, there can be no doubt that enclosure contributed to the general impoverishment of life in the countryside, in its fullest sense, and the drift to the towns which left pauperism and vagabondage in its wake. Indeed, the mobility of rural populations in the 16th century, as a modern computer-based study of the records of Earls Colne in Essex has shown in great detail, was more conspicuous and complicated than was previously thought. Feudal disciplines had already been seriously undermined and in rural Essex numerous families, stimulated by the economic and social factors, were emerging from a formerly peasant status which had tied them to the manors.

During the first half of the 16th century the development of Essex towns appears to have been retarded as a result of neglect and taxation. There is evidence of some depression, particularly in Colchester and Maldon. Later, with the growth of local administrative institutions and the incorporation by charter of several towns, the trend was reversed. Colchester had been the first town in Essex to receive a charter of incorporation. This dated from 1462 and had confirmed the existing privileges of the burgesses. Chelmsford, the present county town, but not then as significant as Colchester, developed as an important market centre and may be seen, literally in profile, on the remarkable Walker map of 1591. In Thaxted, which had thrived in the 15th century, the process was delayed by the decline of the cutlery industry and other economic activities as well as the persistence of manorial constraints. Thaxted was thus newly incorporated as a borough by charter under Philip and Mary in 1556, partly to stimulate the development of the town through economic growth and a new system of public administration. The Thaxted charter speaks eloquently of the town as 'come nowe to great Ruine and decaye by reason of great povertie and necessytie …'. Maldon was chartered by Philip and Mary

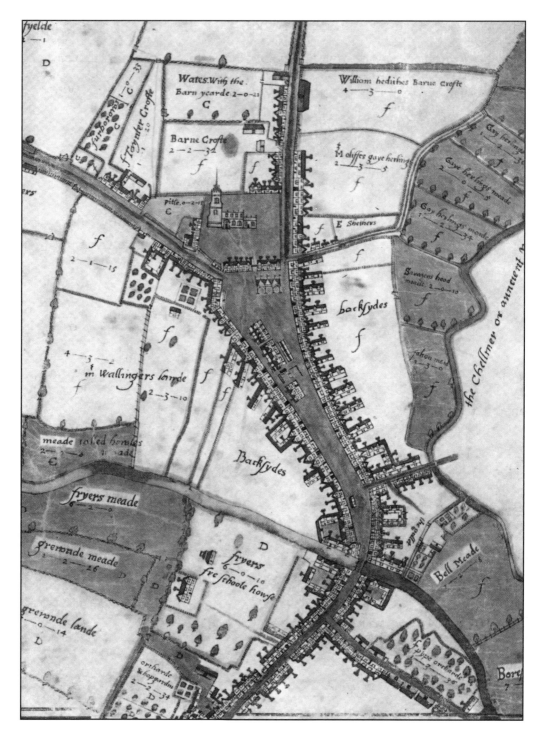

46 *Chelmsford in 1591, mapped and surveyed by John Walker*

in 1555 and confirmed in that status by Elizabeth in 1558. It enjoyed a flourishing role as a port for trade with western Europe. Saffron Walden had been chartered in 1549; Dunmow in 1556. The charters which regulated the customs, jurisdictions and privileges of the boroughs provided also for the appointment of numbers of local officials, by no means popular, and bye-laws. Apart from the encouragement of urban life, much was done to improve the communications of the county. As F.G. Emmison has shown in his comprehensive studies of Elizabethan life in the county, much effort was expended in improving the roads as traffic grew, and people, surprisingly perhaps in view of the conditions, took to travel in the pursuit of pleasure as well as business. Legislative provision was made for the maintenance of the highways and bridges by parish and other local officials out of the proceeds of local rates. Some of the north Essex towns, Braintree, Halstead, and Coggeshall—among others—were beneficiaries, too, of the influx of the thrifty and industrious Flemish refugees from persecution on the continent. By the latter part of the century Colchester had a central role in the clothing industry that hundreds of Dutch immigrants had helped to develop in the town. Wool and silk weaving and the manufacture of worsted, the 'new draperies' and the so-called 'bays and says' all flourished as agriculture was rationalised by the process of enclosure and capitalisation. It was at this time that Walden acquired the affix 'Saffron'. This recognised the town's role as the centre of a relatively small, but locally important cash crop industry that had grown up mainly in the surrounding parishes, although the crocuses from which the spice was derived were also grown in other parts of the county.

For the rich, whose wealth was enhanced by the economic trends then prevalent, and for the new entrepreneurial class, life in Tudor Essex was good by any standards. There were increasing opportunities, too, for the middle-class professional men and the yeoman farmers. At the other end of the social spectrum things were different. One of the consequences of the Dissolution was the loss of the social services in caring for the sick and poor, formerly undertaken by the monastic communities. Furthermore, periodic agricultural depression and the results of the agrarian changes I have described exacerbated the situation and made state action imperative. Unemployment, rising prices and pauperism led also to an increase in crime. The old jingle, 'Hark, hark, the dogs do bark the beggars are coming to town ...' had a serious reality in 16th-century England. The parish book of Great Easton notes, in 1597, that under recently enacted legislation people deemed to be vagabonds could expect short shrift. Among those defined as such were 'Palmesters' and their 'craftye science', idlers, beggars, tinkers, common players and minstrels except those 'lycensed by Barrons or (those) of higher degree'. They were liable to be 'whipped until his or her Bodye be bloudye' and hounded from parish to parish to where they were born or last resided. There had been legislation early in the Tudor period, but it was not until the Beggars Act of 1536 that a formal duty rested upon parishes to provide for the needs of their poor. The system of Poor Relief was further developed under Edward VI and Elizabeth. The Poor Law Act of 1563 placed onerous responsibilities on the manor courts and churchwardens when neither of these authorities had sufficient powers to carry out their duties in this respect. However, the Act of 1597 provided for the appointment of Overseers of the Poor; local resources and competence were further enhanced by the Act of 1601. These acts finally marked the acceptance by government at all levels of a responsibility that had formerly fallen, on a voluntary basis, upon the Church and private charity. This was of

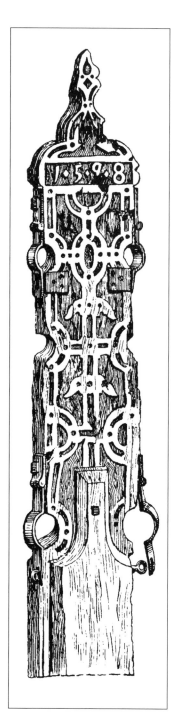

47 *Whipping post and stocks from Waltham Abbey*

considerable social importance and a significant manifestation of the great changes in our national life that occurred in the age of the Tudors. Economic upheaval, political development, the further decay of manorial and feudal institutions, the breach with Rome, and the emergence of a powerful monarchy with popular support were the principal features of a century replete with crisis, triumph, vitality and achievement.

෮෬

'A vestal fire that burns but never wasteth'–so wrote Sir Walter Raleigh, with a typical Elizabethan flourish, of the great Queen who followed her half sister to the throne in 1558. The Spanish envoy saw her 'possessed of 100,000 devils'. She needed all her reserves of intellect, energy, courage and tenacity to grapple with the problems she inherited from Mary's brief but disastrous reign. England, as a result of mis-government and Mary's undiluted bigotry was on the verge of rebellion, financially crippled, and threatened with dynastic war. Elizabeth it is true was vain, tempestuous and parsimonious. She also possessed an extraordinary instinct and an iron will. Above all she was a patriot and enjoyed a magical relationship with the common people that perhaps only a Queen can command. Even a Puritan punished with mutilation doffed his hat with his remaining hand and cried, 'God save Queen Elizabeth'. When she was crowned, wearing the finery she always enjoyed, in gold, ermine and silk, on 15 January 1559, Europe did not expect her regime to last. Elizabeth confounded her enemies as she cajoled, charmed and championed her people. In Essex her prestige stood high; she could rely on Essex hearts; she was part of Essex history.

The defeat of the Spanish Armada, to which we shall come, is seen as the high-water mark of Elizabethan England. Its achievements were in reality more substantial than that as we have seen. The restoration of national prosperity, the settlement of the religious dispute, and the royal succession and cultural advance all rank alongside the successful defence of the realm as the dominating strands in the history of the Elizabethan decades. The Queen's genius for compromise in pursuit of her basic political objectives was apparent in what is now termed the Elizabethan Settlement. In this she resolved the issue of the succession, and by the Act of Uniformity of 1559 the question of the Prayer Book and Protestant supremacy. As time elapsed the wisdom of these moves was fully demonstrated. The Puritans were disappointed, but not disaffected. The Catholics assailed, but not alienated. The people as a whole were generally content. On the one side John Knox saw Elizabeth as 'neither good Protestant nor yet resolute Papist'. On the other the Spanish Ambassador reluctantly reported the unity of Crown, church and people, who found much common ground and comfort in the settlement. The position in Essex was predictable. There was widespread acquiescence if not immediate conformity. Among the moderates the practical dilemma is aptly summed up in an enigmatic entry about a curious little episode described in the church register at St Mary's, Little Sampford at the end of Elizabeth's reign in 1602. The rector, one Morgan Richards, struggling to preserve the unity of his parish and the integrity of his calling, had to record the furtive burial in his church of the recusant but influential Catholic squire, Rooke Green, who could not be brought 'to conformity in religion'. The rector wrote, recording the squire's death, with apparent reluctance: 'And was buried ye next night following by whom I cannot tell'.

Puritanism, slowly gathering strength in the county, was contained if not content. The influx of Flemish refugees reinforced the Protestant cause and it was amongst Puritan elements rather than Catholics that dissent and vigorous criticism of church administration and practices in Essex arose. Indeed, although the cruel harassment of recusants by Elizabeth's ecclesiastical authorities paralleled the atrocities of Mary Tudor's reign, and some 200 Catholics were martyred as 'traitors', only one suffered this fate in Essex. Some, in high positions like William Petre, actually strengthened their social status and political influence. The sole Essex martyr was John Paine, a Catholic priest, who was hideously tortured, hanged, drawn and quartered at Chelmsford in April 1582. At the parish level the Elizabethan settlement, the Acts of Supremacy and Uniformity had added confusion to distress. An Essex tailor and recusant of Finchingfield, William Binkes, remarked in his frustration, 'What manner of religion we have here in England I know not, for the preachers now doe preach theire owne inventions and phantasies and therefore I will not believe any of them.' The Catholic gentry often encouraged the practice of the traditional forms of worship and several clergymen, Thomas Brayne of Cranham for example, were brought before the church authorities 'suspected of papistrie'. The archdeacons' courts heard cases which had failed to carry out the injunctions regarding the destruction of images and rood-lofts. Apart from that, the pressure for religious discipline and conformity in the county was mainly exerted through the courts for offences against the Acts and was manifested in the further destruction of Catholic liturgical imagery.

Foxe's Book of Martyrs, published in 1563, and written at Waltham Abbey, had a considerable influence on the anti-popery movement that inspired much of the Puritan cause. The Bull of Excommunication issued by the Pope under which Elizabeth was declared a heretic also added fuel to the fire of Protestantism and faced English Catholics with the fearful dilemma of treason or apostasy. The general situation was further complicated by the question of the Stuart succession. Mary Queen of Scots, brave, passionate, but, unlike Elizabeth, lacking judgement and fidelity, was drawn inexorably into the centre of the political and religious conflict to die on the block at Fotheringay in 1587. This tragic event, which caused Elizabeth much distress, had less repercussions than it would have done earlier. By then, and despite all the vicissitudes of the religious struggle, the loyalty of Catholics and Puritans alike bore the strain and when the confrontation with Spain finally materialised the would-be conquerors were faced by a united nation.

ஐගෟ

Apart from the deftness of her political touch, Elizabeth's popularity with the mass of the people depended on the assiduity with which she courted their support. She was thus much given to making royal Progresses throughout the country. She had spent various periods in Essex in political hibernation, especially during Mary's reign, and was well known and loved in the county. The Progresses were magnificent ostentations and, for the hosts, expensive affairs. Monsieur de Maisse, the agent of the King of France, described how the Queen on horseback or in open coach was proceeded by the Lord Chamberlain and followed by the nobles, heralds, Gentlemen of the Guard and Maids of Honour. Often, he says, 'near the Queen's person such as the Earl of Essex' who was to suffer execution for his ill contrived and rebellious conduct in 1601. Elizabeth made several Progresses in the county. In July 1561 she left London for Havering, whence she travelled to Loughton Hall where, on 17th, she was received by John Stonard. She was at Ingatestone from 19th-21st, and New Hall for five further days before continuing to Felix Hall at Kelvedon, Colchester and St Osyth. Returning to Colchester on 1 August she then went to Harwich and Suffolk, arriving back in Essex at Castle Hedingham on 14 August, where she stayed till the nineteenth. From there the Progress took her to Gosfield Hall, Leez Priory, Great Hallingbury and back to London in late September. A further shorter Progress was made in the county in 1568

48   *New Hall, Boreham, 1779*

when she visited Gidea Hall and Copt Hall. In 1571 she again toured the county, making her way to Audley End, Mark Hall and Latton. During her Progress in 1578 she was at Horham Hall and it was from there that she sent her refusal to the proposed marriage with the Duke of Anjou. Some idea of the cost and scale of entertainment that burdened the honoured but poorer hosts may be gleaned from the account of the fare provided at Ingatestone in 1561. In a lengthy itemised list are recorded alongside plentiful supplies of beer and fruit such sumptuous comestibles as gurnards and congers, sturgeon, cygnets, egrets, heron, shovellers, and quail–a truly royal collation. These lengthy, well-planned and convivial journeyings of the Queen and her court provided a wonderful focus for loyal demonstration and served to identify the Queen's charismatic personality with the common people as well as the important ingredient in the national unity that she nourished with consummate political skill and regal coquetry.

ഔശ

Elizabeth's personal relations with the Earls of Essex have been well documented and will be familiar to most readers. They are not essentially part of the history of the county. But she was intimate, too, with three men in her personal service whose homes and interests were closely tied to the local scene. In William Petre of Ingatestone Hall we have a remarkable example of one, of Catholic persuasion, who through his dexterity and general administrative ability, managed to survive in the royal service through four reigns. He served Henry VIII, Edward VI, Mary I and Elizabeth I with distinction and without forfeiting the confidence of any. No other high Tudor official shares a similar record. It can be read and savoured in F.G. Emmison's masterly study, *Tudor Secretary,* which also offers a valuable account of domestic life at Ingatestone Hall that no student of Essex social history can omit to read. A more exciting personality, though one less endowed with political acumen, is the great Elizabethan intellectual, Sir Thomas Smith, of Saffron Walden and Hill Hall, whose cultural contribution I have noted. Of interest, too, is Sir Thomas Heneage, his neighbour at Copt Hall, and a favourite of the Queen. I have written of both, inadequately but more fully than is possible here, in the *Essex Journal.* Of relevance to the political theme of this chapter are Smith's personal relations with Elizabeth, whom he served according to his lights, but never fully understood, his impertinent animadversions on the question of a royal marriage, the diplomatic assignments with which he was ungratefully saddled by the unsympathetic Queen, and his sad and exacting spell as

49   *Sir William Petre, 1505-1572*

her First Secretary when Burghley carried the major burden of the administration. Heneage, a lesser man than either Petre or Smith, served honourably and usefully, if not conspicuously. His name is linked erroneously with the Armada Jewel, but whether or not he received this beautiful trinket as a gift from the sovereign for his services during the Spanish war, his career at court offers an interesting example of the relationships of the Queen with her advisers and courtiers and ought not to be neglected by Essex students. He, like other estimable gentry of the county, deserved the confidence and affection of that demanding monarch. For his services he secured the reversion of Copt Hall, land at Colchester, Bretts, and the manor and rectory of Epping. Such was the pattern of service and reward in Elizabeth's England.

⁎⁎⁎

At a moment of high crisis in the history of England and Europe, with the great Armada–in Hakluyt's words, 'so great and terrible an ostentation'–irrevocably committed to its disastrous assault on the English homeland, the effete and dispirited Philip sought solace in the privacy of his personal chapel; England's Queen was on Essex soil inspiring her troops at Tilbury. As preparations were carried out in both countries for the long-awaited invasion, the defences of Thames-side Essex were strengthened, and the navy, to which Essex subscribed its quota of men, ships and money, was fitted out for the impending battle of 1588. At Harwich the artillery was made ready and the *Ark Royal*, Raleigh's flagship, was stationed off the town to supplement the fire-power of the fort. Its master, Thomas Gray, like his brother, John Gray, master of the *Revenge*, which proudly flew the flag of the great Sir Francis Drake, was a Harwich mariner. Among the crews were men of Essex sharing in the dangers and exhilaration of the Channel pursuit of the Spanish flotillas and the destruction off Gravelines that preceded the dispersal and ultimate devastation of the Armada. Alongside the powerful men-of-war were the auxiliaries, ships like the *William*, the *Primrose*, and the *Katherine*, from Harwich. Ships from Colchester

50   Queen Elizabeth at Tilbury, 1588.

and Brightlingsea as well as Harwich took part in the conflict with the Armada. From Wivenhoe came Roger Townshend, knighted at sea for his valour during the struggle.

As the inexorable pressure of the English ships and the great seas of the northern oceans wreaked havoc on Philip's crusading battle fleet, the preparations ashore continued in ignorance of the fate of the Spanish force. More than 4,000 men from Essex joined the vast assemblage of troops at West Tilbury, whose commander, the Earl of Leicester, reported them eager for the contest. Elizabeth, who wished to lead the army in person, was persuaded by Leicester to remain at Havering while the contingents were mustered at East Ham, Stratford and Hackney before moving to Tilbury with, according to John Stow's graphic account, 'Courageous words and gestures their next felicity hope of fight with the enemy'. Among the ranks of the 20,000 men camped at Tilbury by the end of July 1588 were Catholics and Puritans as well as Elizabeth's solid Protestant supporters. In adversity the nation rallied to its intrepid Queen in defence of the liberty and integrity of the Tudor state. As the days passed and news of the struggle in the channel was awaited the Queen visited her troops, staying at Horndon-on-the-Hill. It was for long believed by Essex historians to have been at Arden Hall. Recent research, however, makes it probable that the Queen in fact stayed at 'a proper swete clenly house' called *Cantis* or *Saffron Gardens* in the same parish. It was during her visit to the army that Elizabeth delivered her immortal speech which has echoed across the pages of English history, along with Shakespeare's matchless verse, to enrich the magic quality of Elizabethan England and its invincible people. As she sat, bareheaded on a white charger, her troops thrilled to her challenge, delivered with typical Tudor panache–'Let tyrants fear. I have always so behaved myself that, under God, I have placed my chiefest strength and safeguard in the loyal hearts and goodwill of my subjects; and therefore I am come amongst you ... resolved, in the midst and heat of the battle, to live or die amongst you all, to lay down for my God, and for my kingdoms, and for my people, my honour and my blood, even in the dust'.

It was not until 9 August that the Earl of Cumberland, landed at Harwich by the Lord High Admiral of England, brought the first official news to Tilbury of the decisive defeat that had been inflicted on the enemy fleet. As the troops were dismissed to return to their fields in time for the autumn harvest, the churchwardens of West Tilbury, sadly contemplating, with commendable parochial concern but less than an appropriate sense of history, the conduct of the militiamen, complained that the church furniture and walls were 'much broken down' by the disappointed and frustrated soldiery deprived by the navy and the North Sea of their chance to grapple with the Queen's enemies. This was Gloriana's finest hour. Her end was saddened by the deaths of her nearest friends, and the melancholia of fading health as her great spirit ebbed in the last days of her life. She died on 24 March 1603, in the words of the diarist, Dr. John Massingham, 'mildly like a lamb, easily like a ripe apple from the tree'. She had earned a quiet departure after the tempestuous and precarious events of her glorious reign. If she died like a lamb she had lived like a lion. Nowhere in England was she mourned with greater sincerity than in Essex, whose history is embellished by the lustre of her name and presence. In her last moments she indicated, her imperious voice silenced in extremity, with a nod of the head, assent to her succession by the Scottish king.

Chapter Six
ॐ

STUART ESSEX AND THE CIVIL WAR

'A place of most life and religion'

The death of Queen Elizabeth created a vacuum in the affairs of the nation. The constitutional balances and national loyalties that had developed during her long and illustrious reign were immediately threatened. The growth of parliamentary authority was at once confronted with the Stuart concept of monarchy. The rule of law and English jurisprudence were incompatible with Stuart aspirations; the Queen's death nourished political and spiritual ambitions in Catholic hearts; Protestants prepared to defend their doctrinal and sectarian positions. With the demise of the Tudor dynasts went the attributes of statecraft, leadership and political wisdom. The Stuart sovereigns lacked not only the vital qualities of kingship, but stature and integrity, too. In the 17th century they were to ruin their own cause and squander their inheritance. Not without intellectual talents and courage, history must nevertheless convict them of the most grievous failure in a sovereign; they failed in their duty to the people they claimed the divine right to rule. Alexander Pope referred sardonically to 'The divine right of kings to govern wrong'. The result was rising discontent, revolution and civil war. Yet from this appalling situation the genius and natural instincts of the English people contrived the development of modern political theory and practice. The prestige of the monarchy did not recover until the age of Victoria, when our country was again favoured with the long reign of a queen in whom they could invest their loyalty and affection.

The dour, pedantic James I, 'learned in all things, wise in none' and described as 'the wisest fool in Christendom', had no lack of appetite for power. But he never appreciated the nature and demands of the task of ruling the new English nation-state created by the Tudors. Much as he would have liked to restore the monarchy in its medieval form, he could no more turn back the clock to Bosworth than his grandson could put it back to 1603 on his restoration in 1660. Not even Elizabeth could have done that. It was they, not Elizabeth, 'whom time hath surprised'. His arrogance and obtuseness in public affairs soon alienated Parliament. Catholics and Puritans, too, were deeply offended by the moody monarch–a singular if inauspicious achievement. In Essex the early months of the reign were marked by unrest, and a number of people, mainly of the labouring class, were hauled before the courts for 'treasonable' speeches. Among the minor gentry many refused to comply with the compulsory levy, although it is perhaps of some significance that poverty was pleaded rather than immunity, since the action of the Crown was clearly *ultra vires*. The depth of Catholic reaction was manifested in the abortive Gunpowder Plot, in which a number of Essex men were curiously involved. In 1604 a group of Catholic conspirators inspired by Robert Catesby, and led by Guido Fawkes, a soldier of fortune, resolved to explode a great mine under the parliament buildings during a session at which the King would be present, seize his family, declare a revolution, and enlist the support of Spanish arms to consolidate the plot. An anonymous letter to Lord Monteagle of Great Hallingbury, warning him to excuse himself from attendance in Parliament on the fateful day in November 1605, led to the discovery of the gunpowder and Fawkes and his accomplices in the cellars of the House. Among those questioned in connection with this outrageous plan were several minor characters in Essex, including the vicar of Kelvedon. The immediate, but unhappily temporary result of this attempted crime, was an improvement in the King's relationship with a Parliament thankful for the mutual deliverance from their intended fate.

One of the memorable events of James's reign and one in which Essex figured prominently was the epic voyage of the Pilgrim Fathers in the *Mayflower*. The general background to this episode is one of religious intolerance and the efforts of Catholics and various Protestant sects to assert their freedom of worship and independence. The evidence of the Recusant Rolls shows the pressure that was exerted upon Catholics in Essex to conform to the Protestant settlement. Some found themselves in prison; others forfeited their properties and land. In 1611 the new Authorised Version of the Bible was brought into compulsory use. Among those who worked on its preparation were the incumbents John Overall of Epping, Edward Lively of Purleigh, and Roger Fenton and Roger Andrews of Chigwell. This was but one aspect of the rigours of church doctrine and discipline which also brought the vicars of Little Wakering and St Martin's at Colchester to court for refusing to wear the surplice and breaking the Sabbath. A parishioner at Eastwood was indicted for sleeping during divine service. Bartholomew Legate, an Essex Unitarian, resisted even the King's personal attempts to secure his conversion from heresy and was burnt at the stake for his obstinate refusal to conform.

The Separatists, whose travails eventually brought them together in the *Mayflower*, originated in the northern and Midland counties, migrating to Holland where they hoped, at Leyden, to enjoy the freedom denied to them in England. There they were joined by others from eastern England, including Essex, particularly from the general area of Colchester, Braintree and Witham in the early 17th century. As so often in history the promised land proved illusory, and their lack of resources and international developments soon forced them to move on. They resolved to establish themselves in the New World, leaving Delfshaven in the *Speedwell* in July 1620 for Southampton. In 1619 Christopher Martin of Billericay had been despatched from Leyden to make arrangements for the voyage. Thus the *Mayflower*, which from all the available evidence is virtually certain to have been a Harwich vessel, was chartered to join the *Speedwell* in the enterprise. Martin took over the Mayflower at Leigh and embarked with his wife, and, also from Billericay, John Langemore and Salaman Prower, Dr. Samuel and Susanna Fuller of North Ockendon, and John Bridge from Braintree and others came from elsewhere in the county. The *Mayflower* joined the *Speedwell* at Southampton, and on 5 August 1620 the two ships stood out for the Atlantic. The *Speedwell* was soon found to be unseaworthy and both ships put into harbour at Dartmouth, the *Mayflower* eventually setting forth alone, with 102 passengers, from Plymouth in September. After a tempestuous crossing they sighted Cape Cod on 11 November and gave thanks to God for their deliverance from the storms of the Atlantic. It was in an atmosphere of distress and discontent that they arrived at New Plymouth instead of their intended destination of Jamestown colony further south. Ill-equipped to face the winter ashore, it was not until the following March that the surviving colonists were landed and the *Mayflower* returned to England. The venture as such must be accounted a disaster, and it is of little consequence in the context of the fundamental struggle for political and religious freedom that characterised much of the Stuart century. It has come, however, in the annals of the English-speaking peoples, to epitomise much that is precious to the legacy of English liberties and the American heritage. The place of Essex in the enterprise is permanently enshrined in the prevalence of Essex derivations in place-names of New England today. Thus there is in Massachusetts, Connecticut and New Hampshire the tangible evidence of these Essex folk who faced the rigours of the North Atlantic to found new societies. Colchester, Chelmsford, Braintree, Wethersfield, Epping, Topsfield, Dedham and several others are all to be found on the map of New England. They symbolise the large part that these people took in the brave enterprise. More than that, John Smith, in referring to Stuart Essex as the 'seedbed of American democracy and independence', has demonstrated the importance of the political and philosophical influences of major figures from the Essex homelands. John Winthrop, a charismatic leader, scholar and governor of Connecticut, the clergyman Thomas Hooker, graduate of Emmanuel College, Cambridge and lecturer at Chelmsford and Roger Williams, a prominent Essex divine and a leading New England activist in the cause of democracy were among them. They did much to shape the destiny of colonial America and to define its ultimate values. The links between Essex and the United States can thus be seen to be deep and enduring.

Hooker, a powerful and popular preacher, like others associated with the migrations to North America, had shown his mettle while at Chelmsford in the 1620s. At the time laxity and indiscipline as well as non-attendance at church and misbehaviour on the Sabbath were prevalent in the town. Hooker, who incurred the displeasure of church and government, was removed from office having spoken disparagingly about the authorities of church and state and their, in his view, false and iniquitous adherence to secular power and denial of personal freedoms in worship. But the potency of these strands in political life of England have been subsumed in the popular memory.

The reign of the first of the Stuarts is perhaps remembered more for the Gunpowder Plot and the *Mayflower*–both practical failures–than anything else. Apart from the brief reconciliation following the plot, James's reign was also marred by continuing disputes with Parliament, immorality and corruption at court, illegality and a disastrous foreign policy. His death in 1625 and the accession of his only surviving son held little promise of an improvement in the condition to which public affairs in England had declined.

࿐ఆ

From the outset of Charles I's calamitous reign nothing went right. His determination to pursue the course of personal government further embittered relations between himself and Parliament. His sympathy with the Roman Catholics widened the gulf between him and the majority of his people. In Essex Protestantism remained strong and had been further strengthened towards the end of the previous century by the influx of Huguenots as refugees from Catholic persecution on the continent. Preachers, such as John Rogers, another prominent in the birth of the new colonies in America, whose oratorical fervour raised near hysteria and chaos in Dedham Church, played their part in fanning the flames of popular resistance to conformity. The migration of Puritans in Essex to North America continued.

By 1640 incidents of desecration by dissident Puritan elements were not uncommon. John Walter, Director of the Local History Centre at the University of Essex, has analysed in depth the reasons why the desecration of altars and church furnishings and the assaults on ministers of religion in Essex in the period leading up to the Civil War was so serious compared with much of the rest of the country. He thus argues that this violence, as an expression of deeply-held fears and beliefs, explains the strength of the support for the King as well as the Parliamentary authorities in the county.

In 1631 there were complaints of 'inconformity' in Braintree. The vicar, Samuel Collins, a tolerant man defending his efforts to calm his parishioners and to preserve the authority of the church, opined in response to Archbishop Laud 'My lord's displeasure pierces deepe with me' and refers to 'the error of sundry in my towne which would not be persuaded' and to 'private meetings and schismatic books ... many resolving to goe to New England'. John Bastwick of Colchester was imprisoned and mutilated his ears being cut off in the pillory. The churchwarden of St Botolph's at Colchester, James Wheeler, was excommunicated and incarcerated for refusing to rail in the altar. The dissident clergy and their congregations were vulnerable to repression.

The continued reaction against conformity resulted, on 5 November 1641, in a riotous assembly at Chelmsford when the extremists smashed the images in the windows of the parish church of St Mary's. They returned later, 'a rabble with staves and stones', to destroy the east window of the chancel and to remove the altar rails. After condemning these attacks on the church the rector, Dr. Michaelson, was later assaulted and eventually driven out of the town. In 1643, a Parliamentary ordinance for the removal of images led to the sad destruction of carved wooden angels in the church roof and the removal of the cross from the spire. Many other Essex churches were subject to such desecration by dissident and indisciplined Puritans. Archbishop Laud, supported by the bishops and indeed the King, sought to make changes that Puritans saw as a counter-reformation and akin to popery. The place and status of the altar was particularly sensitive as was the protection or re-introduction of sacred images. There was trouble at Radwinter where Nicholas Drake, the incumbent, was driven from the church by the congregation; and at Kelvedon, Chigwell, Panfield, Finchingfield and at several of the churches in Colchester. Troops mustered in Essex for service in quelling the rebellion in Scotland were much involved in these activities and did much to encourage local people to participate in numerous acts of destruction.

However, along with many of their class in the eastern counties, the gentry of Essex were in the main sufficiently strong and politically so inclined to resist the encroachment of the Crown on their independence and their purses. Some, as did Sir Francis Barrington, who found himself in the Marshalsea, preferred prison to surrender. Economic circumstances also led to discontent. In the political turmoil prices rose and the rural landowners suffered. The de Veres of Castle Hedingham nearly went bankrupt. Many, except those with urban markets for their products, were ruined. This was divisive and damaging to the state. There was resentment, too, as is revealed in the parish records at Maldon, at the impressment of men of the lower classes for service in the barbarous campaigns of the Thirty Years War, in which England had become embroiled as a result of the dispute over the King's marriage to the French Princess Henrietta. The King's reassertion of lapsed and then ancient rights in the forest was bitterly resented in Essex as the whole county, except for the Tendring Hundred, was declared to be afforested and thus within the jurisdiction of the forest courts and subject to the financial disabilities that beset forest communities. It was not until after *c.*1670 that the jurisdiction of the forest courts began to break down, only to be replaced by the increasing severity of the game laws enforced in the ordinary courts to which such powers had been transferred.

Ship money, too, played its part in promoting the ultimate confrontation which the King's reckless policies made inevitable. Although the tax is indelibly linked in history with the name of John Hampden, who declared it to be illegal and unconstitutional, Essex was foremost among those counties where the Crown found it most difficult to collect this unpopular tax, and there were cases of the collectors being molested. But we must briefly retrace the course of the main political events from which these grievances derived during the desperate years that led up to the civil war and regicide. In June 1628 the grievances of parliament and people were put formally to the King in the Petition of Right. It was concerned specifically with illegal taxation, compulsory billeting, and the exercise of the prerogatives of the Crown at the expense of liberty. I have already observed that the Stuarts lacked the advantages enjoyed by the Tudors. Their pursuit of absolute monarchy was incompatible with the penury of the Crown. The sale of Crown lands, begun in Elizabeth's reign, and continued by the Stuarts, diminished the ability of the Crown to raise money. Thus it became more and more reliant on Parliament to vote taxes known as subsidies. Furthermore, the debts inherited from Elizabeth had been vastly increased by the mismanagement of the Stuart kings, and although the issues were basically political and social, finance was the crux of the practical difficulty between the King and Parliament. In March 1629 the King's folly led him to prorogue Parliament which did not meet again until 1640, when his financial position made it inescapable. Meanwhile he had sealed his fate.

The Long Parliament was strong and resolute. Events moved fast. The impeachment and execution of Strafford was followed by the Grand Remonstrance of 1641 and the polarisation of the Royalist and Parliamentary factions. The failure of the Stuart kings to come to terms with the parliamentary developments that had taken place under their predecessors now brought the situation to a head. The crisis over the revolt in Ireland in October 1641 led to the raising of armed forces by King and Parliament. Charles, in an attempt to reassert his dwindling authority, committed his final blunder in violating parliamentary liberties in attempting to arrest the Five Members. With tension rising in the capital, London's decisive weight was thrown in favour of the people as represented by Parliament. Charles was forced to leave the city. His queen fled to the continent with the crown jewels.

When the civil war broke out it ended a period of 150 years during which English soil had been free of war. Although they were not unevenly matched, neither side was fully prepared for war on the scale that ensued. On the King's side his commanders included the Marquis of Newcastle, Hopton and Rupert. The parliamentary leaders were the Earl of Essex, Waller, Fairfax, and, pre-eminently, Oliver Cromwell. There was no clear social or geographical division in the country. Broadly speaking Parliament held London and the south-east, though there were royalist supporters in the area. In the end the discipline and organisation of the parliamentary forces were decisive, but at the outset the King's cause was by no means hopeless. He scored an early marginal success in the indecisive battle at Edgehill in October 1642, where the famous physician, William Harvey, who discovered the circulation of the blood and now lies buried in Essex soil at Hempstead, was present and attended to the King and his senior officers. After the battle a considerable assembly of Essex gentry and farmers at Chelmsford, anxious about royalist intentions after Edgehill, resolved 'with one consent' and remarkable if commendable ambivalence to unite in defence of King and Parliament. A large force was raised in the county and the resolution, which bore names significant in Essex history, such as Mildmay, Barrington, and Grimston, besought God to 'prosper their designs and good endeavours'. There was, in fact, no doubt where the loyalties of Essex mainly lay. Sir Thomas Barrington was told in a letter from Hampden, seeking material support from Essex, that the power of the county was 'great, a place of most life and religion in the land ...' The situation demanded more than good intentions. The immobility of the trained bands and local militias, their poor equipment and scant administration, rendered them largely ineffective. The war would be won by professionals, and it was the Parliamentary leadership, inspired by purpose and unerring faith in their cause, that saw what was needed. The Royalists suffered heavy losses at the hands of Fairfax and Cromwell at Marston Moor in July 1644, and after Naseby in June of the following year their position was beyond restoration.

Despite the parliamentary successes the seeds of future discontent were already apparent by mid-1647. Parliament was nervous about the growing power of the New Model army which had won the war. The army had grievances about their pay and conditions of service. A restless parliamentary force stationed at Saffron Walden, where they used the church as an officers' mess, was visited by a parliamentary deputation led by Cromwell and Ireton to deal with what threatened to become a mutinous situation.

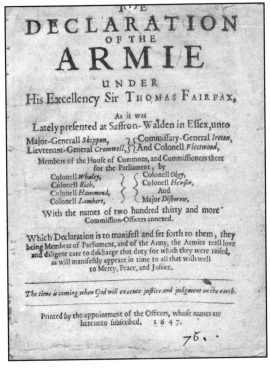

Meetings with the army officers and General Fairfax took place in the church on 21 and 22 March. Assurances were sought about arrears of pay, the appointment of officers, terms of service in England and indemnity. After reporting to Parliament Fairfax was ordered to reject the petition and discipline the officers who had signed it. The situation became tense and efforts were made to persuade the troops to volunteer for service in Ireland. The Parliamentary Commissioners met with Fairfax, probably at the *Sun Inn* in Saffron Walden, but the meeting was abandoned. By May Cromwell was again in Saffron Walden and further meetings were held in the church. Eventually after a long and heated altercation in the church an accommodation was reached. It was agreed

51 *Declaration of the Parliamentary Army at Saffron Walden, 1647*

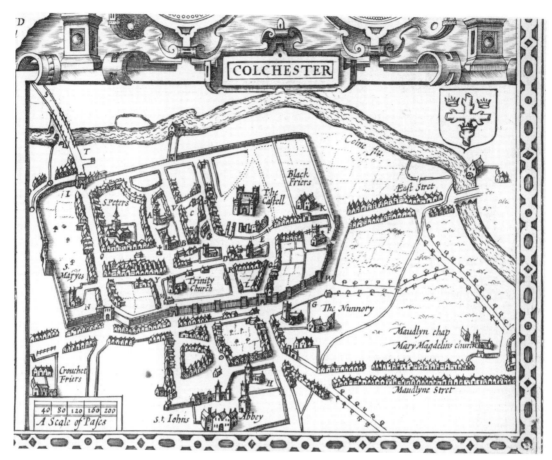

52   *Speed's map of Colchester, 1610*

that the army would not go to Ireland but would disband if satisfied with the conditions of demobilisation. Parliament agreed but would only grant eight weeks pay. Fairfax returned to Saffron Walden and then transferred his headquarters to Bury St Edmunds. The situation was gradually resolved in the context of wider proposals and actions. A compromise worked out at Newmarket narrowly averted civil strife.

The action of Charles himself prevented the strained situation from developing further. The King had surrendered in January 1647, but escaped from captivity and fled to Carisbrooke, only to find himself once more in Parliament's power. Charles still nourished hopes of retrieving his authority, and while at Carisbrooke Castle plotted the resumption of hostilities and entered into secret arrangements with the Scots. Amidst growing political confusion Royalist factions in Kent, Hertfordshire, Wales, and Essex joined with the Scots in support of the King. This wanton, unco-ordinated and hopeless violation of the welcome peace convinced Cromwell and the other parliamentary leaders that no reconciliation was possible with 'that man of blood'. They reacted quickly and decisively. Cromwell first destroyed royalist resistance in Wales and then marched north to settle with the Scots. Fairfax crushed the insurrection in Kent and destroyed the Royalists at Colchester. Charles was at their mercy.

Essex, although deeply committed to the parliamentary cause, was not, until the siege of Colchester, directly involved in the hostilities. Along with the East Anglian counties, Hertfordshire, and Cambridge, Essex formed part of the Eastern Association where Cromwell's support was strongest. His wife in fact was an Essex lady, daughter of Sir James Bourchier of Felsted, and the future Lord Protector looked to the county for a significant contribution in men and supplies for the parliamentary forces. The leading families, among whom personal loyalties were strong, were more divided. We find the Tyrells, Ayloffes, Nevilles and Fanshawes generally in the royalist camp, whereas the Barringtons, Everhards, Lumleys and Mildmays of Wanstead were for Parliament. Some families were even divided amongst themselves as the harsh realities of this fearful situation engulfed them in passion and blood.

A few cases will exemplify the tangled web of conflicting loyalties that rent the upper echelons of Essex society asunder. Sir Benjamin Ayloffe, an ardent Royalist of Great Braxted, was confined in the Tower for several years for his 'Contempt and Neglect of the Orders of the House; and for being, aiding and assisting to the war raised against the Parliament'. More precisely, as High Sheriff of Essex he had obstructed the supplies requisitioned by the Parliamentary army. Whilst imprisoned his horses, valuables and money were seized for the use of the Commonwealth. A family was divided when Sir Henry Mildmay of Danbury Place, was fighting for the Royalists. The Barringtons of Hatfield Broad Oak were strong Parliamentarians and supporters of Cromwell. Sir Thomas was a member of the Council of Divines, composed of both clergy and laity and formed to appease Puritan feelings.

Generally the people of Essex, with their strong Puritan instincts, were firm supporters of the parliamentary cause. But not everyone supported Cromwell. A Wimbish labourer, Christopher Emberson, was brought before the Quarter Sessions at Chelmsford charged with 'not having the fear of God in his heart but with a devilish malicious mind against Cromwell'. Among the Clergy the Royalist rector of Great Parndon, William Osbalston, was deprived of his living in 1643 for neglect of his duties and having 'offended in his lack of preaching', encouraging football and other sports on Sundays and 'for liturgical aberrations'. He was replaced by Jeremiah Dyke but was later restored to his cure. However, Edward Spranger at nearby Harlow was an 'able and godly preaching minister' as was his neighbour William Haughton of Little Parndon. Sussex sources contain an interesting reference to the state of opinion in Essex during the civil war, when after a fracas at Pulborough one 'R.T.' of Horsham reported to the royalist leaders that unless more troops 'be sent down presently they are like to be as high here as in Essex'.

It was the relatively minor incident at Colchester that brought violence and war to Essex and marked the end of Royalist resistance in that county. The campaign that ended at Colchester began in Kent where Fairfax defeated the Royalists at Maidstone on 2 June 1648 and thus frustrated their intention to march on London. A large body of survivors made their way to the Thames at Woolwich, pursued by the parliamentary cavalry. After suffering some losses in the river crossing they arrived at Bow Bridge where they were rejoined by their leader, George Goring, the Earl of Norwich. After a minor clash with a small parliamentary force under a Colonel Whalley, during which they incurred some casualties, the cavaliers quartered at Stratford. Again harassed by Whalley, they left for Chelmsford where they were to rendezvous with other

53   *Leez Priory, 1818*

royalist contingents, by way of Ilford and Romford. At Romford on 7 June there was some indiscipline and Marks in Romford was attacked, although Carew Mildmay, its parliamentary owner, had made good his escape before the Cavaliers arrived. The discipline and general demeanour of the psalm-singing parliamentary troops who arrived in Romford close on the heels of the Royalists has been noted in local annals. Pressing on to Brentwood the Royalists were joined by another force led by Sir Charles Lucas. On 9 June they were at Chelmsford and were reinforced by a party from Hertfordshire under Lord Capel. Marching towards Braintree, en route for Colchester, the Royalists took Leez Priory, the home of the Earl of Warwick who was then serving at sea with the Parliamentary navy. After looting the Priory, seizing weapons, horses and other military equipment, they reached Braintree and marched overnight, arriving in the vicinity of Colchester on the morning of 11 June. After a brief skirmish at the gates the combined Royalist force entered Colchester on 12 June.

Meanwhile Fairfax had occupied Rochester and moved on to Tilbury where his troops are said to have desecrated the church. From there they went to Billericay and

54   *Billericay, 1833*

were at Brentwood on 11 June, but a few days after their quarry. Some 2,000 volunteers from Coggeshall under Sir Thomas Honywood of Marks Hall met up with Fairfax at Brentwood. The day after the Royalists had forced their way into Colchester the parliamentary army was outside the walls of the town. The Royalists, some 4,000 strong, held out for about twelve weeks, during which they and the besieged citizens of Colchester suffered severe privation from lack of food, even domestic animals being eaten before the end of the siege. Sporadic fighting took place

55   *Colchester Castle*

during the siege with many sorties and skirmishes mounted by both sides. The town was also subjected to bombardment by the Parliamentary artillery to which the Royalists could make little reply. All hope was abandoned by the defenders when news of Cromwell's victory over the Scots at Preston reached the town. With a hostile, hungry and restless populace in their midst there was no alternative to surrender on 28 August. Fairfax dealt harshly with the Royalist leaders. Although Sir Bernard Gascoigne was reprieved at the last moment, Sir Charles Lucas and Sir George Lisle were shot in Castle Park. Their bearing and gallantry when facing the firing party only emphasised the frightful waste of the civil war to which the King, in his folly and wilfulness, had condemned his country. As John Milton wrote in reference to the siege at Colchester 'for what can war but endless war still breed'. Thus ended in tragedy another episode in the story of the historic fortress town, the walls and fortifications of which were largely demolished on the orders of Fairfax after the siege had been raised. A similar fate awaited the King. It was one of Colchester's notable citizens, Sir Harbottle Grimston, who had knelt before Charles at Newport begging him to seek a basis for peace for the benefit of the country. He pleaded in vain. The King continued on his disastrous course, and following the defeat of his dwindling forces was brought to trial in January 1649. The man, against whom in Cromwell's eyes 'the Lord hath witnessed', was found guilty, though he had refused to plead, and was executed in Whitehall to the horror of Europe and many in England. Ralph Josselin, Essex-born at Roxwell, the son of a farmer and Puritan vicar of Earls Colne, caught the mood of the people when he noted the event in his diary. He was much 'troubled with the black providence of putting the King to death'. There was little love for Charles but even in Essex there were many who found regicide hard to stomach.

England had been ruled for more than a decade without a Parliament; for a decade the country had been locked in civil war; a third decade was to pass without a King. The Commonwealth was declared shortly after the execution and the country was to endure a constitutional experience which it soon found it did not like. The rightful king, eldest son of 'the royal martyr', was crowned as Charles II at Scone and almost at once led an invading force into England. Heavily defeated by Cromwell's troops, he fled to France. Cromwell, who became Lord Protector, having refused the Crown, raised the prestige of the country abroad to heights to which the Stuarts could never aspire. But he was gradually forced along the road of unconstitutional government until he lost the support of all but a small minority of opinion. The military rule of the Major-Generals following the dissolution of the Commonwealth fostered the desire for a restoration of the monarchy. Oliver Cromwell, in many ways an estimable and remarkable man, died in August 1658, unlamented by all except his intimate colleagues. Once again we may turn to the pages of the Essex parson's diary for an authentic note of the reaction of the ordinary people to the news of Cromwell's death—wrote Josselin, 'Cromwell died, people not minding it much'. His son, Richard Cromwell, lacking the prestige and will of his father, soon abdicated his responsibility and the stage was set for the Restoration of 1660.

⁎⁎⁎

It says much for the vitality of English life when in an era of revolution and despotism such as that experienced in the 17th century, intellectual achievements of timeless expression and value enable us to think of it as the age of Milton, Newton, and Wren, as much as that of the Stuarts and Cromwell. It was only to be expected that in the doctrinal confusion and political ferment of the time theorists such as Locke and the materialist, Hobbes, should focus their attention on what they saw as the central issues of social organisation. The horizons of literature and science were extended, too. Milton's majestic prose and glorious verse ranks with the language of Shakespeare, whose own life extended into the period, although he belongs generically to the immediate Tudor past. In the *Areopagitica* John Milton uttered one of the most powerful political statements of all time. Newton's towering intellect elevated the range of scientific thought and gave it an impetus never exhausted. Wren bequeathed to posterity the classical splendour of his prolific and creative reign as England's premier architect. All in all perhaps the most significant legacy of this turbulent century was the rise of constitutional government and rational thought from the struggle between bigotry and dissent. It was aptly epitomised in the pregnant words of Bishop Laud to an Essex farmer in 1631, when he opined that 'last year's famine was made by man and not by God'.

Throughout the 17th century the population of England grew but slowly, though London, to which the economic health of Essex was largely tied, expanded as a centre of commerce and government. The fortunes of the county as a whole were naturally influenced directly by the effects of foreign war and domestic strife. The Puritan movement and the efforts of the Stuart kings to impose their will upon the country were inspired not primarily by economic or social factors, but motives of a political and religious nature. The results were profound and permanent and the whole fabric of English life was affected. The economic setback caused by the wars was followed by a measure of revival until after the Restoration, when there was again a depression in trade during which the gulf between rich and poor was widened. Not until after the wars of Anne's reign were brought to an end by the Treaty of Utrecht did some prosperity return and England experience the benefits of commercial expansion and the rewards of maritime enterprise.

In Essex the economic situation was broadly similar to that in the country generally, though some areas of activity were especially vulnerable to general trends and, as at Colchester, local events. In the early years of the century the historian and topographer, William Camden, described the Essex marshlands:

plentifull in grasse, and rich in Cattaile, but Sheepe especially where all
their doing is in making of Cheese: and there shall ye have men take the
womens office in hand and milke Ewes: whence those huge thicke Cheeses
are made that are vented and sould not onely into all parts of England, but
into forraign nations also…

During the period with which this chapter is concerned we may think of Essex as
primarily relying on mixed farming, its maritime produce and in certain areas the manufacture of textiles. The urban population began to expand at the expense of the countryside. The growth of road communications and water-borne traffic reflected the emerging
patterns of diversifying economic activities. But there were also serious social problems
other than those attributable to political or religious conflict. Poverty and malnutrition
among rural workers and their families and in some of the manufacturing industries were
among the factors which encouraged emigration to North America. Bad harvests, rising
prices and competitive markets led to beggary, rioting and crime promoted by hunger
and distress. Charitable trusts, although important in relieving some of the worst problems locally, could not resolve them. Colchester, the county's only sizeable town, was
developing, as is clear from the Ship Money assessments in payment of which Essex was
described as obstinate. In Braintree, Thaxted, Maldon and Harwich on the other hand
there is sufficient evidence of economic stagnation. At Dedham the signs of decay in the
clothing industry, important in that part of the county, were apparent by 1641 when the
local clothiers petitioned the King, who received a deputation at Greenwich and was told

56   Dedham, 1832

that trade had declined and 'the cryes for food of many thousands of poor ... do continuously press us'. Colchester's prosperity was for a time shattered by the siege and the town never recovered its former prominence in the cloth trade. The situation in the industry was further exacerbated by the loss of foreign markets in the Spanish wars. As we shall see when we come to Hanoverian Essex, the decline would never be reversed. John Evelyn in his diary refers to Colchester in 1656, eight years after the siege, as 'this wretchedly demolished town'. In 1678 the Dutch in the town instructed the mayor and corporation that they were in difficulty in sustaining the needs of the poor within their community, as they had traditionally always done. In agriculture, except in south-west Essex, there was a general drift away from dairying to arable, particularly corn, for which the soils and climate of the county are most suited. Hedgerows were grubbed-up, as has again happened in our time to enlarge the wheatfields to satisfy the demands of agrarian economy. Thomas Fuller, in his *Worthies of England*, saw Essex, which he knew well, in 1662 as 'a fair county ... plentifully affording all things necessary for man's subsistence'. Fisheries were an important industry in the coastal and estuarine towns of the Crouch, Colne, Blackwater and at Barking on the Thames. Essex was famed for its oysters–the 'Colchester natives'– and the quality of its turbot, cod and sole supplies. The fish trade naturally fostered a sizeable ship-building industry in ports such as Harwich, Maldon and Wivenhoe.

Towards the end of the century steps were taken under the turnpike legislation to improve the road systems which had fallen into decay. There were regulations, too, which governed the weight of vehicles and general usage of the highways. Before the central authorities took the situation in hand the condition of many main roads was extremely bad. In September 1621 it was necessary for the Essex justices to order special measures for the repair of roads 'especially ... where the king may have occasion to pass'. Even as late as 1660 Samuel Pepys, whose diary reveals him as a frequent visitor to Essex on social occasions and in his official capacity to Waltham Forest to secure timber for the navy, found the road through Epping good 'only in one path'. It was well into the following century before the turnpikes could be said to have created a satisfactory road system in the county generally.

It is hard now to understand the credence that was given in the 11th century to witchcraft which attracted one of the most obnoxious manifestations of social injustice and cruelty that history has to record. Essex was especially involved, the Puritans perhaps associating the evils of the craft with Catholic rites and practice. Before his native intelligence finally overcame his propensity

57 *The frontispiece of Matthew Hopkins'* Discovery of Witches, *1644*

for superstitious practices, James I himself had spent several years in researching for a book on *Daemonologie*, which he published in 1597. Under an Act of 1604, early in his reign, the penalties for practising the evil arts were heavily increased and many were convicted and executed before he realised the cruel nonsense that was being perpetrated in his name. Later, in the mid-century, a witchfinding campaign that mesmerised the justices and public opinion in the eastern counties was conducted by one Matthew Hopkins, a lawyer from Manningtree, his assistant, John Stearne, and a woman whom they employed to search for the supposed 'witch marks'. Between 1645-47 they accused some hundreds of people and many were executed. Of these, a number met their death in Essex, mostly in the Tendring area. Among those who were condemned to this awful fate and thus subscribed their sad and humble names to Essex history were Elizabeth Clarke, Elizabeth Gooding, Anne Leach, Susan Cock, and Rebecca Jones of Manningtree, Mistley, St Osyth and elsewhere in the county. Not until 1675 was the last case of alleged witchcraft heard in the Essex courts.

The 17th century was not, in Essex, an age of high achievement in the arts. Only in London where Wren was at hand to repair the ravages of the Great Fire was the period a vintage one for ecclesiastical architecture. In Essex there is little of outstanding interest, but in Audley End and the fort at Tilbury the county still possesses two surviving examples of the time that merit our attention. Otherwise there are but such as the pleasant

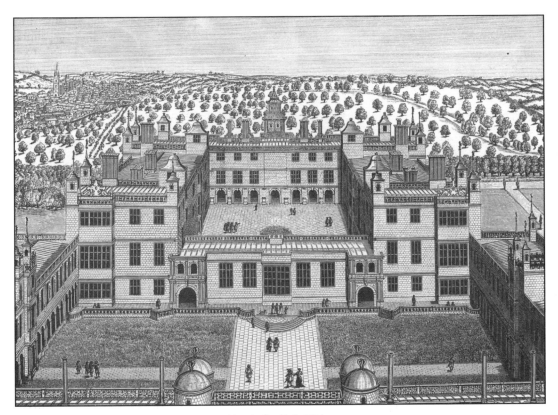

58 *Audley End, 1688*

brick houses of Bois Hall, near Navestock, Dynes Hall, at Great Maplestead, the fire-place of 1620 at Langleys and the pargetting of the period as may be seen at Crown House, Newport, and the former *Sun* inn at Saffron Walden. The fine Jacobean frontage of Audley End in its park by the River Cam may be seen to advantage today from the Cambridge road. It was built between 1603-16, on land originally granted by Henry VIII, for Thomas Howard, the Earl of Suffolk and Lord Treasurer. Although considerably altered and diminished from its original grandeur it is still essentially Jacobean. Suffolk himself told the King it had cost £200,000 and prompted the response that it was 'too much for a king, but might do very well for a Lord Treasurer'. It was bought back by Charles II in 1669 for £50,000 and called New Palace, but when it was returned to the Suffolks in 1701 the purchase price had still not been fully met. Tilbury Fort is perhaps the best example of 11th-century military architecture in Britain. It was reconstructed in the 1670s by the Chief Engineer of the King's household, Sir Bernard de Gomme, after the incursion by the Dutch into the Thames. Its military virtues were never put to the test, but the brick-faced ramparts and the fine classical water-gate with its semi-circular pediment and voluted pilastered columns surmounted by a variety of carved military impedimenta make it a notable landmark on the southern river-boundary of Essex.

୫୬୯୪

Sir Harbottle Grimston, elected Speaker, was in the royalist mission to Holland sent to invite Charles II to return to his kingdom, and it was he who delivered the speech of welcome to the King in parliament. In the immediate wake of the Restoration, hope was uppermost in the hearts of a people instinctively monarchist, though wearied by the events we have recalled in this chapter. In the first delirious moments when the return of the maypoles to the village greens symbolised the overthrow of the Puritan yoke expectations were high. But the issues were far from being settled by the return of Charles to a gladdened people; the ambitions of a Catholic king were then incompatible with the aspirations of a Protestant kingdom. Charles was not long in undermining his own position with the characteristic malevolence and obstinacy of his house.

The years between the Restoration of 1660 and the Glorious Revolution of 1688 were ones in which the Dissenters suffered severe persecution. The Acts of Uniformity the so-called Five Mile Act, the Test Acts and the Conventicle Act failed to restrain the rising demands for freedom of Worship and liberty of conscience. The Dissenters in Essex, it was said, 'spoke of their faith, if at all, in bated breath'. However, in 1689, the Act of Toleration relieved the constraints on freedom of worship although the dissenting nonconformists continued to suffer civil inequalities for almost 150 years.

Ralph Josselin, having prayed for the restored King, soon noticed the varying fortunes of his fellow clerics for their past loyalties and practices. Clergymen who refused to conform were driven from their livings and religious meetings broken up by the constables. Many incumbents of the established church like those at Shenfield, Rayleigh and Rettendon faced difficult dilemmas of conscience and were ejected. Others, like Israel Edwards of East Mersea, sequestrated in 1651, were restored. Samuel Johnson of Corringham was inducted in 1670 as 'the friend of Liberty and Defender of true religion'. Emanuel Uty of Chigwell, deprived in 1643 as one of the 'superstitious, innovating, scandalous and malignant clergymen', was restored, only to die in a year.

A poignant token of this turbulent century for the church may be seen in the parish register of St John and St Giles at Great Easton. In 1653, the rector, Thomas Leader, who served there from 1648 to 1678, had recorded his appointment as 'civil register' under the Act of Parliament that authorised him to perform marriages and baptisms. At the Restoration in 1660 he intruded the words 'the wicked' before 'Parliament'. His belated protest after the anxious years has echoed down the ages in this evocative entry which must have reflected the mood of many of his fellow Essex clergymen of the time.

The restored clergy faced serious inherited problems, especially the nearly impossible task of re-establishing the prestige and authority of a church discredited and in doctrinal confusion after the fluctuating fortunes of the previous half-century. The desecrations of the Commonwealth period were purged. During that unhappy time 'superstitious' pictures and crosses were defaced and 'Popish' inscriptions removed. In 1661 we find sexton Francke at Danbury receiving payment of a shilling for painting out the arms of the Commonwealth. Laymen, too, faced the consequences of the Restoration. Sir Henry Mildmay, Master of the Jewel Office to Charles, and a judge at the King's trial, was tried for having yielded the treasure to the unlawful Commonwealth authorities, though he can have had little option in that matter. He suffered imprisonment, loss of title and honours and personal degradation in the retribution exacted at the King's command. Hezekiah Haynes, Major General for the Eastern Counties, was imprisoned in the Tower, but later petitioned successfully for his release. Conversely the royalist hero's sister, Mary Lisle, was granted £2,000 in recognition of the sufferings of her family for the Stuart cause, her brother having been 'murthered for his Loyalty to our Royall Father of glorious memory'.

In national affairs Charles lurched from disaster to disaster. The humiliation of 1667 when the Dutch destroyed English shipping at Chatham led Pepys to recall the triumphs of Cromwell's reign. The King's prestige was seriously damaged and his intrigue with France which culminated in the Treaty of Dover has been regarded by historians as one of the most discreditable acts of English diplomacy. He was unlucky, too. The year 1666 saw the Great Fire of London, when for a brief moment he identified himself with his people in the hour of danger. Also the Great Plague descended on the land. It spread from London to Essex and northwards. In Colchester 4,500 people, half of the town's population, died between the summer of 1665 and the end of 1667. The definitive *Victoria History of Colchester* describes this calamity as probably the most destructive outbreak of plague in any large town in modern England. Despite the remedial measures that were taken in regard to the burial of the dead, the provision of pest-houses and financial support, the immediate impact was profound. The population and Colchester's economy, apart from the textile industry, nevertheless recovered with unexpected rapidity. Ralph Josselin does not fail to record this disastrous event–'At Colchester it spreads exceedingly, this week buried 188', and there were fears for the surrounding towns and villages though his own 'Colne, sinful Colne' was spared. Pepys, too, noted the virility of the pestilence in Colchester, where 'it rages mightily'. Nearly a third of the population of Braintree succumbed, and at Harwich, Epping, Brentwood, Romford and Barking the archives mark the suffering of the afflicted people. Curiously, other towns, Chelmsford and Saffron Walden for example, escaped the worst horrors of the outbreak.

ೞೞ

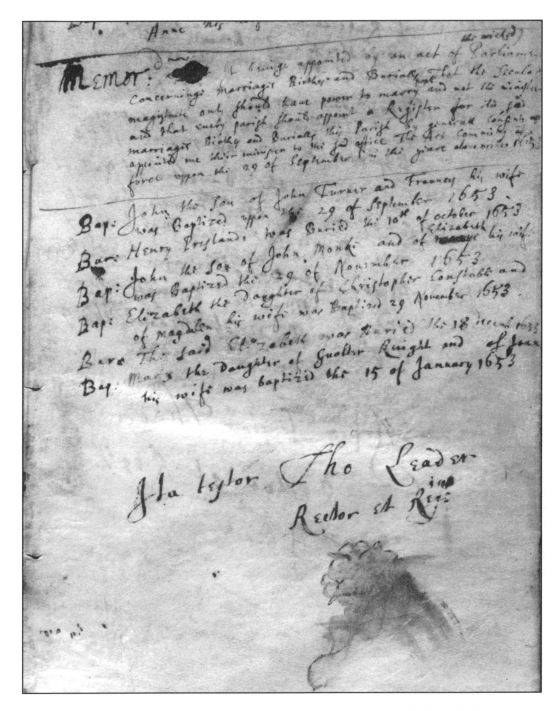

59 *Parish register, Great Easton, 1653: note the post-Restoration insertion of 'wicked' before 'Parliament'*

At the death in 1685 of Charles, whose selfish and salacious conduct earned him no affection nor respect in the still puritanical hearts of the people of Essex, he was succeeded by his younger brother, James VII of Scotland. As James II he was as unfitted to assume the responsibilities of the Crown as his predecessor had been. The brief episode during which this bigoted religious zealot, who thought himself above the law, occupied the throne offered no relief to the pattern of self-indulgence and self-destruction the English people had come to expect of the House of Stuart. A strong Protestant king was a national necessity and the swift and bloodless character of the deposition of James in favour of Dutch William and Mary, the daughter of the Stuart king, testifies to the mood of the nation. William of Orange landed in Torbay on 5 November 1688. James fled and despite his efforts to stir up revolt in Ireland, where he was supported, and Jacobite intrigue, he never recovered his throne and died at St Germain in 1701. William had been invited to accept the Crown in the name of liberty and the Protestant faith, but he never succeeded in winning the hearts of his subjects. Sensible, industrious and cool, he survived the early troubles of war with France and the uncertainty surrounding his tenure of the throne. Mary died in 1694 and William in 1702. With the accession of the last of the Stuarts, Anne, Mary's younger sister, national fortunes took an upward turn. Marlborough's great victories at Blenheim, Malplaquet, and Oudenarde restored the country's prestige in Europe. The union of England with Scotland in 1706 was of immense and lasting benefit to both peoples. Across the seas the birth of the first British Empire was marked by settlement and military success in North America, the Caribbean, Gibraltar, and the Far East. At home prosperity returned. The Queen herself, a sad, uninspiring, somewhat domesticated figure and the last of her line, died, gladly it was said, in August 1714.

And so a new age would dawn with the advent of the Hanoverians. Essex, as has been noted, had been closely identified with the issues of a period during which the fundamental basis of our constitutional future was hammered out in civil strife. The direct involvement of the county was relatively slight, but the people of the county made their contribution to the eventual success of the causes to which most Englishmen subscribed–parliamentary government and the Protestant succession. In their support of the Cromwellian revolution and their share of the burden of wars and natural disasters they were in the mainstream of English history. There remained at the end much still to be resolved in the course of time and in the wisdom of man. In retrospect one feels that the nation's uncharacteristic lapse into irrationality and the social, political and religious labyrinth that tormented its people ought to have been avoided.

I shall leave the last words of this chapter of our story to the sagacious and estimable Thomas Fuller whose place in Essex history has been so elegantly inscribed by William Addison:

> All things are not to be found out in one age,
> as reserved for future discovery; and that
> perchance may be easy for the next, which seems
> impossible in this generation.

Chapter Seven

ℰᎧℭℬ

HANOVERIAN ESSEX

'No very considerable Disturbances'

The period–1714 to 1837–with which this chapter is concerned has attracted much attention from historians as the age of transition. To many it is Georgian, but that is too narrow a term adequately to describe an era that spans the time between the Stuarts and Victoria, and marks the end of absolutism and the advent of constitutional monarchy in a context that would eventually admit democracy. It saw also the last abortive gestures of Jacobitism, the political domination of the Whigs and such figures as the hard-headed Norfolk squire, Robert Walpole, and the remarkable Pitts. It was an age, for all its social problems, of relative tranquillity after the upheavals of Stuart England and, on the whole, one in which there was a growing spirit of toleration. For the rich, who relished and exploited their leisure as never before or again, life was never sweeter. For the ordinary folk life was arduous and mundane. Long hours and poor wages were the lot of a people who, at the mercy of the harvest, aspired to share the political power of the country gentlemen on whom they depended. In Essex the wealthy families of Dacre Barret, the Mildmays and the FitzWalters typified the influence and social prestige of the Whig aristocracy in that mobile age of contrasts. Of social excesses and affectation there is ample evidence, but, despite the contrived ostentation and epicurean fancies in which the rich could indulge, there was also a real consolidation of the economic base of the nation which eventually made possible the unprecedented growth of Victorian industry and commerce. Triumph and disaster abroad, in India, Canada, and the 13 colonies that formed the United States, were followed in Europe by the drama of the Napoleonic Wars, and at home, Reform. Dull and unattractive though the Hanoverian monarchs may have been, a lack of lustre after the brittle Stuart monarchy was no bad thing. They provided the breathing-space the nation needed before the trial of strength with France and the subsequent political crisis in Britain. The interests and experience of Essex, inevitably Hanoverian in sympathy, were engaged in all these facets of the life of an England that was beginning to glimpse the promise and perils of modern society.

ℰᎧℭℬ

With the accession of George I, who was succeeded by his son in 1727, England settled down, under her alien princes, to a somewhat featureless regime and a humdrum court. Neither evinced much interest in Britain, and with their German mistresses neither sought nor attracted popularity. There was indeed a good deal of public resentment, especially over George II's ill-treatment of his queen. However, national unity and the further development of parliamentary government, including the genesis of our cabinet system under Stanhope and Walpole, sufficed to ensure general support for the

Hanoverians, and where there was not support, apathetic acquiescence. The first two Georges reigned for almost half a century during which the dominance of the Whigs was the paramount feature of the political scene, although the sovereign was still an important factor. The major figure was Walpole, whose own relations with the sovereign were not good, but he did win the confidence and active support of Caroline of Ansbach, George II's queen. Until 1742 when, as his parliamentary support declined, he resigned, Walpole's was the guiding hand in national policies. Not until Clive's victories in India at Arcot and Plassey, Wolfe's success in Canada, and the victories over the French at Minden and Quiberon Bay in 1759 at the end of the first Georgian period, was the nation's appetite for foreign adventures re-kindled. At home there were the alarms of the '15' and the '45'.

In restrospect it is clear that neither of these ineffectual Stuart bids for their rightful, but squandered, inheritance posed a serious threat to the stability of the Hanoverian throne. At the time it was by no means clear that the Jacobite campaigns would fail. The rising of 1715 followed a period in which there had been fairly widespread riots, and when James Stuart landed in Britain he may have had high hopes. Many thousands of highlanders joined his colours at Perth and the situation in Scotland was serious for the government of George I. The Stuart forces in the south-west were, however, ineffective, and the main thrust from Scotland was defeated at Preston. After the surrender of the Jacobites there the Stuart prince had no option but to return ignominiously to France. Most of the ringleaders also escaped; only two, Lord Kenmure and the young Lord Derwentwater, were executed. Faint echoes of the '15' come through to us from the Essex archives. Prior to the attempt there had been minor disturbances in Hanoverian Essex, and one unfortunate Jacobite, Christopher Layer, was executed with the usual barbarities for his part in a 'conspiracy' that was alleged in court to have involved also Lord North and Grey, who lived at Epping, and to have been conceived at the *Green Man*, Leytonstone. A few other Essex people were indicted at the Assizes for disaffection, the squire of Gestingthorpe, John Elliston, for example, being convicted, fined, and whipped at Chelmsford for his offence. When the invasion took place the authorities took into custody a number of known Stuart sympathisers in the county. Samuel Tufnell of Langleys, captain of a troop of horse in the Essex militia, was ordered to round up several prominent Jacobites. When arrested in October 1715 they were escorted to the *Black Boy* inn at Chelmsford and committed to prison. Among the 15 arrested were members of prominent Essex families who had supported the Royalists during the Civil War. They included Anthony Bramston of Roxwell, a Waldegrave, a Turner, a Searle, a Windus, and a Petre, all of whom were taken into custody 'upon suspicion of being disaffected to K. George'. In December they were released by Order in Council, pending their appearance at the Assizes, on recognizances being lodged by their families, who had clearly looked after their interests well during the period of confinement. In the long inventory of the provisions sent in, as a privilege of untried prisoners, by their well connected families and friends, the Harveys of Chigwell, the Lethulliers of Aldersbrook, and Lady Petre of Writtle among them, were game and venison, lobsters and oysters, fruit, brandy and punch. Hardly a Barmecidal diet; loss of liberty it would seem was not accompanied by loss of appetite. It was all little more than a precautionary gesture, for these people had no power in the circumstances and when brought before Mr. Justice Tracy in March 1716 they were discharged 'noe person appearing to alleadge anything against them'. It was all symptomatic of a state of nerves for which there was little substantive reason.

The '45' was no more successful, and its total failure marked the end of Stuart ambitions to recover the British Crown. With the British army heavily committed on the continent Charles Edward Stuart, the 'Young Pretender', made his futile gesture. Landing in the Hebrides he rallied the clans at Glenfinnan and plunged into England, driving south through Lancashire, where he tasted military success at Preston Pans, to Derbyshire, but here, lacking support, the campaign petered out. Retreating to Scotland the forces of the courageous but forlorn young scion of his House were destroyed by the royal army at Culloden Moor on 10 April 1746, a victory followed by shameful atrocities. A graphic, if partisan, account of this crushing debacle for the Stuarts is contained in the Mildmay archives. Like the '15' before, the '45' created alarm in sensitive official circles. The High Constables of the Essex Hundreds ordered local parishes 'to keep a Watch Day and Night upon suspicion of an Invasion'. The squirearchy of Essex, with resolution and loyalty, formed an 'Association of the Noblemen, Gentlemen, Clergy, Freeholders and Inhabitants', which in pledging its support for George II condemned Charles Edward as a 'Popish Pretender and Tool of France'.

At the Quarter Sessions the Essex Whigs expressed their 'abborrence' of his 'insolent and rebellious designs' and the Lieutenancy records contain a long subscription list which demonstrates the readiness of the local gentry to put their hands in their pockets for the benefit and comfort of the Hanoverian forces.

Yet these events were but ephemeral ripples on the surface of history and, by 1768, already largely forgotten. The Essex historian, Philip Morant, could write, 'Since the Restoration, no very considerable Disturbances … have happened in this County; and may it always remain quiet and peaceable'.

೮೦೮

If the period of the Hanoverians is convenient as a basis for describing a further phase in the political evolution of England, it is all too long to encompass with facility the far-reaching changes that took place between 1714 and 1837 in the economic condition of our country. Until now, in the age of the New Scientific Revolution, the pace of change had never been so fast. Inescapably the effects were felt in the county. Yet in the Essex countryside the momentum of change was real, but less apparent. The Industrial Revolution left its mark on the future metropolitan areas of Essex, and agriculture and the cloth trade were significantly affected. The county remained a largely rural and farming area. John Wesley, in 1758, saw Essex as 'an extremely pleasant and fruitful county'. He was much taken by Colchester, though Morant, not long after, deplored the town 'running to ruin'. As early as 1722 that most percipient observer, Daniel Defoe, had appreciated the growth that was taking place in the Hams, at Leytonstone, Ilford, Stratford and Barking which, under the influence of the expanding capital, were beginning to respond to its demands. He noted the considerable estates of the London merchants and tradesmen who set the fashion, revived again in our own generation, for the country retreat from the daily round in the city.

Arthur Young, to whose industry and wit we owe much of our knowledge of the time, writing in 1767 mentions the 'very magnificent palace', Wanstead House, but asserted that husbandry in the county afforded him 'a pleaure superior to that which any palace could confer'. He waxed enthusiastically about the view across the Thames valley from Horndon-on-the-Hill: 'I never beheld any thing equal to it in the West of England, that region of landscape'. Chelmsford he considered 'a pretty, neat, and well built town'. Lest it be thought that the famous Secretary of the Board of Agriculture was free with praise be it noted that just across the border in Suffolk he found Sudbury 'an exceeding dirty, but a great manufacturing town'. All in all 18th-century Essex must have presented to the privileged traveller a pleasant rural landscape with good small towns and Thames-side, as yet not despoiled, an active, thriving infant of the industrial transformation to come. The homes of the rich, landed gentry and London merchants, embellished the countryside. In reality there was another side to the picture. The process of assimilating change was, as always, painful. An expanding population could not all enjoy the fruits of commercial enterprise, and unemployment caused by the decline of the cloth trade in north Essex led to much distress. The public authorities which had replaced the old shire organisations and the Hundreds, of which only vestiges remained in the manorial courts and parliamentary representation, were not strong enough to cope. Local government was now vested in the officers of the Vestry, the overseers of the poor, the surveyors, constables, churchwardens, and the Justices in Quarter Sessions. The local historian is fortunate in the survival of so much of the documented evidence for increasing activity of these all too weak, but generally active and worthy servants of the public. The local impact of the trends and events in a society in transition will be found in prosaic but often engaging detail in the parish records. But it is essential for a valid perspective to evaluate history in a broader context.

Before the decennial census began in 1801 historians must rely for their statistics on estimates based on various demographic indicators and contemporary evidence. When the Hanoverians came to the throne the national population was about six millions. Until well into the 18th century it rose slowly, and by 1760 has been estimated at no more than seven millions. Thereafter, social and economic factors continued to cause an acceleration in this growth. At the national census of 1801 some 9.2 millions were recorded. This figure climbed steeply and doubled to about 18 millions by the end of the period. In Essex there were perhaps 130,000 people at the beginning of the 18th century, and this figure, too, had reached well over 300,000 when the Princess Victoria succeeded. Within this considerable demographic growth was concealed a significant migration from country to town, especially London, which attracted a great many people from Essex. The influx of Irish immigrants to Lancashire, the west country and the Essex farmlands was also important and not without direct consequences for the rudimentary social services then existing. Cobbett asserted, in *Rural Rides*, with his familiar sweeping judgement, that all the mowers in the country were English and all the haymakers Irish!

The upheaval caused by the rapid and profound changes that were taking place in the structure of society was beyond the resources of the authorities to contain. Among agricultural families in particular, distress was widespread by the end of the 18th century. The Vestries, dispensing poor relief, were incapable of meeting the demands of a problem on this scale. The situation was held only just short of a social disaster. In Essex, apart from the future metropolitan area, one-sixth of the population was in receipt of poor relief at the turn of the century. The standards of living of the agricultural labourer and his family inevitably declined and many were sustained only by the Poor Law.

RULES, &c.

CONCERNING THE

MASTER AND MISTRESS

Of the Workhouſe at ROMFORD, in the Liberty of HAVERING atte
BOWER, in the County of ESSEX, made at a General Meeting
of the Directors and Guardians of the Poor, held the 3d Day
of *November* 1787, and confirmed at a General Meeting held
the 1ſt Day of *December* following.

Firſt, THAT the Maſter do regiſter in a Book the names of all the Poor,
their age, and the times of their admiſſion, and diſcharge by death or
otherwiſe.

Second, That he muſter them every morning at ſix in ſummer, and at ſeven
in winter, and at one o'clock all the year.

Third, That he keep a regular and fair Daily Account of all Proviſions,
Stores, Clothes, Goods, Materials, Tools, or Things, which ſhall be
received into the Houſe, and of all Work done therein, in ſuch form
as ſhall be directed; and he is ſtrictly to examine all Goods and Proviſions received, and make a faithful report to the next Committee of
any deficiency in weight, quantity, or quality.

60   *Poor Law Rules, Romford 1787*

The basis on which this was operated was changed fundamentally by the historically famous decision of the Berkshire magistrates at Speenhamland in May 1795.
When, in the wake of the worst winter in that century, they realised that the distress in
agricultural areas could not be relieved effectively by the provisions of the existing Poor
Law, they enforced the responsibility of the parish authorities. Under the 'system' they
initiated, low agricultural wages were supplemented by a sliding scale of poor relief
related to the price of bread. Their action was reinforced by legislation in 1796 and
generally implemented in the south of England. In 1800 parliament enacted the Bread
Act 'for making better provision for the Maintenance of the Poor'. The state had officially recognised the seriousness of the position. Under the Poor Law Act of 1834 the
Speenhamland system was abolished and the process of transferring responsibility from
the parishes and justices to the state was given formal sanction. The Speenhamland

system had not been uniformly applied in every locality. Generally it took the form of a kind of family allowance. At Wickham Bishops, for example, it was available to families with four or more children. Elsewhere in Essex the authorities at Thorpe-le-Soken paid the allowance according to the size of the family without specifying a minimum qualification. In these circumstances it is hardly surprising that there was trouble. In the years of bad harvests there was rioting and arson in Essex. A food riot at Saffron Walden in 1795 led to some of those concerned in the 'Riot and Confusion from the general Insurrection of the lower class of inhabitants' suffering trial and imprisonment. A local butcher had been intimidated by a mob into lowering the prices of his meat. Similar occurrences at Harlow, Boreham and Halstead were typical of a pattern of discontent bred of poverty and desperation. But the Berkshire magistrates had promoted a basic premise, that of the duty to establish minimum standards, a concept that prevails widely in European jurisprudence and social policy.

As a farming county, Essex was especially sensitive to these problems. In the van of progress in agricultural techniques, Essex farmers were yet vulnerable to the pressure of economic fluctuations and the labour problems associated with migration to industrial areas and social penury. The process of enclosure, although it enhanced the efficiency of farming and the productivity of the land, left social problems in its wake that were permanent in their effect. Generally, however, the development of more advanced crop rotations, selective breeding, the practice of seed drilling and horse hoeing, and the introduction of the turnip and other fodder crops such as lucerne, heralded an Agrarian Revolution almost as significant as that in industry. Larger farms, improved tools and farming implements, and capital investment all contributed to the progress of British farming.

Essex, still a county of small towns and villages, experienced a modest level of prosperity in the early years of the century. Largely an arable county with a small dairying industry devoted mainly to supplying the capital, it was well placed to lead in experiments with rotations, manuring, drainage, and farm management. The small specialised crops such as saffron, caraway and teazle, for which the county had long been noted, had practically disappeared by mid-century. Lord Petre was experimenting with new ploughing techniques. Lewis Majendie and Thurlow are Essex names famous in the record of progress in general farming practice, and Sir Richard Neave of Dagnams followed in the paths trodden by Lord Townshend in pioneering the new approach to soil fertility problems. One interesting but short-lived experiment was Lord Clare's use of oxen as draught animals in his park at Gosfield. These he brought from Gloucestershire and their advantage over the horse on heavy clay soils was reluctantly applauded by the hard-headed Essex farmers who had abandoned this useful animal long before their fellow agriculturalists in the Cotswolds and in Sussex, where this beast survived at work until the 1920s. By 1800 wheat, the most valuable crop in the county, was widely grown. In south Essex dairying was the main occupation on the low-lying flat pastures along the riverside. Arthur Young noted in 1807 that Essex farms were generally of moderate size, although some 400- and 500-acre farms were among the largest in England. Barley he found cultivated to the 'highest pitch of perfection' by John Yeldham at Saling. But amidst the advantages of technical progress labour problems dogged the industry throughout most of the period. Defoe had drawn attention to the 'poor women in Essex' who were attracted from the farms to spinning at which they could earn 1s. 0d. to 1s. 6d. a day. Ploughmen, he said, did the same, and made their ways to Bocking, Braintree and Colchester. The significance of these industrial wages while the cloth trade flourished may be seen in the rates quoted by Young. In winter the male agricultural worker could expect 1s. 0d. a day and small beer; at haytime a dinner, too. At harvest the daily rate was 2s. 0d., and reaping was rewarded at 4s. 0d. an acre. Some indication of the value of these wages may be inferred from the price of bread which cost 2d. a pound in 1772; butter was 6½d. a pound; beef 4d. a pound; and cheese 3½d. a pound.

Arthur Young, to whom so many county historians are indebted for his agricultural surveys merits, in view of his Essex connections, a paragraph in this book. Writing at the *King's Head*, Tilbury, in June 1767, he evinced a proper appreciation of the quality of Essex farming which would find a legitimate echo today:

> An Essex-man would hear you with scorn talk of any farmers being equal to theirs and they certainly have some reason for this boasting.

And he, in turn, was appreciated by no less than George III–'Farmer George'– who at Windsor proclaimed, 'Mr. Young I consider myself as more obliged to you than any other man in my Dominions'. The famous Secretary of the Board of Agriculture

61   *Spains Hall, Finchingfield,* c.1905

was born in 1741, the second son of an Essex parson. The family seat was at Bradfield Hall in Suffolk, and Young himself farmed, unsuccessfully as it happened, 300 acres near Thaxted, more precisely, at Sampford Hall, Little Sampford, where, at the age of 26, he 'fixed upon a very fine farm'. Nevertheless, owing to lack of capital, the farm failed, but he published a treatise on his experiments in Essex farming in 1770. Later, he was able to renew his Essex connections, with the revival of his friendship with an old schoolfellow, Thomas Ruggles, of Spains Hall, Finchingfield. He is now best remembered for the county agricultural surveys carried out for the Board which, though not always reliable, are among the standard sources for 18th-century English economic and social history.

Young's robust common sense was, consistently with the policy of the Board of Agriculture, brought to bear in support of the enclosure movement which became inevitable and, on balance, desirable. Prior to the Enclosure Acts the process of enclosure had generally been by private agreements which were subject to confirmation in Chancery or the Court of Exchequer. Earlier experience, despite the social disadvantage, had demonstrated the importance of enclosure to agricultural development. In the 18th century Parliament was invoked to give legislative authority to the rapidly growing process. Before 1700 enclosure by Act of Parliament was rare. In Essex it was not until late in the century that we find enclosure taking place by this process. Between 1700 and 1750 there were, nationally, barely 100 such Acts. Later the process gathered pace, almost 2,000 Acts being made in the next half-century, and about another 1,000 in the first decade of the 19th century. Thereafter enclosure by legislative consent was the normal procedure. It was during the period of parliamentary enclosure that the common-fields in west Essex were largely extinguished.

Another aspect of agrarian life resented, as was enclosure, by those who were its victims was the long-standing question of tithes, which was only dealt with by commutation in 1836. From time immemorial the payment of tithes had been a matter of complaint and grievance and even disorder. Its original purposes, under which the income was largely distributed to the parish poor and needy, were useful and commendable. Latterly, when it became entirely a source of income to the parson, it was paid under protest. William Cowper, the Georgian poet, in verses reminiscent of Tom Hood's later work, so familiar to lovers of Epping Forest, puts the issue lightly but unambiguously in an Essex context. I came across this extract by chance when pursuing local research into the Cowper family estates in Slinfold, where I then lived. In a deliciously amusing poem, published in 1779, and entitled 'The Yearly Distress or, Tithing Time at Stock in Essex', he makes a serious point:

> For then the farmers come jog, jog,
> Along the miry road,
> Each heart as heavy as a log,
> To make their payments good ...
> One wipes his nose upon his sleeve,
> One spits upon the floor ...
> One talks of mildew and of frost,
> And one of storms of hail,
> And one, of pigs that he has lost ...

How many chords, I wonder, does this jolly and pointed rhyme still strike in Essex farming hearts!

ಬೃಃ

It was not only tithes that gave grounds for complaint. Arthur Young in touring the southern counties in 1768 found 'of all the cursed roads that ever disgraced this kingdom in the very ages of barbarism none ever equalled that from Billericay to the King's Head at Tilbury'. Overgrown with trees, it took 20 to 30 horses to pull out from the mud the waggons carrying chalk from the quarries at Purfleet and Stifford on Thames-side to Essex farms where it was spread on the land. For nearly 12 miles, says Young, the roads were so 'narrow that a mouse cannot pass by any wagon ... ruts are an incredible depth'. In truth the situation was not generally that bad and the turnpikes did much to improve and develop the road system needed to support the growth of commercial and industrial activity. Parson James Woodforde, whose intimate and felicitous diary we still relish, noted on 13 April 1775, when he travelled more than 100 miles to Norwich, changing horses at the 'bull faced Stagg', via Epping Forest, Harlow and Stansted 'the best roads I ever travelled'. Indeed by then Essex roads were as good as any, having been repaired and improved partly as a result of the stimulus provided by trade with the capital and the need to service the seaports on the Essex coast.

The first of the Turnpike Trustees Acts was passed into law in 1663. Under the Acts trustees were appointed and empowered to erect toll-bars and levy tolls for the maintenance and up-grading of inadequate roads. The responsibility thus effectively passed from the parish authorities to the turnpike trustees and the road-using public. In establishing a turnpike the first step was to find satisfactory local financial resources as a necessary preliminary to the promotion of an act of parliament. The tolls were varied according to local circumstances, and from season to season, in winter the rates usually being raised. The clergy, soldiers and sailors, mail coaches and church-goers were exempt from the charges. The farming community were not, and deeply resented the tolls, and local opposition often placed the trusts in financial jeopardy. Corruption, wasteful competition between neighbouring trusts, and toll evasion all placed severe constraints upon the trustees. They also lacked technical expertise, as few competent surveyors and engineers were available until Telford and McAdam pioneered their new techniques much later. By the mid-18th century there were over 500 turnpikes in England, and eventually more than a 1,000 were authorised administering some 23,000 miles of roadways. The first Essex turnpike was constructed at Mountnessing in 1695. Other, more important, turnpikes were established on the Great Essex Road between 1721 and 1725, and to Bishops Stortford and Cambridge from the same time. The road to Epping was turnpiked in 1721 and later was taken on to Ongar. The Chelmsford, Colchester, Harwich route was turnpiked in 1725.

One effect of the turnpikes was, inevitably, in view of the heavy burden of improvement, to increase the cost of travel. Some idea of the rates may be gauged from these few examples. In 1770 a carrier, John Church of Chelmsford, was transporting goods to London at 1s. 0d. per cwt. From Colchester in 1769 it cost 3d. per mile per person by the 'New Post Coach' to the capital, and Mr. Mellor at Romford carried his passengers at 6d. per mile. The service was on the whole impressive. Regular schedules were maintained, and the 'Chelmsford Machine Fly' starting from the *Coach and Horses* at 7 a.m., reached the *Spread Eagle* in Gracechurch Street at noon, having changed

62 *Chipping Ongar, 1832*

horses at Romford. From the coast there was a thrice-weekly service on the 'Maldon Machine' to Whitechapel. The 'Royal Mail' ran in Essex from 1785. Apart from accident there were other hazards, too. In particular the sordid scourge of highwaymen, like the Essex-born Dick Turpin, who plagued the forest parishes to die eventually on the scaffold at York for the murder of his accomplice. The necessity in those days of transporting cash and valuables to the city led to the attempted concealment of such tempting cargo. In 1736 Samuel Tufnell of Langleys secreted 100 guineas and other corn in a hamper of pork in the 'Dunmow Waggon', a matter of anxiety to him as well as the unfortunate travellers who risked attack from such rascals as Turpin, Everett and Bird, who terrorised the Essex highways.

The Essex ports developed markedly during the 18th century under the stimulus of expanding trade. River transport, too, was enhanced by the construction of canals, now again attracting public favour as important environmental assets, having been usurped by the railways for a century or more. As part of the major canal system that was created in the 18th century the Essex rivers were improved to carry extra traffic. Some of the early projects in the county collapsed, but in 1797 an ambitious venture succeeded in the opening of the Chelmer navigation which linked Chelmsford to the Blackwater near Maldon. The canals were extensively used for the transport of manufactured goods, coal, timber and agricultural produce, and were of much economic value at first in providing an essential and cheap transport service from the countryside to the towns. For people in general it was the horse-drawn vehicles that provided the normal mode of long-distance travel before the railways which had a decisive impact in Essex in the Victorian age. They were to bring cheap mass travel and to revolutionise the county's basic communications which were so vital to the growth of the agricultural and manufacturing industries. But in Essex the important cloth industry died before the railways came.

At the beginning of the 18th century the cloth industry, for long of major economic importance in England, was centred on the north, south-west, East Anglia, Kent and Essex. In an age when the names of Arkwright, Hargreaves, Crompton, Watt and Wedgwood symbolised the modernisation and expansion of the manufacturing industries, the cloth trade in Essex went into decline. Even before mid-century the early momentum of the Industrial Revolution, yet to reach full flood, was apparent. New markets were being exploited at home and abroad, and their demands stimulated technology, investment, and a marked increase in the migration of the working population and dependents. The decline of the cloth industry in Essex continued throughout most of the Hanoverian century. At the outset there were major centres at Colchester, Braintree, Bocking, Halstead, and Coggeshall. Further afield in the smaller towns such as Dedham, Dunmow, Witham, and Saffron Walden the industry was established as a significant part of the local economy. Minor cloth trades were in operation also at Waltham Abbey, Billericay, and other villages in the south, but the real centre of gravity lay in the north of the county. At the height of the trade there were not less than several thousand weavers in Essex and well in excess of 10,000 spinners in the county. Colchester was the main seat of bays manufacture, containing the largest community and being mainly dependent on the industry. The bays and says which accounted for the bulk of the Essex trade in cloth were shipped to Spain, Portugal and Latin America, where they were used to make clothing for the well-to-do, the military and religious orders. Little was consumed by the home market. Colchester's produce was noted in

63   *Witham, 1832*

Europe for the excellence of its quality. A minor trade in broadcloths and silks was also carried on in some parts of the county. Many of the workers were women who span the yarn in their homes. In the worksheds and mills were the weavers, combers and fullers, who, earning relatively good wages, provided a steady market for the agricultural producers and market gardeners.

The first real signs of pressure on the industry came in about 1715 when the Spanish market was undermined. The trade, always responsive to international events, recovered slightly after the Seven Years' War, but by 1760 it was in such serious difficulty that its future was already in doubt. Capital began to move into farming and real estate. The smaller centres were the first to abandon the industry and the Napoleonic wars sealed the fate of the remainder. When the end of the war came at Waterloo, the cloth trade in Essex, apart from the small silk industry established in the Braintree area by George Courtauld, was nearly at an end. Wages were depressed and, as Philip Morant remarked, 'what employment … could be immediately substituted in its room'. The last factories closed in the 1830s, victims of the war and their own failure to broaden the base of their operations and to keep pace with the technological advance taking place elsewhere in England. The industry in Essex appears never to have progressed significantly from the guild system on which it was originally organised. It simply could not compete in the economic circumstances created by the Industrial Revolution.

ಶಂಗ

In his long and chequered reign George III excited much public emotion and if, on the whole, it must be counted as undistinguished and even humiliating, his moral rectitude and sad illness did, in the end, attract some sympathy. The King in his early

64 *The Corn Market, Colchester, 1831*

years tried to establish a political role for the Crown which was not only anachronistic, but seriously weakened the government and gave rise to public dissatisfaction. After the loss of the American colonies the monarchy and the effete administration were completely discredited. Furthermore, parliamentary jobbery, the consolidation of rural landed interests and urban oligarchies in the midst of the social upheaval of the Industrial Revolution and the rumblings of revolution abroad, first in America and then in Europe, created a new and dangerous political climate. It was an age in which government agents, like John Roberts the M.P. for Harwich, could feather their own nests and acquire a local influence that was altogether unhealthy in a country at long last beginning to aspire to a democratic way of life. On the credit side it saw the rise of philanthropy, the abolition of the slave trade, economic progress and the assertion of cultural values. Over all hung the shadow of the French Revolution and Napoleonic Europe.

Essex saw less of the Hanoverians than their predecessors who had been attracted to their residences in the county and the delights of the royal forests. George III's interest in the new fashion for sea-bathing, however, brought him to the coast where the new resorts grew up to meet a public demand for the 'sea-side' that shows no sign of exhaustion. When 'Farmer George' took to the sea it was a truly royal affair. He would leave his bathing machine to be greeted with flags and cheering crowds enlivened by the efforts of the specially assembled bandsmen. It was all, said the medical men, good for body and soul. We shall come again to the seaside in Victorian Essex, but one or two other royal visits to the county should be mentioned before we turn to more serious matters. To Harwich in 1761 came the Princess Charlotte Sophia of Mecklenburg-Strelitz, where she was met by the royal coach to be taken to London for her marriage to the reluctant George III. It was not a festive occasion, but a happier note was struck in October 1778 when the King and Queen visited Lord Petre at Thorndon Hall which at that time the family preferred to Ingatestone. The royal couple received a warm welcome from the Essex villagers who lined the route, and at the

65   *Southend, 1831*

fireworks display organised at the royal levée in the evening. On 20 October the King reviewed his troops at Warley. The sordid affair after the death of his daughter-in-law, queen to George IV, was later to excite hostile emotions in the county. It all demonstrated that, with all his failings, George III was able to come closer to the English people than the remainder of his dreary House.

From the time of the Conquest these islands have been confronted periodically with the military threat posed by ambitious dynasts, who have succeeded in imposing their wills on much of Europe thereby dangerously upsetting the balance of power on which the strategy of our foreign policy relied until modern science made it obsolete. Thus it was with Philip of Spain, Louis XIV, and Adolf Hitler; and in Hanoverian Britain, Napoleon Buonaparte. The potentially disruptive danger to society of the revolutionary ideas that erupted in France exercised men's minds greatly throughout the country. The rise of the military power of a France bursting with dynamic energy and the emotions unleashed by the national trauma of the revolution cast Europe into war and despair. Britain was directly challenged, but despite her inferior resources, sound strategy and superior naval and military leadership enabled her to lead an allied coalition to victory over Napoleon which was decisively endorsed at Waterloo in June 1815. The highlights of this long and exhausting struggle were the brilliant campaigns in the Peninsula, Lord Nelson's dazzling naval victories at Copenhagen, the Nile and Trafalgar, and Wellington's *coup-de-grace* in the farmlands south of Brussels.

Of all these stirring events Trafalgar was that which captured the imagination of the people and, because of the heroic tragedy of Nelson's death, provoked a wave of national emotion that the most mundane historians cannot wholly suppress even today. As Essex men were at sea with Howard and Drake, so they were to be found in Nelson's ships off Cape Trafalgar. In command in the *Temeraire*, immortalised in Turner's great painting and Newbolt's poetry, was Captain (later Admiral Sir) Eliab Harvey of Rolls Park, Chigwell. With Nelson's reluctant agreement the *Temeraire* led the line of attack, but at the last moment was ordered astern of the flagship, which was at

66   *Chelmsford from Springfield Hill near the gravel pits*

once engaged by the French. The *Victory*, heavily damaged and in the forefront of the engagement, was locked in battle with the *Redoubtable*, which was almost destroyed by broadsides from the *Temeraire*. In his despatches Admiral Collingwood described the valiant part played by Harvey's ship in the most famous victory in naval history. Nelson, shot by one of the marksmen in the *Redoubtable*, lay in the cockpit of the *Victory* tended in his dying moments by Alexander Scott, his friend and chaplain, who was later the vicar of Southminster. After the victory Harvey was fêted at a Trafalgar dinner arranged in his honour at the *King's Head*, Chigwell. Scott and Harvey were thus prominent among many men who brought to Essex tables first-hand accounts of this thrilling and poignant success for British arms. They would never have lacked loyal and enthusiastic audiences in a county whose links with the sea were second only to its basic commitment to agriculture.

So much for the image of war; the reality is less agreeable. The geographical position of Essex meant that the threat of invasion was of practical consequence. The Essex militia was therefore strengthened by the mustering of local Volunteers who were established in camps at Warley, Epping, Danbury, Clacton, and other centres. The local gentry and farmers enlisted in the Volunteer Cavalry, supplying the horses at their own expense. Colonel Montague Burgoyne of Mark Hall, Latton, raised the Loyal Essex Light Dragoons, which mustered more than 200 men. The Yeomanry and other cavalry units were raised at Chelmsford by Mr. Tufnell, at Coopersale by Mr. John Conyers, and on Thames-side. The volunteer infantry were mustered at Colchester. After the Peace of Amiens the Volunteers were stood down, although, along with the Essex Sea Fencibles who had been raised to man strategic points in the coastal defences, they were recalled in 1803 when invasion was again thought to be imminent. Altogether several thousands were enrolled in the local defence forces.

A system of beacon signals was established, the straw, wood, tar and other combustibles being stored ready on the hilltops at Colchester, Langdon Hills, Danbury, Wethersfield, and other vantage points. The burning off of weeds and crops was forbidden. Church towers, too, were designated as flag-stations to give warning of the approach of the French. These local forces suffered from the weaknesses of all such volunteer bodies in that they were immobile and ill-equipped. But the readiness with which the volunteers offered their services is evidence of the fundamental loyalty of Essex folk, which was acknowledged by the Duke of York when he inspected the Volunteers at Chelmsford in 1803, although those who bore the cost of billeting the men were not always equally enthusiastic. The Essex shipyards made their contribution in building men-of-war. The *Irresistible*, a third-rate of 74 guns was built at Harwich in 1782, and with the *Terrible*, also a Harwich ship, was at St Vincent. Another Harwich vessel, the *Conqueror*, was commanded at Trafalgar by Captain Israel Pellow.

Along the coast from Suffolk to Sussex the defence forces constructed a series of Martello towers, a name borrowed from Cape Mortella in Corsica, to serve as strongpoints in the event of invasion. Between 1804 and 1808 some 103 were constructed, of which 11 were in Essex. Each cost more than £5,000, and hundreds of men were employed in building them; 500, for example, at Grays alone, in making bricks. Some were heavily armed. That at Harwich, a veritable fortress, carried 10 mounted 24-pounder guns as well as a secondary armament in 18 bomb-proof casements. Others at Walton, Jay Wick, Lee Wick, and Brightlingsea Creek were equipped with small howitzers. Of those in Essex seven still intrigue visitors to the coastal resorts, particularly in the Clacton area, where three still stand as redundant reminders of a danger that never materialised. Before the first one was finished Nelson had destroyed at Trafalgar the French prospects of a seaborne landing in Britain. More than that, the victory ensured to the British fleet 100 years of supremacy on the oceans of the world. 'I don't say the French won't come', said the Earl St Vincent. 'I say they won't come by sea.'

ஐ௸

67   *Tilbury Fort, 1831*

68 *Harwich, from the sea, 1831*

By the end of the war with France George III, an old man of 77 and his mental faculties seriously and irrevocably impaired, was no longer coherent. His heir, the Prince Regent, and from 1820 George IV, had formally assumed the Regency in February 1811. If the father was mad he was at least, unlike his son, moral and not without virtues. The Prince Regent, pleasure-loving and clever, was also idle, mendacious and selfish. His attitude to his wife and cousin, Caroline of Brunswick-Wolfenbüttel, was outrageous and deeply resented in Essex. The future Prince Regent had contracted a morganatic liaison in his younger days with a Mrs. Fitzherbert, and married Caroline in 1795. In 1806, when relations between them were strained, he had the impertinence to bring damaging charges against her for misconduct. On investigation they were not proved; nor were suspicions completely dispelled. Court factions supported either side, but popular opinion sided mainly with Caroline, who was conspicuously ill-used by her reprobate husband. At George's coronation she was refused entry to the Abbey and died, rejected, a month later. As the funeral cortège processed from London to the coast en route for burial in her native land there was demonstration and disorder among sympathetic crowds. At Romford large and excited crowds turned out to pay their respects to the uncrowned Queen, to express their opposition to the government, and condemnation of the King's conduct towards her. The procession was escorted from Kelvedon to Colchester by leading county Whigs and their tenantry. At Colchester as the coffin lay at rest in St Runwald's in the High Street there was a riot in which leading citizens of the town took part. William IV's brief reign, dominated by the struggle over parliamentary reform, did nothing to restore the monarchy to popular favour.

In the arts and sciences the great names of the age were numerous and it must suffice to mention only Gainsborough, Constable, Kent, Handel, Dryden, Johnson, and

Dalton as evidence of the wealth of cultural excellence in which the Georgian kingdom revelled. Consistent with the great agrarian and industrial changes that were taking place was a renaissance in design and thought that has elevated the period to the dignity of an age of elegance, taste and transition. Such men were its mainspring and there were many others. In Essex those who stand near the pinnacles achieved by this company were James Bradley, curate at Wanstead and Astronomer Royal from 1742-62, who defined the nutation of the earth's axis and discovered the aberration of light, and William Derham, the rector of Upminster and scientist.

Essex at the time was beautifully depicted by none less than John Constable himself, whose painting of Dedham Vale is his tribute in oils to the lovely valley-country that is shared by East Anglia and Essex, and which he knew from birth. In a very different way, but of immense delight and value to Essex historians, the county was delineated by John Chapman and Peter André in their wonderful map for which they surveyed the county in 1772-74. Printed in 1777, it was the first to show minor roads, bridges and such detail as milestones and toll-bars. It is itself a fine example of the cartographer's art and an essential source document for local history. The significance of their choice of illustration for the title page which showed a fulling mill and cloth-beaters at work will not be lost on readers of this chapter. In the field of ceramics the Bow pottery was making its contribution to the development of fine English porcelain and its wares are collectors' pieces today.

Of all the arts it is in architecture and landscaping that we have the most conspicuous legacy of past taste and opulence. The Georgian period represents the highest peak of disciplined and formal classicism in the development of English architecture. It was an era at once creative and prolific. Within reach of the capital, Essex and the other home counties provided the sites for the fine new mansions of the prosperous merchant and commercial families. A number of Essex towns, notably Colchester, Thaxted and Dedham, took on their mantle of Georgian elegance which remains an agreeable feature of the townscapes in those favoured localities today. In rural Essex there arose small and charming country houses like that built for John Harle at Rainham in 1729, and the magnificence of Wanstead House, which rivalled any other in Britain. Of the great names of the period the architects Sir John Vanbrugh and Adam worked at Audley End, the stone screen and staircase being the product of Vanbrugh's heavy hand. Robert Adam was also responsible for the fine church at Mistley of 1776 now, alas! but a partial relic, only the towers remaining. Earlier in the period was Langleys, at Great Waltham, the home of the Tufnells, of *c.*1719, and built to an H-plan in brick. Also early was the pleasant Bower House at Havering, the product of Henry Flitcroft's competent mind. There is good work of the period, too, at Kelvedon Hall and Thorndon Hall, the work of James Paine. Bradwell Lodge, the former rectory, with its charming belvedere on the roof, is a graceful feature of that remote and interesting part of the county. Of churches I have already mentioned Mistley. Wanstead, by Thomas Hardwick, also merits attention and still survives as a tasteful product of that lesser-known Georgian architect. It was the county surveyor, John Johnson, who left his mark most widely—and agreeably—in the county's Georgian inventory. His was the Shire Hall built in 1789-91 at Chelmsford in the Adam idiom. He also conceived Terling Place in 1772-80 in white brick, and the Moulsham Bridge over the Cam in the county town. It was Wanstead, however, that dwarfed all. Begun in 1715, it was

designed and constructed by Colen
Campbell for Sir Richard Child at a cost
of £300,000 an amazing sum at today's
values. Its style was pure Palladian and its
great colonnaded facade was a Georgian
tour de force. Unfortunately, the family over-
reached itself in investing in such a mansion, and its upkeep and the profligacy of
a later member of the family brought about
financial ruin and the demolition of what
ranked among the finest houses in Britain;
virtually nothing remains.

In landscaping the period was led and
dominated by 'Capability' Brown and
Humphry Repton, the latter an East

69 *Shire Hall, Chelmsford*

Anglian who spent much of his life at Romford. Brown's contribution to the environmental aspects of architecture had a European quality and was of much importance in
the development of taste in England. His known work in Essex is to be seen in several
parts of the County. Audley End, where his conception of the fine frontage that extends
to the banks of the diverted Cam still provides, from the Cambridge Road, one of the
most spectacular roadside vistas in England. He worked also for Lord Petre at the now
ruined Thorndon Hall and at Coopersale, Navestock, Hallingbury, and Belhus. Contemporary and surprisingly original in view of Brown's dominance and their earlier
associations was Humphry Repton, whose best known work was at Hill Hall, the characteristic 'red book' for which is still extant. He carried out some competent landscaping also at Highams at Walthamstow, Rivenhall Place, and Stubbers, North
Ockendon. Repton's work is certainly to be ranked high in the whole range of Georgian
art in Essex, but it is only in comparatively recent years that his reputation has been
sufficiently detached from his former colleague's for it to secure appropriate recognition
for its own intrinsic merits.

༺ଔଔ༻

After Waterloo there was a general collapse in the demand for manufactured goods
as markets at home and abroad were glutted. A series of bad harvests added to the
economic dislocation caused by the market situation. Social conflict, in the shadow of
the French Revolution, therefore seemed inevitable, and it is a miracle that in England
it was generally, though not without difficulty, contained within the constitutional process. Neither George IV, nor his brother William IV who followed him to the throne in
1830, were of the calibre to make a useful or constructive contribution to the Great
Debate of their time.

At the expense of strict chronology I would mention here an event, still not
without significance in industrial relations today, in which Essex was eventually involved.
In February 1834 six agricultural labourers were arrested at Tolpuddle in Dorset and
charged with administering illegal oaths in forming a trade union to protect agricultural
wages. The trial, a travesty of justice, led to their being sentenced to suffer transportation
to Australia for seven years, and they were shipped to Botany Bay before the gathering

public protest could be made effective. After months of bitter debate in Parliament and demonstrations the 'Tolpuddle Martyrs' were granted full pardons in March 1836. Because of local feeling it was thought desirable to re-settle them far away from their old homes, and so they were established in Essex at New House farm at Greensted Green, near Ongar, and at a farm near High Laver. It was not long before they made their radical views heard in the locality and the political agitation they led incurred the wrath of local landowners. They eventually left for Canada, although some did later return.

The struggle over parliamentary reform led to a major constitutional crisis and outbreaks of rioting and violence epitomised by the irony of 'Peterloo', which, though it has been misrepresented, was nonetheless serious and a tragic affair. The anxiety of the authorities was evident in the efforts made to reinforce the local defence forces. The Volunteer Cavalry in Essex was re-formed and enlarged in response to the threat of disorder and not, in fact, disbanded for another half-century. The constitutional background was complicated, but what is obvious in restrospect is that the religious and dynastic issues that had bedevilled political life for centuries had at least been laid to rest and replaced by the question of electoral and parliamentary reform. The inadequacy of the arrangements for representation, and in particular the franchise as manifested in the scandal of the 'pocket' boroughs, had become intolerable. Parliamentary seats were controlled by rich local gentry whose wealth put power into their hands. In 1727 the Earl of Egmont spent a great sum in securing control of the seat at Harwich and the Whigs, in their heyday, had consolidated their corrupt monopoly of such seats in the pursuit of political power.

By 1830 Grey, the prime minister, was lurching from crisis to crisis and violent public protest had led to the execution of several agitators and the imprisonment and transportation of many others. The middle and labouring classes of Essex were strongly in support of the Reform Bill that was laid before Parliament in 1831, and its defeat caused much public concern. After the rejection by the Lords of the second Bill the situation was grave. More than 100 influential gentlemen in Essex signed a formal protest against the Bill, but hundreds more subscribed to a petition designed to bring pressure on the Lords to accept it. The High Sheriff, William Davis, refused to convene a meeting to sponsor the campaign against the Lords' rejection of the Bill, but it was summoned by Lord Petre and others instead. The third attempt to secure the Bill was made in December 1831 after a general election. The King was finally persuaded to agree to create sufficient peers to carry it in the Lords, and this resulted in enough abstentions to get it through and the ultimate crisis was averted.

Although of limited scope the Reform Act of June 1832 was of the utmost importance to the course of constitutional advance. It did not provide for a secret ballot; nor did all the pocket boroughs and burgage-tenancies disappear. The county constituencies were still deprived of adequate representation and only under the pressure of public opinion throughout the 19th century was this eventually remedied. Even at the end William IV refused to attend Parliament and gave his reluctant assent to the Bill by commission. Prior to the Reform Act two knights of the shire represented Essex in Parliament together with two representatives from each of the boroughs of Colchester, Harwich, and Maldon. Elections, if corrupt, could also be amusing and somewhat bizarre. One candidate in Essex, Mr. Conyers of Copt Hall, Epping, in addressing the electors as 'brother calves' barked like a dog on the platform and roared 'Tally-ho' at frequent intervals during his speeches. Lasting up to two weeks or more, the polls were the occasion for violence, demonstration, graft, and jollification. Much money was expended. One Whig candidate is said to have laid out more than £20,000, but was absent from the hustings as he was in hiding from his creditors. The three candidates at the election at Maldon in 1826 spent almost £50,000 between them. Under the Reform Act the county was divided into two double-member constituencies, Northern and Southern Essex. The representation of the three boroughs was unchanged, leaving Essex with 10 members. The actual changes affecting Essex boroughs were thus marginal. It was not until the later Acts of 1867 and 1884 that the old basis of borough representation was significantly altered, and the secret ballot introduced. The Reform Act was, however, a popular and long overdue measure and in the county there was much rejoicing. Villages and towns were decorated by their delighted citizens, who could not have fully understood the limited nature of the reforms. There were illuminations, bonfires, bell-ringing, and enthusiastic oratory. Typical of the celebrations in Essex was the dinner given at the Bower House, Havering, to mark the great event. The owner, Mr. Edward Robinson, and his neighbour, Mr. John Rogers of Bedfords, shared the cost of a gathering of several hundreds of the labouring poor of the village, who were regaled with mutton and beef, pies, and plum puddings, beer and punch. A special feast and entertainment was arranged separately for the village children. The people, it was believed, had at last crossed the threshold of democracy; the age of transition was reaching fulfilment.

In sum the century during which the Hanoverians occupied the throne was perhaps one in which economic and social circumstances were more profoundly changed than in any other in history until now. Industrial advance and military success had raised the British from the status of a small, if influential, people, to a pre-eminence in world affairs that they were to retain for another 100 years. In the summer of 1837 William IV died, and a young, untried and apprehensive girl learned that she was Queen.

Chapter Eight

☙❧

ESSEX IN THE AGE OF VICTORIA

'Never such a May-day and never such a Queen'

For Essex the changes that transformed the face of the county and the life of its people in Victoria's England were more far-reaching than in any comparable period in its history. Through all the vicissitudes of time from the arrival of the Roman legions, through the Anglo-Saxon colonisation, the Norman usurpation, and the disasters and tribulations of the medieval and post-medieval eras, nothing as profound or swift overtook the county as the urbanisation of Thames-side and the migration of people from the countryside to the towns. When the plain, but gracious and self-conscious little Princess Victoria, granddaughter of George III, was told by Lord Conyngham, the Lord Chamberlain, at dawn on a summer morning in 1831 that she was Queen, she had already resolved to 'be good'; she was good. Her maternal influence was to be shed on a period remarkably free from major wars abroad.

At home it was one in which an intense spiritual investment in religion and family life was complemented by the necessity for private philanthropy and state agencies to grapple with the horrors of degrading poverty and cruel and inhuman indifference. If

70   *The Eastern Counties Line on the Stratford Marshes; the earliest Essex railway*

71 *The Whitsun Fair at* The Bull, *Great Sampford, c.1900*

the 18th century was an age of transition, Victoria's century was an age of contrasts. The industrial pulse of the nation, beating vigorously and indiscriminately, was nowhere more in evidence than in south-west Essex, where industry, railways, and modern dockland were created to handle the rapidly increasing seaborne trade of the world in which Britain enjoyed its lion's share. In the countryside the large estate owners and the last generations of the ancient squirearchy were comfortably ensconced in their well-serviced households, while the Essex farm workers were forced to seek their livelihood in the mushrooming slumdom of the new boroughs that London would eventually engulf. All over the county there was progress and decay; people came and people went. And when Victoria departed the old Essex had gone, too. The evolution that we have traced through the chapters of this book was not completed; evolution never is. It had, nevertheless, matured to the point where Essex folk could no longer readily recognise more than a tincture of life as experienced from time immemorial; they belonged at last to a dynamic modern and democratically orientated society.

At 18 the young and hopeful Queen leaned naturally on tried and trusted men. So she looked to Lord Melbourne and King Leopold for the steadying and perceptive guidance that was later provided by the Prince Consort and Lord Beaconsfield. She was never, however, a cypher, and in the long run her own name would be regarded as that which best exemplified the 19th century. In attempting an evaluation of this unique period in our history in national terms it is still too near our own time to bring it definitively into focus. At the local level we may see more clearly what occurred and the significance of these events on the topography of the county and the structure of Essex society.

The first real political crisis to confront the Queen was the issue of the repeal of the Corn Laws about which feeling in Essex was strong. It is interesting, too, that it brought Disraeli, who was at school in Essex at the Unitarian Eliezer Cogan's academy for the sons of gentlemen at Walthamstow, into the political limelight, though the aura that was latterly to illumine his personal relations with the sovereign had yet to descend on his eager shoulders. At the time of Victoria's accession a series of bad harvests and distress among the artisan classes revived earlier demands for the repeal of the Corn Laws in the interest of cheap food. Despite the energetic campaigning of the anti-Corn Law League, the improved harvest yields of the early 1840s weakened the demand for a while. The subject was an emotive one and part of the general issue of Free Trade. It thus attracted the support of those ardent campaigners, Richard Cobden of Midhurst, and John Bright, the Lancastrian quaker and mill owner. Peel, the Prime Minister, with such forceful allies at his back, had already determined his course, and the failure of the Irish potato crop in 1845 provided the occasion to force the issue in Parliament. In a bitter struggle against the Protectionists, reinforced by the brash effrontery and dazzling oratory of the flamboyant Member for Maidstone, Benjamin Disraeli, the future Lord Beaconsfield, Peel resigned after being defeated on the Irish Coercion Bill, but was recalled to carry the repeal in June 1846. Essex farmers, who had organised themselves in defence of the Corn Laws, and had contested the matter through public meetings, propaganda and petition, were alarmed and, like their fellow-farmers in the corn-growing areas, prepared for the worst. In the event the direct and immediate effects were minimal. Other factors, such as economic trends abroad and the rising demands of the growing population at home, delayed the impact until the great agricultural depressions in the next generation. Essex farming had certainly not escaped.

While in agriculture the controversy raged over Free Trade and the Corn Laws, in industry *laissez-faire* was accompanied by the rise of a significant trades union movement and the passage of legislation which afforded some measure of protection to factory workers against the worst abuses of commercial exploitation. Indeed, in the manufacturing industries, mining and ship-building wages rose. But in the more numerous fields of employment, which were conspicuous in Essex agricultural work, minor domestic industries such as match-making, cobbling, textiles, tailoring and straw-plaiting the constraints of economic and social realities prevailed. The state, averse to interference in the entrepreneurial role of private industrial enterprises, was taking a yet firmer grip on its corporate responsibilities for the welfare of the indigent. Abroad, the Crimean War provoked a public reaction against the hardships endured by the British forces. National pride was evoked by the heroism of the troops at Balaclava and Sevastopol. The medieval panache and tactical absurdity of the famous cavalry charges stirred the imagination and incipient Jingoism of Victorian England, but contributed nothing to unlock the stalemate in the peninsula. In India, Cawnpore and Lucknow excited similar emotions. From 'darkest' Africa reports of the dedicated explorations of the intrepid David Livingstone must have aroused special interest in Ongar, where he had lodged with the local pastor in the High Street during his training for the priesthood. It was a link with the wider horizons of an expanding imperial role. Colchester was honoured by the presence of the Prince Consort in 1856 when from the Moot Hall he went to Wivenhoe Park to inspect the garrison and the combined militia of the eastern counties, thus stamping the seal of royal approval on the contribution of Essex men to these historic events in the far corners of the new British Empire. So passed the first phases of the Victorian decades. Victorian England was flexing its muscles across the oceans and mobilising its economic resources at home with a confidence and conviction that was to make Britain, for a moment in history, the most influential nation in the world.

℠℞

It is in terms of the Royal Navy, and the raj and a maternal sovereign that we tend to see Victorian Britain in the near historical perspective of 100 years, but in truth it is in its socio-economic aspects that the period will, in due course, be seen to be the most significant. The demise of the cloth trade in Essex in the last years of the Hanoverians was followed, in Victoria's time, by fluctuation and decline in agriculture, and the eventual rise of an industrialised region east of the Lea by comparison with which the textile enterprises were not much above the level of cottage industry. Never was the interdependence of London and the county more in evidence. The industrial expansion on Thames-side in the future metropolitan boroughs of Greater London was phenomenal and was a prime cause of migration from the Essex villages further north. As farming sank, others sought their fortunes further afield in the developing countries of the Empire though the evidence suggests that it was to London and the south-west of Essex that most were attracted. Many former Essex farmworkers crowded into the human rookeries that sprang up in the slums of East London. There, some still practised rural crafts, and the basket-makers of Bethnal Green continued to gather their raw materials from the marshlands of the Hams. Nevertheless, the majority of working people in Essex was still engaged in agriculture or in the allied industries which expanded in response to the demands of a rapidly rising population. The small enterprises, such as local milling and brickmaking firms, were gradually superseded by larger concerns as the realities of economics favoured the more highly-capitalised and broadly-based industries.

As we have seen, the severe agricultural depression that followed the Napoleonic wars lasted well into the 1830s. The campaign for the repeal of the Corn Laws also cast its shadow over farming prospects, and a series of bad harvests and blight led to discontent and genuine distress. Poor yields and falling returns were reflected in appeals in many Essex parishes for abatements of rent and tithes. Although by 1840 the beneficial results of experiment and the spread of new techniques had put Essex farmers among the best in England, only the most efficient weathered the storm without a serious lowering of their standards of life. After 1850 there was a recovery and Essex farmers no doubt drew some comfort and, one hopes, inspiration from the Great Exhibition of 1851 at which the latest machinery, including much from America, was on display. The fore-runner of the tractor that eventually ousted the fine old draught horses from our farms, steam-ploughing tackle, was among the advanced and exciting equipment on show. Steam-ploughing in Britain was developed by Albert Fry at Bristol, and he brought his patent mechanical devices to Essex where he worked on drainage schemes in Hainault Forest. Everywhere, in the field of technology, things were on the move, and progressive Essex farmers, hard-pressed on their heavy lands, were of necessity in the van.

At Witham, Hutley, interested in the substantially increased yields to be won with the use of South American guano and other farmyard manures, demonstrated their value,

DARBY'S DIGGER

Is Made of the Best Steel.
Is Strong and Durable.
Will Last 20 Years.
Is the Lightest Machine per inch width used in the cultivation of heavy land.
Covers 21 feet each journey.
DIGS Two Rods in One Minute.
Gives a greater depth of Moulds for Roots than other Implements.
Minimizes the cost of Manure.
Improves the Land every year.
Raises the yield of Wheat Twenty per Cent. beyond any other mode of cultivation.
Farms the Subsoil without pressing it.

The Digger can now be worked by One Man and a Boy.

Full particulars of the Darby Digger system of Farming may be obtained of T. C. DARBY, Pleshey Lodge, Chelmsford; or at the Digger Office, Crane Court, High Street, Chelmsford, Essex, England.

72   *The Darby Steam Digger*

in combination with break-crops, in maintaining the fertility of the land. Already farmers were creating a market for Chilean nitrates and the superphosphates that became commonplace and indispensable a generation later. An Essex stockman, Fisher Hobbs of Boxstead Lodge, did important work in improving the strain of Essex pig breeds which are still prized for crossing today. The enormous Darby Digger, though not a complete success, was to be seen steaming as it grappled with the Essex clay at Pleshey, and farmers struggled to stay on terms with the economic challenge. Some, like Lord Rayleigh's second son, the Hon. Edward Gerald Strutt of Terling, proved, as had Mechi, that farming was no longer simply an inherited art, but a matter of business acumen and managerial skills. Strutt, who took over the management of his brother's estate of some 17,000 acres in 1882, demonstrated that despite the severe agricultural depression efficiency could be the key to success. With indefatigable energy, good hygiene, expert husbandry and shrewd marketing 'Lord Rayleigh's Farms' set new standards. Strutt eventually became the Chief Agricultural Adviser at the Board of Agriculture, and his work is still remembered in the county. Perhaps the most remarkable character in Essex farming in the 19th century was, however, John Joseph Mechi, son of an Italian refugee. After a short career in business without any knowledge of farming, he purchased 170 acres of derelict marginal land at Tiptree Heath in 1840 for £3,400. It was from books and treatises that he learned his trade and through the alacrity with which he grasped new ideas and was prepared to experiment he attracted much interest. American machines from the Great Exhibition were demonstrated publicly at Tiptree in 1851, and Mechi immediately invested in them. His book on *How to Farm Profitably* was published in 1857 and ran to three editions and 10,000 copies. He acquired Tiptree Hall, and his fame spread far beyond the borders of Essex as he came to be regarded as one of the giants of Victorian farming.

In the dry Essex climate corn was the favoured crop, but it is vulnerable to the weather and the diversification provided by stock was essential in bad times. 'Down corn, up horn' was the slogan of farmers who reacted to spread their losses one year with another. The depression of 1875 was disastrous for Essex. The larger estates of the county in the hands of important landed families like the Mildmays, Petres, Tyrells and Tufnells came under pressure and began to fragment as rents and values declined, while death duties exacted an increasing levy from each generation. After a period of moderate prosperity since the repeal of the Corn Laws there were two disastrous periods for British farming, from 1875-1884, and again from 1891-99, during which the area under cultivation fell from 8 million acres to less than 6 million. Underlying the depression was the vast production of cheap prairie-grown wheat in the New World and the import of refrigerated meat from South America and Australasia. To cap it all the bad summers and cruel

73   *Tiptree Hall farm in the 19th century*

winter of 1878-80 made it the worst period that British farming had ever known. Indifferent landlords, debt, mortgage, and inhospitable markets drove tenant farmers and agricultural labourers off the land. Established farms, where families had toiled for generations in Essex, failed by the score, and the land reverted to rough, uncultivated pasturage. Neglected farm buildings, unkept hedges, deteriorating farm paths, falling gates, and land invaded by weeds was a common and 'melancholy sight'. Only the large and efficient farmers or those sustained by the richest soils or the proximity of good markets escaped the worst consequences. The Richmond Commission touring rural Essex in 1881 reported on the distress in the farmlands. In the area bounded by Rochford, Chelmsford, and Maldon, and in the Rodings they reported that formerly cultivated land was then derelict. Lord Petre's agent, F.J. Coverdale, reporting on the necessary reduction of rents and the abandonment by tenants of their holdings confirmed that the position was no better in 1893. Attracted by low rents hardy immigrants from Scotland and the north, experienced in marginal farming, took up abandoned farms in the county, and by dint of hard graft and tenacity made them viable. Some Essex farmers turned, with profit, to stock, poultry, dairying and horticulture. But prejudice and the commitment to corn was a major impediment. Such shifts of emphasis were regarded as 'a necessary evil' and corn was seen as 'the chief end of farming'. A Commission of 1894 saw this attitude exemplified in Essex in neglected cattle sheds alongside barns and granaries in good repair. Not until the First World War did Essex farming recover from the effects of the decades of despair that depressed the countryside after 1875.

Generations of Essex men had also farmed the seas. It is not generally appreciated that in mid-19th-century Britain Barking ranked as its most important fishing port and harboured one of the world's largest fishing fleets. Barking's maritime role had been its mainstay since the 12th century, and as a result of the rising demand of London's growing population the fishing trade in the town reached its peak. Yet soon it would be gone. From the 18th century the development of this important Essex industry was given impetus by the imaginative management of the Hewett family, whose Short Blue Fleet pioneered new techniques and a fleet operating system that gave them a supremacy in the trade. They built ice-houses on the Essex marshlands and introduced fast, small boats to ferry the fish haul from the larger seagoing 'well-ships' that had been designed to carry live fish in the central compartment of the hull until off-loaded into the smaller craft. As did agriculture, this stimulated the ancillary trades in the area, but Barking's remoteness from the North Sea fishing grounds, the development of refrigeration, and finally the construction of the east coast railway routes undermined the economy of the trade. By the end of the Victorian age the industry had been transferred to the North Sea ports.

Simultaneous with the decline of agriculture there was the growth of metropolitan Essex which we shall consider later. At Colchester new industries in light engineering, iron founding, garment manufacture and wholesale trading were developed at the end of the century, and although, as a market centre, it reflected the debilitation of agriculture, the town enjoyed a measure of prosperity and the population grew apace. There was also rising activity in the county town and one name, that of Guglielmo Marconi, is prominent. Colonel R.E.B. Crompton had established an electrical industry at Chelmsford which still remains an important part of the town's economy from about 1878. Marconi carried the development forward when he set up his factory at Chelmsford in 1898. This followed his patent for electrical transmission and signals, and the formation of the Wireless Telegraph Company in 1897 which led to the world-wide system of telegraph services. Paramount, however, in the field of communications was the contribution of the railways and no history of Essex can ignore the impact that they made on the topography and economic development of the county.

The speed and scale of the effort that was mounted to create the great Victorian network that is still the basis of rail communications today was prodigious. It had a profound influence on all aspects of national life and was an achievement of organisation and engineering unparalleled in the world in the 19th century. In the spheres of technology, finance and labour it raised issues of social and environmental significance. When the Stockton and Darlington railway was opened in 1825 a new age was announced. Within half a century the main lines of the country-wide system were complete, and over 15,000 miles of track had been laid. Britain, then 'the workshop of the world', had invented the railway to sustain the vigour of her industries. The people have had a classic love-hate relationship with it ever since. In Victorian England it was a mania and Charles Mackay's poetry–'Lay down your rails, ye nations, near and far'– reflected the enthusiast's uncritical view. As so often the highest hopes and worst fears were both confounded.

The Bill for the promotion of the Eastern Counties Railway was enacted on 4 July 1836. It was an event of cardinal importance in Essex history. Its later reputation, quoted by D.I. Gordon–'Notoriously there is no railway system in the empire as badly worked as the Eastern Counties. There is no system on which the passenger trains are so few or so irregular; none on which the rates for passengers and goods are so expensive; and few, if any, where accidents are more plentiful'–does not detract from this, and due allowance must be made for the natural and immoderate prejudices of the pamphleteer. The Act provided for the construction of a railway from Shoreditch via Romford, Brentwood, Chelmsford, Colchester to Norwich and Yarmouth. Landowners on the route were served with notices for the compulsory acquisition of the land needed for the rail path. There was, naturally, some resistance and opposition, based on alleged loss of amenity and farming efficiency, which came from important landowners who complained also about inadequate compensation when, as usually happened, they lost their case. Nothing could stop the railways, supported as they were with capital amounting to hundreds of millions of pounds and stimulated by intense commercial rivalry. The first section of the E.C.R. (later the Great Eastern Railway, then the L.N.E.R., and ultimately British Rail), from Mile End to Romford was officially opened to the accompaniment of music by the band of the Coldstream Guards on 18 June 1839. It was extended to Brentwood by the following summer, reached Colchester in 1843 and Norwich in 1849. During roughly the same period Robert Stephenson's E.C.R. line to Cambridge which traversed west Essex via Bishops Stortford was also brought into operation. Ceremonial openings with celebration luncheons, military bands and formal and symbolic acts heralded the new lines. In 1854-6 the rail route to Southend by way of Tilbury, with its growing dock traffic, brought the seaside within short reach of Londoners. The further link from Barking to Pitsea, which provided the more direct route to Southend was not built until 1888-9, by which time the rail had been extended beyond the resort to Shoeburyness. Subsidiary lines through the Stour valley to Colchester and to Clacton were completed in 1869 and 1882. By then the basis of Essex rail communications was firmly established, but there had also been, as elsewhere, abortive schemes as when, despite fierce inter-company rivalry, the General Railway failed to secure the Southend traffic via Tilbury and the proposed South Essex Railway.

The railways naturally made a direct impact on road travel. By mid-century the stagecoach had largely gone, and the turnpikes were neglected as capital and public enthusiasm were transferred to the railways. The last coach on the London-Norwich route ran in 1846, though a number ran as far as Chelmsford, Colchester, and the Essex coast for a year or two longer. A few local short-distance services survived until about 1865, by which time the motor car, which would eventually reverse the drift from road to rail, was in sight. As early as 1829 George Shillibeer, in whose honour there is a brass memorial tablet in Chigwell church erected by London busmen, had promoted a horse-drawn bus service. These vehicles were superseded by steam carriages, but when in 1885 Gottfried Daimler patented his internal combustion engine the railway train was at last challenged. Panhard built his first car in France in 1894. A young Walthamstow engineer had put the Bremer car on Essex roads in 1892; in the 20th century, after Fords came to Dagenham, Essex became a major contributor to man's newest transport mania.

ᔥᏗᎶ

The social problems of Victorian England are near enough in time to cloud political attitudes today. The rapid industrialisation, the unprecedented growth in the population and migration created poverty and squalor on a scale that was quite beyond the resources of the authorities to control. The conscience of Victorian society thus turned to philanthropic activity with an urgency now evoked by the relief agencies in the modern world. Despite the emergence of a strong and stable middle class, the gulf between the relative affluence of these people and the penurious condition of the lower orders of society remained obstinately unbridgeable. The wealth created by industrial enterprise and commercial expansion was insufficient to relieve the destitution, degradation and delinquency that contrasted with the proud achievements of the world's leading trading nation. In 1837 there were 14 million people in England and Wales. By 1901 about 33 millions lived in the two countries. The population of Essex over the period of the Queen's reign grew from about 330,000 to over a million. There were 250,000 in the County Borough of West Ham alone, which area had contained but a few thousand only a century before. This rate of growth was simply beyond the capacity of inexperienced social authorities and private philanthropy. Within this massive demographic explosion there was more mobility than ever before. An analysis of the population of Chingford in 1851 found that after 20 years the total was static—as a result of local conditions—yet of 963 people in the parish more than half had been born elsewhere, and of those born in Chingford (440) some 229 were under 13 and mainly children of immigrant parents. Only 31 of the total of Chingford born inhabitants were more than 50 years of age. Yet Chingford was a parish which at that stage had not fully experienced the impact of the agrarian and industrial changes that were taking place or received any significant number of the destitute Irish whose migration into England was not of inconsiderable proportions. All of these factors exacerbated the social instability of lower Victorian society and it is hardly surprising that Edwin Chadwick's horrifying report shocked a complacent nation.

Despite the economic theories of such as Bentham, Ricardo and Mill, state action in the social field was seen as an inescapable duty by the progressives. Public concern led to an investigation by Edwin Chadwick, Secretary of the Poor Law Commission in London, into the 'Sanitary Condition of the Labouring Population' in 1842. It was issued in his own name out of deference to the wishes of the Poor Law Commissioners who preferred that, and spoke of 'prevalent misery', 'hot-beds of disease' and the 'wretched condition of a large portion of the labouring population'. A Benthamite as well as a persistent advocate of action by central government, Chadwick in his report referred to inadequate housing, appalling working conditions, dangerous water supplies, and rudimentary drainage systems. His trenchant prose was reinforced two years later by a Royal Commission report on the problems of 'Large Towns and Populous Districts'. There were 50,000 children in Poor Law institutions. *Oliver Twist* symbolised them all for a conscience-stricken nation. In Essex Charles Dickens's brother Alfred, a senior official of the General Board of Health, found the same dreadful conditions in the slums of West Ham. As late as 1871 Dr. Thomas Barnado could describe similar squalor and neglect in his *Out of the Gutter*. This famous philanthropist established the village homes for destitute children at Barkingside in what is now one of the best residential areas of south-west Essex. The homes are still run by his successors, who continue to provide the caring shelter for needy children that Thomas Barnardo's energy and humanity demanded.

In more hopeful vein Victoria's reign saw real and lasting improvements in the education services. At the beginning of the 19th century village children in Essex could at best expect to receive some education in the charity schools, Sunday schools, or the Dames' schools, which were not much more than child-minding institutions. Then came the British and National schools. The privileged few went to private day schools or the grammar schools, where they experienced the discipline of a classical education. By 1850 public funds were supporting education, teaching standards were rising, and a system of inspection had been provided. In August 1870 W.E. Forster's Education Act was a major advance since it placed education on a national footing and set the stage for the introduction of compulsory education shortly afterwards. Before the end of the century the newly created Essex County Council assumed full responsibility for public education in the county.

Alongside the struggle by the indigent for human dignity, the means of subsistence and an elementary education, the rising standards of the working and middle classes encouraged the use of leisure. Of interest to Essex history is the development of the seaside resorts in response to a public demand for holidays, which was a new Victorian conception made possible only by economic progress. A visit in 1801 by Princess Charlotte had given the 'South End' of the ancient parish of Prittlewell a cachet as a desirable resort. By 1830 its credentials as a fashionable venue for the well-to-do were well established. The attractive sea-front of 1850 looks well in contemporary prints, and when the London, Tilbury and Southend railway arrived in 1856 its future was assured. Public demand was stimulated by the second line via Shenfield in 1889 and Southend was well on its way to becoming the Londoner's favourite destination for excursion parties. By 1863 steam vessels arrived daily at the old wooden pier, and the 'front' was extended towards Cliff Town as the resort's popularity increased. After Southend, Clacton-on-Sea is the principal holiday resort of the Essex coast. Here the pier was opened in July 1871 and served by the Woolwich Steam Packet Company, which also participated in financing the development of Clacton as a seaside vacation town. Later

74 *Walton-on-the-Naze, 1831*

75   *Saffron Walden, 1831*

the first of the 'Queens', the *Queen of the Thames* and *Queen of the Orwell,* plied daily from London Bridge and Ipswich, and a few shillings took thousands of delighted passengers to the seaside then and for generations to come. Clacton's population grew rapidly after the railway arrived in 1882. It was almost quadrupled in 20 years, reaching 7,500 by 1901 and, like Southend, mirrored in a minor key on the Essex coast the great upsurge of population that was taking place on Thames-side. Similar expansion was also evident at Walton-on-the-Naze, and, later, Frinton. Thus Essex, extending the Londoners' playgrounds from Epping Forest to the coastal venues, contributed its share to the development of leisure pursuits that, in late Victorian England, made the picnic and the day in the country or at the seaside part of our way of life.

෭෮

The most conspicuous factor in the history of Essex during the 19th century was the creation, east of the Lea and along Thames-side, of metropolitan Essex. The boroughs of this now populous and urbanised area are today part of a Greater London that continues to make its demands on the Home Counties. Middlesex it has wholly engulfed. Kent, Surrey, Hertfordshire, and Essex have all made their sacrifice to the capital's territorial appetite. At the dawn of Victorian Britain the urban population was expanding at a significant rate. In south-west Essex, even before the railways, West Ham, Leyton and Walthamstow had already grown beyond their former village status. Further out, East Ham and Dagenham and the forest-girt villages of Wanstead and Chingford were, however, as yet insulated by their local geography from the impact of London

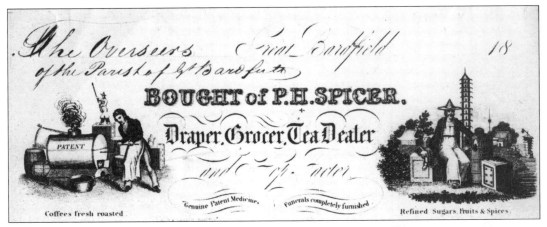

76 *Billhead from Great Bardfield Overseers' accounts, 1834*

and industrial growth. The course of events was irreversible, and by mid-century London had become the commercial capital of the world. South-west Essex, bordering the river-artery on which the capital's seaborne trade relied and sufficiently proximate to serve as a growth area for industry and in a dormitory role, was a logical reception area for London's overflow. Therefore all the elements of industrial urbanisation, roads, docks, railways, factories, housing, and people encroached on the woods and pastures of what ceased within the span of a man's life to be an authentic part of rural Essex. Insofar as the economic development of the area spared that corner of the county the tribulation of the agricultural depression of the later decades of the century it was a gain. But, as in London, the social and environmental crisis that accompanied an expansion too rapid and profound for the weak and unco-ordinated public services to contain bequeathed a legacy of problems still unresolved. There is indeed evidence to show that the local authorities in the boroughs and parishes of south-west Essex were slower than those in the more highly developed areas of London's East End to appreciate the evils of the situation and serious weaknesses in housing, public health and the provision of basic utility services aggravated the declining social standards. It was not until the emergence of modern local authorities from about 1890 that the situation was brought under adequate control.

From about 1860 the main growth points in south-west Essex were at West Ham and along the banks of the Lea. Roads and railways were built and the rivers dredged and banked to facilitate local communications with new factories. At Stratford and Silvertown, encouraged by the policy of the authorities at West Ham, whose lower rates and standards attracted commercial enterprises from London, there were established the nuclei of major industries. Paint and varnish, chemical and rubber, soap, sugar and confectionery, and ships, were among the products of the industries that forced their way onto the local scene. Further heavy industry was developed at Barking and concentrations of light industry sprang up at Leyton, Walthamstow and Romford. Later, footwear, electrical components, wire and cables, furniture and instrument-making were added to the growing industrial capacity of the Hams, Ilford, Romford, Barking, Leyton, and Walthamstow. As Britain's overseas trade expanded and the strident industrial empire on the Essex riverline burgeoned, so the great complex of the London docks

77   *King George V Docks, c.1970*

was constructed. The West India Dock had been built in 1802. On the Essex side of the Lea in what is now Newham, the port system was extended from 1855, when the Royal Victoria Dock was declared open by the Prince Consort. Later, in 1880, the Duke of Connaught inaugurated the Royal Albert Dock, the vast Thames-side installations being further augmented in 1921 by the King George V Dock. The grasslands of the former Essex marshes had disappeared under a sea of concrete, bricks and metal. The agrarian parishes of the Thames-side levels and the secluded forest hamlets of this part of the county found themselves, in less than a lifetime, part of the largest industrial complex in Britain. A vital factor was the Thames, but it was the proximity of the capital, with which the fortunes of Essex have been so often involved in history, that was decisive.

Over-population, burgeoning industrialisation and inadequate public services made it imperative that more strongly-based local authorities should be formed. Vestry government could not survive the changes that took place. In 1834 Boards of Guardians were appointed to carry out their duties under the Poor Law Amendment Act. In the same process Local Boards of Health, Education Authorities, and Highway Boards assumed responsibility within the widening scope of public administration needed to grapple with the pressing social problems of the urban areas. It was not enough, and the ill-co-ordinated jungle of local authorities that were set up under piecemeal legislation in the London region led to public concern, and an enquiry by Royal Commission that resulted in the establishment of the County Councils, including that of Essex, under the Local Government Act of 1888.

Concurrently the local government status of the parishes of south-west Essex developed under the stimulus of industrial growth and enlarging populations. East Ham, West Ham, and Little Ilford were, at the beginning of the period, united as the West Ham Union, together with some outlying areas that now form parts of Redbridge and Waltham Forest. By 1856 West Ham boasted a Local Board and was incorporated as a Municipal Borough in 1886. County Borough status came in 1889 as an acknowledgement of the phenomenal growth of the area. In East Ham a Local Board was created in 1879, municipal progress being marked by the formation of the Urban District Council in 1894, Borough and County Borough status following in 1904 and 1915, by which time the Hams were populated by well over 400,000 people. To the north of this area where London had made its first and most decisive impact on rural Essex, in Woodford, Wanstead, Ilford, Leyton, and Walthamstow, a similar, if less spectacular development was simultaneously taking place. Between 1854 and 1901 when Queen Victoria died all these areas advanced in municipal status. Further east Barking and Romford were embraced in the same process of urbanisation and industrialisation with the appropriate development of local government institutions. It was a complicated and significant evolution which I have described in more detail in *Discovering Essex in London*. During this period the structure of administration in the area assumed its basic modern forms as the old organs of local government were consumed in the tide of history as London overflowed. That the area would eventually be lost to Essex in the administrative sense was perhaps foreseeable but not then foreseen, and the county continued for another 60 years to contain these ancient parishes within its boundaries.

For metropolitan Essex, and indeed, nationally, the victory of the Victorian conservationists in preventing the final destruction of Epping Forest was a dramatic and decisive endorsement of environmental values. This lovely and historic forest was almost on the point of extinction when action was successfully taken to halt and reverse the march of enclosure and despoliation. For centuries the Forest of Essex had exerted its influence on the quality and nature of society in rural Essex. In the course of time, under the pressure of economic and social trends, it dwindled to become the Forest of Waltham and finally to its present area and designation of Epping Forest in which Londoners and the people of the forest parishes of Essex rejoice. As early as 1793 the Land Revenue Commissioners, although primarily interested in the physical state and economic health of the forest had, in advancing the case against further enclosure, stressed the amenity value of such natural woodland and heath to the London conurbation. Enclosure had by then, with official acquiescence if not encouragement, reduced the afforested area to no more than 9,000 acres. By 1850 the area had shrunk to but 6,000 acres and the remainder was seriously threatened by utilitarianism and private greed. Arthur Young, whose perspicacious mind we met in the 18th century, had considered the forest to be an impediment to agricultural progress and strongly advocated its enclosure and redevelopment for farming. Sir Walter Besant, the historian of London and its environs, inveighed powerfully against the enclosure with bitter and cogent irony. More was needed, and Hainault Forest, another remnant of the vast Forest of Essex, was virtually swept away following its disafforestation by Act of Parliament in 1851.

It was necessary that the weight of organised public opinion be brought to bear before the powerful interests that were impoverishing the forest landscape could be frustrated. In 1865 the Commons Preservation Society was founded to fight the issue of Commons versus Enclosure at the national level. In Epping Forest several Loughton villagers presented the movement with its *cause célèbre* and the opportunity to bring the matter into the legal arena. The Willingale brothers and a relative, William Higgins, were charged and convicted in the police court at Waltham Abbey in March 1866 with malicious trespass in exercising their common right of lopping. Their father, Thomas Willingale, had previously been before the court for the same offence. The court case was, in itself, unimportant, but it focused attention on the issue of principle and precipitated the litigation successfully conducted by the Corporation of London whose competence to intervene rested on their status as forest commoners by virtue of the ownership of a few hundred acres of land in the forest parish of Little Ilford. This costly and public-spirited legal action pressed forward over several years ended with a verdict against the enclosures, of signal importance in commons litigation, that saved the forest from further depredations and resulted in much formerly enclosed land reverting to the forest. The Epping Forest Act of 1878 has effectively safeguarded the forest from serious encroachment. Under it the Corporation of London were appointed as Conservators and, having deserved public approbation for their service in rescuing the forest from

78   *Queen Victoria visiting Epping Forest in 1882*

enclosure, have since enhanced its physical condition through wise and responsible management, to the public benefit. The last major occasion on which the forest attracted royal patronage was when Queen Victoria formally opened the forest in 1882 and dedicated it to the use and enjoyment of the public for all time. Arriving at Chingford in a royal blue train, she was received by other members of the royal family and tens of thousands of visitors. At the station was erected a welcoming flower-bedecked arch on which were inscribed appropriate loyal greetings, including the legend 'Never such a May-day and never such a Queen'.

The forest has been a decisive factor in preserving a rural environment on the northern periphery of the former Essex boroughs of Redbridge and Waltham Forest. It has effectively prevented the further sprawl of London towards Epping. It thus has a vital environmental role in metropolitan Essex elsewhere in which no similar barrier to London's expansion exists. The new boroughs are at once a monument to progress and the price that must be paid by rural communities for the amenities and benefits of modern life. Nothing as dramatic as this Victorian phenomenon has occurred in Essex to transform the landscape and lives of hundreds of thousands of people, over such a relatively short span of time, in all history. The old Essex is now unrecognisable, except for vestigial fragments, in the new boroughs. And, as we shall relate, the same process has continued into the 20th century.

൬൭൫

The aesthetic values of Victorian society are a matter of legitimate public debate. That some debasement of the refined public taste of the Georgian period occurred is undeniable, but the condemnation of that has tended to obscure the merit of much Victorian art and architecture. The stature of Victorian literature cannot be seriously challenged. In science progress was stimulated by public and commercial need. The townscapes of metropolitan Essex and the larger county towns, despite the ravages of war and re-development, still testify to the vigour, civic pride and relative affluence of Victorian Britain. The terraced streets of the older Essex boroughs still exhibit their Victorian frontages, monotonous rooflines and modest garden patchworks. Some have degenerated to the point where they inevitably qualify for inclusion in slum-clearance programmes. Others continue to serve as neat, if generally featureless, residential districts overlooked, all too often, by cranes, factory chimneys or railway embankments embedded as they are in the industrial maw. In the outlying areas of 'Essex in London' and in the towns of the Essex countryside Chelmsford, Colchester, Braintree and Halstead, over-large but serviceable and dignified Victorian housing serves as modern apartments or public offices for the overflow staff from outgrown administrative centres.

The significant names in Victorian architecture in Essex are Sir George Gilbert Scott, Arthur Blomfield, and Norman Shaw. C.F.A. Voysey, who emerged at the end of the 19th century as the foremost practitioner of domestic architecture, is represented in a pleasant house, 'The Homestead', at Frinton-on-Sea, and his stylistic features are also present in the old Chingford Nursing Home which was built in 1905. Scott was responsible for the splendid Victorian church of Holy Trinity, Halstead, but his most important work in the county was carried out at the Royal Wanstead School, then an orphan asylum, at Holly Bush Hill. It typifies the Victorian predilection for revived period styles and its Jacobean elevations are much admired in the lakeside setting at Snaresbrook. Norman Shaw built Chigwell Hall in 1876 in a confident and inventive Victorian idiom. Eden Nesfield, in the neighbouring parish at Loughton Hall, contributed a house of comparable vintage. However, his most important work in Essex is probably that to be seen in the market square at Saffron Walden and in the reconstruction at Radwinter after a major fire in 1874 that destroyed much of the village centre. But, aside from Victorian housing of the boroughs, the villas of surburbia and the gentlemen's country houses, it is in the churches of the Gothic revival and in municipal architecture that we now encounter the most conspicuous architecture of the period. Much of the building and re-building of medieval churches in the county was disastrous, but some was good. I have already invited attention to Holy Trinity at Halstead. At Romford Johnson built St. Edward the Confessor; and at Chingford 'the church on the green', Saints Peter and Paul, is a fine conception by Vulliamy and Arthur Blomfield. Although not strictly Victorian–it was rebuilt in that idiom in 1904–St Mary the Virgin at Great Warley is a stunning manifestation of Art Nouveau decoration and as a postscript to Victorian architecture and design as splendid as anything that can be found in the county or, indeed, in England.

The civic arrogance of much of the public building of the era can be forgiven. Time's patina has blunted the edge and the utilitarian virtue of such architectural Victoriana as the West Ham College of Technology, Library and Museum by Gibson and Russell in 1896-8, Newham's town hall, and the old town hall and central library at Leyton has been fully vindicated. The Victorians built well, and Essex has a generous range of the architectural product of the period in town and country. At village level there are some handsome, even delightful, schools and chapels, like the Victorian ensemble at Great Sampford for example, that equate the Victorian increment with other period architecture in that environment. Some must yet go in the interests of planning and public taste. But there is much that merits retention and I would include both civic and domestic building in this plea for judicious conservation. Whatever the view taken of the art and

79 *William Morris (1834-1896)*

architecture of the age nobody questions the undoubted contribution made to English literature by the Victorian novelists and men of letters. Pre-eminent in that distinguished company were such as Dickens, Trollope, Macaulay, Tennyson, Ruskin, and Kipling. Of these Dickens knew and loved his Essex haunts–'Chigwell, my dear fellow, is the greatest place in the world'–he wrote to his friend. Tennyson lived for a time at 'Beech Hill House' in Epping Forest and in *In Memoriam* inscribed the bells of Waltham Abbey–'Ring out, wild bells'–in the poetry of his age. John Clare, the pastoral poet, was also, in the unhappy circumstances of his infirmity, lodged in a private asylum at High Beach in the care of a Doctor Allen. To the east the rector of East Mersea, the Rev. S.B. Baring-Gould, who wrote with such felicity of the marshlands and the estuaries as well as dabbling in county history, struck an authentic Essex note. Charles Haddon Spurgeon, the dominant figure of Victorian Nonconformity and pastor at the London Tabernacle, was born at Kelvedon and went to school at Colchester. His wit and powerful prose made him an influence of national importance in the intense religious debate of the 19th century. Spurgeon's books commanded a wide and ready audience; today we would call them best-sellers. From Woodford came Coventry Patmore, the moralist, whose esoteric verse found favour with Ruskin and Carlyle, but never commanded general popularity. The most outstanding Essex name in art and literature was, however, that of William Morris, whose aesthetic genius is still potent today. Born at 'Elm House', Walthamstow, in 1834, Morris lived also, in his boyhood, at Woodford Hall. His father, a wealthy city merchant, brought up the Morris family in the beautiful forest whose charms William Morris never forgot. Versatile, sensitive, and naturally endowed with great artistic talent, he was among the leaders of Victorian culture. His delicate and expressive prose and verse found visual expression in his inspired designs and exquisite craftsmanship. As a political thinker he was less important, but he must stand with the highest of the personalities of Essex art and literature of any age.

In science, too, Essex had its great men. Darwin and Faraday are names with which everyone is familiar. Lord Lister's name is less famous, but hardly less illustrious, for the work of this eminent surgeon conferred immeasurable benefits on mankind. His birthplace was at 'Upton House', a modest and, sadly, now demolished Georgian home at West Ham. His practice and enunciation of the principle of antisepsis in 1865 and painstaking development of modern surgical techniques was fundamental, along with anaesthesia developed from 1846, in minimising the risks and horrors of surgery. Lister's professional approach to his subject and the technical competence and authority that he brought to it earned him the acclaim of his contemporaries and the respect of his successors in the field of hospital surgery. His, and the contributions of Morris and others like Elizabeth Fry the prison reformer, whose home lay near to Lister's, must be cast in the balance in any evaluation of good and evil in the experience of Victorian Britain.

ဆၢၵ

The later decades of Victoria's reign were ones in which her own matriarchal authority was strengthened as public admiration for her standards and devotion rose. Abroad she witnessed, and relished, the imperial role of the puissant nation over which she ruled and increasingly influenced as her stature grew. In Britain politics, in which she was deeply interested, were dominated by Gladstone and Disraeli. Economic growth continued apace and government, at all levels, gradually got to grips with the social problems which caused Victoria much concern. The period from 1867 can be seen as one in which the organs of national and local administration were developed as one of the principal activities of successive governments. In 1867 a further instalment of electoral reform enfranchised the artisan populations of the growing urban areas. It was significant and doubled the electorate which then totalled about two millions. The redistribution of seats under this measure left Essex with six representatives in Parliament, two each from the three geographical divisions of the county, west, east and south. The election that followed in 1868 was the last at which Essex voters participated in the hustings, which had hitherto caused much excitement and spectacle in the election centres. The Ballot Act of 1872 replaced the open bidding by secret voting which was another step in the direction of truly democratic government and long overdue. In 1884 another extension of the franchise in rural areas gave Essex eight seats as well as a number of borough representatives. The process towards representative government was carried a stage further in 1888 when the County Councils Act, piloted through parliament by C.T. Richie, the President of the Local Government Board, created 62 county councils, including Essex, with wide administrative powers. In 1894 the pattern of parish, rural and urban councils was consolidated to put control over roads, sewerage and other public utilities firmly out of central and into local hands at appropriate levels.

There were administrative changes, too, in the ecclesiastical sphere. For more than a millennium Essex had been governed within the bishopric of London. Largely because of the growth of metropolitan Essex which imposed considerable administrative burdens on the diocesan authorities, the future metropolitan parishes were separated from the other parishes in the county when, in 1846, the remainder of Essex was transferred to the see of Rochester. This was perhaps the first governmental signal of the eventual excision of the area from the administrative county, but the problems of the London diocese led to the assignment of south-west Essex to Rochester, also in 1863. In 1877 Essex joined Hertfordshire to form the Diocese of St Albans. It was not until 1914 that the county, including the metropolitan parishes, was created as the Diocese of Chelmsford. Essex, after a vote in the parishes that favoured Chelmsford over Colchester, West Ham and several others, at last had a cathedral. All was part of the great issues of governance and effective control of the social and administrative problems of this strident and fluid age.

When the princess came to the throne in 1837 the prestige of the monarchy was seriously diminished. The Hanoverians had bequeathed a legacy of public contempt and apathy. Victoria's sense of duty, youth, and the strength of her family life commanded the love and loyalty of her people, engaging first their sympathy and then their emotions and interests. She arrived on the royal scene as a determined, but hitherto sheltered princess. She rose in public esteem and self-dedication to the role of Queen Empress in her own right. She was beset not by treachery, though she was not unacquainted with attempted violence, or intrigue, but by the pressures and responsibilities of world power and influence that none even of her greatest predecessors like Alfred and Elizabeth had to bear. Her life was not without personal tribulation following the death of her beloved husband, and she felt deeply the anxieties posed by war, Ireland, South Africa, and the social problems of industrial Britain. Her steadfast resolve, application to filial and national duty, and indeed much of her personality was typical of the best traits of Victorian Britain. The people of Essex rejoiced with her at the celebrations held throughout the county on the occasion of her Diamond Jubilee in 1897. But her last days were clouded by the distress caused by events in South Africa and family problems. She died after the longest reign in English history at Osborne House in the Isle of Wight in January 1901. It was as if her great spirit could not face the century then dawning and to which she did not belong. Queen Victoria epitomised 19th-century Britain in which Essex was re-defined in all its social, economic and administrative dimensions. If Essex was created by the Anglo-Saxons it was re-created by the Victorians over 1,000 years later. As we shall see in the next chapter, modern Essex is indebted to every past age; but to none more so than that of Victoria.

Chapter Nine

৪০০৪

MODERN ESSEX

'The essential England'

At this point of our story the historical quality of the book is diluted by reportage and description as events of the recent past perhaps loom too near to be focused in a perspective context. The convulsions of two world wars, in which Essex was wholly involved in the national cause, have distorted the amazing advances that science has made possible in social and economic terms. The true evaluation of this fluid age of technical progress, violence, dissent, consensus, relative affluence and the caring soci-

ety, lies beyond the parameters of contemporary history. But some account, at the county level, is demanded by the concept of this book which has envisaged the continuity of Essex life from the gravel terraces of the prehistoric river valleys to the 20th century. In essence the story of modern Essex is that world wars, modern science, natural disaster, evolving international trading patterns, European agricultural policies and major residential developments in the new towns, the massive investment in communications at Stansted, Dartford and in the county's road systems have fuelled unique sequences of human drama and achievement.

Since King Edward VII followed his mother to the throne in 1901, Essex has witnessed the consummation of the changes so dramatically launched in her time and shared with the nation the experience of conflict, crisis and deliverance. In one war the humble, Leyton-born boy seaman, Jack Cornwell, immortalised his name in the annals of Essex by his steadfast devotion to his duty at Jutland. In the other, Sir Winston Churchill's famous name and lineage honours the county in which he represented the Epping and Woodford constituencies during most of his parliamentary

80 *Jack Cornwell*

155

life. In an age which we readily assess in material terms, the county has still had its heroes and the mettle and aspirations of its people have been demonstrated to be not so different from those who lived at *Camulodunum* and those who colonised the Anglo-Saxon kingdom.

The casualties of both wars were borne by families in every town and village in the county. The people of Essex took their place in the struggles at home and abroad. At sea, on land, and in the air men and women of the county were engaged in these great and tragic conflicts.

The First World War, which erupted in 1914 and engulfed Europe in desperate conflict, found Britain ill-prepared and without credible air defences. However, the sea power deployed by the Royal Navy meant there was, as in previous European wars, no serious threat of seaborne invasion. The Essex coast was secure and harboured a destroyer flotilla at Harwich. A motor torpedo boat squadron was based at Osea Island just downstream from the legendary Northey Island where Byrhtnoth had challenged the Danish invaders in A.D. 991, in the broadening waters of the Blackwater estuary. But Essex lay on the flight path of the marauding German Zeppelins which were attacking London, their main target. The capital's air defences were at first ineffective but had been developed by 1916 with a shield of fighter bases in Essex and an anti-aircraft network of guns and searchlights in the Epping Forest area. Sea-fighting took place off the Essex coast and there was combat in the Essex skies. Bombs fell on those areas of urban Essex in the vicinity of London like Ilford and Leytonstone and elsewhere in the county at Chelmsford, Maldon, and Heybridge causing casualties and damage. Essex countryfolk saw a Zeppelin destroyed at Great Burstead and another shot down by fighters at Little Wigborough. The involvement of civilians in this way gave war a new and then modern dimension. It inevitably gave rise to rumour and alarm. One elderly woman claimed that during a raid in September 1916 a Zeppelin passed so low over Little Sampford that the German crew could be heard talking!

Experience in the county during the Second World War was even more immediate as the reality was brought nearer home by air-power and the threat of invasion. Essex, facing the continent and exposed by its numerous estuaries which open onto flat, low-lying terrain was vulnerable to attack. In fact, as in the First World War, naval supremacy and, this time, air battles that diminished the German capacity for air-cover and assault, frustrated the invasion strategy of the enemy forces. But the Essex coastline had been prepared for a dogged resistance should the challenge materialise.

The German armoured divisions after a swift and successful advance through the Ardennes and northern France were poised on the Channel Coast. Despite the losses at Dunkirk where much equipment and transport had been abandoned, a memorable rescue operation for the recovery of the British land forces was mounted. Many of the small craft employed came from the Essex estuarine harbours, especially of Mersea and on the Colne. Britain was ready. The Essex coastline was mined and defended by gun emplacements, anti-landing obstacles below the tidelines and rapidly constructed fortifications. Regular troops and Essex Home Guard battalions were deployed to oppose and harass invading forces in depth. Just inland from the coastal barrier was the Colchester Stop Line. Further west, the GHQ line ran roughly from Saffron Walden via Chelmsford to the Thames near Canvey Island. The last line of defence in Essex before London was the Outer London Defence Ring. All of these defensive barriers were

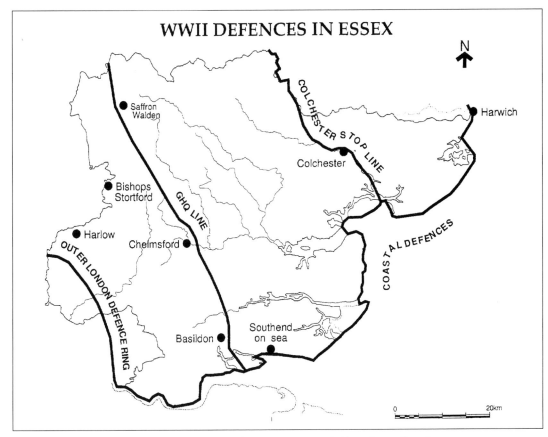

81 *The World War II Defence Lines in Essex.* © *Essex County Council*

buttressed by hundreds of pillboxes and anti-tank defences. Happily, these dispositions were never tested. The Home Guard (originally the Local Defence Volunteers) was mobilised in July 1940, conjuring faint echoes of the Anglo-Saxon Fyrd and the Essex Trained Bands and Fencibles of former days. It was an amateur force and not equipped with modern battlefield weapons until later in the war. The Essex Home Guard nevertheless supported the excellent county emergency and medical services in coping with the casualties and disruption caused by the often continuous air raids.

The county was attacked on numerous occasions. In metropolitan Essex in particular, where the docks and industry were prime targets for enemy air-raids, there was great destruction, and thousands of people were killed and injured in the devastated areas.

Throughout the county the larger towns, Colchester, Chelmsford, Harwich and even villages suffered in the aerial bombardment of England. Later in the war hundreds of the V.1 flying bombs and the long-range V.2 rockets caused more loss of life and destruction in the county.

Now, half a century on, local memorials in the county's towns and villages record the names of Essex men and women who, at home and overseas, died as their ancestors had in defence of the realm. After the wars the paths of progress were resumed and the scars of war removed. Here and there, along the coast, and in the fields and at the roadside there are still the sad, ugly, concrete reminders of the days when Essex was at war. In time, they will mostly disappear; but some are being preserved for historical record.

෨෬

Despite the industrialisation of Thames-side and the growth of manufacturing enterprises in the larger towns of the county, Essex still sustains a strong agricultural economy. If the communities of south Essex are becoming orientated to London, the rural heart of the county still beats strongly. Its people have seen agriculture recover from the trauma of the late-Victorian decline to find a viable level in the economic society stimulated by European policies and markets in which we now live. Corn, cereals and vegetable crops have yielded something to market gardening, soft fruit, poultry, and the garden centres, but the fields of Essex still, in the main, submit to tractor-drawn ploughshare, harrow and cultivator. It is still a seed-sowing county. It is not yet, north of the Southend arterial road, fully conscious of its industrial role despite the strong and growing concentrations of industry at Colchester, Chelmsford and lesser manufacturing centres such as those at Billericay, Wickford, Harlow and Saffron Walden. Thames-side, however, is almost wholly committed to 20th-century commerce and constitutes one of the major industrial regions of Britain. Shipping, oil storage, chemicals, heavy engineering and power production were supplemented by electronics, photographic assembly, clothing and consumer products in the metropolitan boroughs. All are exemplified by Fords. When Fords came to Dagenham they placed the hallmark of the 20th-century world on the Essex landscape. In 1909 A.V. Roe made the first flight in Britain in a British aeroplane over the Walthamstow marshes by the banks of the River Lea, where he had his workshops under the viaduct that carries the Chingford railway line. Ford cars were already running on British roads, and by 1912 were being manufactured in a new plant at Manchester. The growth of demand for the motorcars led Fords to establish their principal works on the marshes at Dagenham where the site was purchased in 1925. By 1931 the plant was in production and road and rail communications in the county had been further enhanced to serve this and the other enterprises that had been expanding their activities in step with the growth of the whole industrial complex of which London and the Thames were vital elements.

Simultaneously one of the most significant rehousing schemes in the world was planned and implemented in the same part of the county. Fords and Becontree as much as anything else typify the changes wrought in Essex in modern times. People, homes and work are the essential ingredients of modern society. The marshlands of Essex west of the Lea and extending northwards from the riverline of the Thames received them all in unprecedented circumstances as thousands of Londoners were, from social necessity, moved to peripheral localities to relieve the pressure of population in the over-crowded boroughs. The Housing and Town Planning Act of 1919 provided for central government finance in support of local authority housing and under it the London County Council was empowered to develop estates beyond the boundaries of the administrative area which it governed. Some 3,000 acres were consequently acquired for this purpose in the Dagenham, Barking and Ilford districts by compulsory purchase between 1920 and 1922. And so Becontree was born to provide decent homes at rents that working-class people could afford on the so-called cottage estate that was created on the deteriorated farmlands and in place of the decaying

82   *Becontree, c.1970*

homes of agricultural labourers and marginal farmers. Becontree was developed, not as a model town with a balanced sufficiency of all the amenities of life, but as a housing estate for workers who in the main still travelled to the capital for their daily work. It was, at any rate at first, a dormitory for the London artisan classes, and until the retail trades and local services were developed only road-work and building offered employment in the vicinity. In the first phase, from 1921-1924, some 28,000 people were re-housed in almost 6,500 new homes. By 1932 some 22,000 houses provided good reasonably-rented homes for more than 100,000 people. Over three-quarters had moved from the metropolitan boroughs, particularly Poplar, Stepney, Hackney, and Islington. Most of the remainder originated from the Greater London area, including East and West Ham, still part of the geographical county of Essex. Only a handful came from elsewhere. A social survey carried out in 1934 for the Pilgrim Trust showed that most of the tenancies were taken up by workers in the manufacturing industries and transport. The estate was not beautiful or, by the standards of the New Towns, comprehensively conceived to conscious environmental norms. Professor C.E.M. Joad spoke disparagingly of 'these architectural monstrosities', but it is only fair to concede that the L.C.C.'s architect, Mr. G. Topham Forest, was a pioneer, and that the homes he devised elevated the conditions of life for thousands of Londoners whose sub-standard dwellings in the dreary streets of the capital were gladly abandoned in favour of the anticipated salubrity of Becontree.

The development of public services at Becontree was at first retarded by the divided control exercised by the local authorities in whose administrative areas the estate was sited. The formation of the Urban District Council at Dagenham in March 1926 meant that for the larger part of the new urban community services could then be provided on an appropriate scale. This was followed by the establishment of some light industry to

83   *Municipal architecture at Waltham Forest*

supplement the limited local employment opportunities in the area, but the new estate still remained basically a dormitory town. It may also be seen as tangible evidence of the concern that post-war society in England had for the living standards of its urban populations. The degradation of an over-crowded and dispirited existence in London's decaying Victorian streets was exchanged for the decency, dignity and relative comfort of the new suburbia.

The creation of the London County Council's estate at Becontree between the wars and the New Towns after the 1939-45 War have clearly been important factors in the build-up of the population of the county. It is now about 1,500,000 in the administrative county alone, with more than 1,000,000 in metropolitan Essex, which includes Becontree. The new communities at Harlow and Basildon have outstripped the populations of all the other major Essex towns outside metropolitan Essex and Southend. The New Towns were built with the help of central government under the supervision of Development Corporations set up with the authority of the New Towns Act of 1946. The building of these towns with the main object of relieving congestion in the cities by creating comprehensive independent communities away from existing urban concentrations has been a major achievement of social policy. In Essex the Harlow Development Corporation was established in 1947. The site on which the New Town, one of eight new planned communities in the London regions, was to be built was situated within the rural parishes of Harlow, Netteswell, Great and Little Parndon.

84   *Water Gardens, Harlow Town Centre*

Never before had towns been planned in such carefully evaluated detail for long-term development and a robust community life of their own.

These imaginative planning concepts envisaged residential areas designed to provide a healthy living environment, the basic amenities of life and ample scope for employment and recreation. Described as 'a leap into the unknown', the Ministry of Town and Country Planning saw it as planned decentralisation, not 'satellite' but 'new' towns—and not derived from the 'garden city' image of pre-war experiments. Each was to have its own identity, social and environmental characteristics. Necessarily it was a compromise that was 'neither better nor worse than other towns, but different'. As the new homes, shops, factories, churches and social centres spread through the 'neighbourhoods' that clustered around the town centre at Harlow, the new people of Essex found themselves in an environment of an entirely novel conception. Garden cities there had been before, but this pioneering venture was conceived in more advanced terms. A traffic-free town centre, master-minded by the architect Frederick Gibberd, was dominated by the water gardens, a fine town hall and 'The Lawns', which was the first tower block to be built in Britain. In the amenity areas orthodox ideas of urban statuary commemorating local dignitaries or heroes made way for the controversial creations of Rodin, Henry Moore who sculpted 'The Family Group' and Barbara Hepworth who subscribed 'Contrapuntal Forms'. There had naturally been anxiety and even opposition to the project at the outset, but even the severest critics had to admit that it was new; and most would concede that it was exciting. At all events Harlow, like Basildon which came a few years later, added a new dimension to the topography of the county. Becontree, ahead of its time 30 years before, was already an anachronism.

Basildon, under the Basildon Development Corporation, commenced in 1949, grew even faster than Harlow. Here it was planned to house 70,000 people on the lands described as a 'rural slum' to the west of Laindon, some five miles south of Billericay. This had its origins in the agricultural decline caused by the arrival of cheap wheat from North America in the late 19th century, a process accelerated by the difficulty of cultivating the heavy Essex soils and consecutive seasons of inclement weather. This led to the purchase of failing farms by speculators who acquired them at low market prices and sold off small building plots which were virtually without main services or even tolerable access roads. Thousands of inadequate dwellings were erected on the derelict farmlands and the local authorities in that part of Essex had neither the powers nor the resources to cope with the environmental problems that resulted especially during the period between the wars. It was not until the post-war period that serious solutions could be developed. The New Town concept was one. It was a major enterprise involving extensive land acquisition, careful planning and development. Public finance, as always, was limited and the inevitable changes in approach took place as circumstances fluctuated over time. The original concept, which envisaged Basildon as a self-contained community,

85   *Basildon, New Town.*

came under pressure and had to be modified. Those who have criticised the result under-estimate the scale and complexity of the problem and the political and procedural difficulties of responding to changing social, industrial and environmental imperatives and aspirations.

Unlike Harlow which was virtually a virgin site, Basildon was thus sited on countryside extending through seven parishes and already containing some 25,000 people in sub-standard, mainly bungalow, housing, who had been tempted to the area by cheap fares and the opportunity of a life in the country away from the noise and smoke. Unplanned, and to a large extent uncontrolled, the result was an environmental disaster. Basildon was perceived as the answer to more than one problem. Today, the formerly degraded landscape presents a bold modern countenance with a country park and well-contrived townships purposefully disposed in relation to the splendid central facilities and the inevitable high-rise profile of modern architectural horizons. There are, of course, social problems in both of these Essex New Towns today, in common with urban experience throughout the world. It is perhaps too soon for an historical verdict on the success of this bold social experiment. But, by any reckoning, much has been achieved and many of the original objectives have been satisfied. Each is a significant community in the Essex scene. Basildon District including the New Town and older towns of Billericay and Wickford, which form a part of it, has a population well in excess of 150,000 people: Harlow about 80,000. Both will continue to expand and are among the largest of the eight New Towns built on the outer circumference of the London region since the war— only Crawley and Stevenage being of comparable scale.

ಸಂಆ

London had already, in the 19th century, staked a considerable claim to the Essex countryside in the south-west. It had created Becontree within the eventual perimeter of the expanding urban area and later poured more of its people into Harlow and Basildon. The same process, on a less ambitious scale, but attractively conceived, took place at Harold Hill, near Romford, and at Debden between the forest town of Loughton and the Rodings. In metropolitan Essex the ultimate step was almost a formality. The continued growth of population and industry in the area and the parallel development of local government was common to the whole London periphery and culminated in the Local Government Act of 1963 under which Greater London was created. Thus the capital engulfed what remained of Middlesex and other large and populous areas of the Home Counties. In Essex, although only six per cent of its land area was involved, more than half of the population of the county and rateable value was transferred to the new super-authority in London in April 1965. The former Lea-side, Thames-side and forest parishes of Essex, by then major urban communities, became administratively a part of London and 'Essex in London' was an acknowledged reality.

The territorial demands of local government development were, however, by no means satisfied. Modern problems, the needs of social administration and economics led to the postulation of a 20th-century solution that had little regard for history and the integrity of the ancient boundaries of the county. Everyone agreed that local government was ripe for further reform as it had been in the 1880s; nobody could agree on what form the new authorities might take or where the geographical boundaries of administration should be drawn. At one time the proposals for Essex, in visualising the establishment of major new district authorities with enhanced powers, postulated also the excision of a large area in the north-east, including the historic towns of Colchester and Harwich, which would have been attached to an enlarged Suffolk county. But the only result was the withdrawal of county borough status from Southend which was equated with the other local authorities in the county. In 1989 the Essex County Council celebrated the centenary of the English county councils which had been created under an Act of Parliament of 1888 consistently with Victorian zeal for the reformation of local government. It began with a flourish. The new County Council met for its first formal meeting in the Shire Hall at Chelmsford in April 1889. Provisional meetings had been heralded by the bells of the parish church and the White Ensign was hoisted on the tower. County Boroughs within the boundaries of the geographical and then administrative county were established at West Ham in 1889, Southend in 1914 and East Ham in 1915. The creation of the Greater London Boroughs in 1965, as we have seen, further diminished the scope of the County Council's responsibility. Surviving the proposals of 1974, as indicated above, the county and its council were faced in the late 1980s with the possibility of fundamental change when the Local Government Commission was charged to review the structure of local government. The eventual result of this, after protracted and complicated consultations on the various options, was the emergence of recommendations to establish Southend-on-Sea and Thurrock as all-purpose unitary authorities. Basildon was considered for this status but, in the end, the recommendation was not made. This did not mean that the districts administered by the new unitary authorities would cease to form part of Essex. It was recognised by the Commission that entrenched traditions and loyalties that bind people to the ancient counties were too valuable to yield. The history of the Metropolitan boroughs of south-west Essex has exemplified this as I tried to demonstrate in *Discovering Essex in London*.

Essex as a maritime county, whose low-lying shores rarely present a cliff barrier to the sea, has always been vulnerable to the high tides. Along the North Sea coast, in the tidal estuaries and on Thames-side there has, over the centuries, been a constant struggle with the incoming sea which has shaped much of the Essex shoreline. From time to time the defences have been overwhelmed, and episodes such as the Breach of 1707 at Dagenham have found their way into local history. In 1953 occurred a tide that penetrated the shore defences all along the county's seaward boundaries from Suffolk to the Lea on London's border. It has been chronicled with great literary panache in Hilda Grieve's monumental book, from which this brief account was culled. It is a story of peril, heroism and resource in which the county rose to the challenge of the tides. 'There has surely been', wrote Miss Grieve, 'no more extraordinary or spontaneous mobilisation, in so short a time, in the whole history of the county'.

Towards the end of January 1953 fierce gales blowing down the North Sea and the build-up of storm conditions led, on 31 January, to the issue of routine warnings. No-one foresaw the disaster that was imminent. By nightfall there was some anxiety, but no alarm. In the early evening it was realised at Harwich, Walton, Clacton, Maldon, and other coastal stations that an ominous situation was developing. At midnight the sea had broken through the sea-defences and a number of serious breaches had been made; the position was by then seen to be perilous. During the night the rising tide and relentless waves battered through the walls and overran the saltings and the coastal islands. The whole county was confronted with an assault from the sea beyond the experience of any

86 Foulness: The Great Tide, 1953

living person in Essex. Harwich was inundated; Clacton pier was largely submerged. At Foulness the sea walls failed and the Colne and the other estuaries were flooded as the inexorable tides rolled in to the point of danger and beyond. The High Street in Old Leigh was under water; Canvey Island, itself won from the sea, was seriously threatened. As far upstream as Tilbury the defences were breached. Before the tide turned at 2 a.m. on 1 February the riverside areas of much of south Essex were awash and there was flooding as far up as Bow Creek and Canning Town. In a natural disaster of international proportions–the North Sea coasts of Eastern England and the western European countries were even more seriously affected–the seaward periphery of the county had proved vulnerable to the seas which, in a night, had reoccupied the Essex marshlands that had been reclaimed and maintained by human ingenuity and industry centuries before. In 308 miles of tidal defences 155 had been topped, demolished or weakened to the point of failure. Fifty thousand acres were affected and more than 12,000 homes flooded, leaving over 20,000 people homeless. When the human toll was counted it was found that at least 119 Essex people had died. There was high mortality, too, among farm animals who clustered hopelessly during the night on higher ground as the waters rose around them.

The catastrophe encompassed the whole coastline. From Harwich and the Stour, down to Walton, around Bramble Island, Horsey and Landermere Creek on past Clacton, Jaywick, the Colne, West Mersea, Bradwell, and the Dengie Peninsula the waters found their ways over Essex soil. The Blackwater, Foulness, Wallasea, the Crouch, Great Wakering, Southend, Canvey and Tilbury all felt the brunt of the Great Tide. Along

Thames-side at Thurrock, Dagenham, West Ham, and to the Lea at Bow Creek the waters had risen with devastating effect. The county emergency services, police, fire, ambulance, the armed forces, and the people throughout Essex were equal to the task and rallied, in defence of their homes, as they had done before in times of peril. There were numerous acts of heroism and endurance. Morale remained high and human generosity was typically part of the response one expects when England is under threat. After the hour of trial came the period of reconstruction. Thousands needed to be re-housed, the land rehabilitated and, if the sea was to be successfully resisted, the defences restored. Between 1953 and 1957 concrete, stone and steel were poured into the rebuilding of the new sea walls on which Essex will rely if ever the sea should again mount an assault as violent as that which arose from the North Sea on that calamitous night of 1953.

‎‎‎

The tragedy and drama of the Great Tide was followed in the summer of 1953 by the joyful celebration in all parts of the county of the Queen's coronation. Towns and villages were decorated in festive mood and loyal and happy events organised to mark the great occasion. Memories were evoked of the county's past associations with the Crown and particularly with the great queens, Elizabeth I and Victoria. A new age was contemplated with a glow of excitement and expectation. No-one could foresee the future but the county was quietly confident of progress and at least a modest prosperity. The New Towns were symbols of a happier future and the age of planning.

An important hallmark of the county's status and its commitment to the value of its cultural and academic resources was the inspirational decision to establish a University of Essex. Proposed in 1959, it all came to fruition at Wivenhoe Park on the fringe of Colchester in 1964. Since then, despite some inevitable problems, the University has established its academic credentials and, in particular, pioneered work in a number of important scientific fields and made valuable international contributions to contemporary thought. It has thus a special role in enriching the life of the county.

The beneficial influence, in town and country, of a more significant public conscience in regard to amenity and environment began to manifest itself in tidier, cleaner towns and better ordered roadsides. At a high level great planning issues like the third London airport that was initially frustrated at Stansted and was once destined for Foulness excited public emotions. Following the Roskill Commission of 1968 it was proposed to reclaim thousands of acres of the Maplin Sands for the creation of a great air and sea terminal complex that would have had considerable implications for Essex generally. Road and rail communications would have had to be further developed and the enterprise was expected to attract people to the county, which, according to the census of 1971, was already one of the fastest growing in population in Britain.

This major issue was subsequently decided in 1985 when the old wartime United States Air Force base at Stansted became the chosen site. Development of the runways and the building of new terminal facilities commenced in the following year. London Stansted was formally opened in 1991 with a projected capacity of 15 million passengers a year. Already employing 5,000 people and having promoted a local road and rail network with ready access to the motorway system that services London, the North and the Channel ports, it was a major investment. A positive approach, with landscaping, the creation of ponds and massive tree and shrub planting to encourage wildlife, was followed

87 *Essex landscape: Passingford Mill, near Abridge, photographed by Jeffery Whitelaw*

88 *The award-winning terminal at Stansted Airport*

to minimise the environmental impact on the Essex farmlands and villages that were engulfed by this project. The terminal building, an exciting essay in modern architecture, has won several awards for design and the standards of comfort and amenity offered to passengers and visitors to the airport. The sophisticated navigational aids and landing systems were installed to satisfy its operational roles and air safety standards. It has already become a major county resource with international dimensions.

In recent decades the Essex road networks, in an age when the railways have declined, have also been extensively developed to improve standards as part of a county-wide communications policy. The proximity of Essex to the European trading routes and economic growth have demanded this. The strategic trunk routes and the 'feeder' networks to service Stansted, Harwich and other outlets have attracted massive investment. Chelmsford now has by-pass routes, as have other Essex towns, which also provide traffic relief to numerous villages that were traversed by the old roads. In the same context the Dartford crossing has been complemented by the opening of the fine new Queen Elizabeth II bridge linking Essex with Kent. Another 20th-century manifestation of modern science and engineering is the nuclear power station at Bradwell which has been in operation since 1962. Inevitably controversial, it is planned to provide nuclear energy into the 21st century and is an important part of the nation's electricity generation resources. This giant installation, sited not far from St Cedd's humble chapel, makes it hard to think of anything more symbolic of the leap that mankind in Essex has made over the intervening centuries. All of those developments, demanded by the norms and aspirations of contemporary society, cannot but have serious environmental implications.

Presently, however, the county of Essex—once seen as 'a landscape in decline'—still offers a fair prospect in the forests and in the farmlands north of the industrial base. The loss of trees and hedgerows is worrying, but agriculture, for long the mainstay of the county's economy, is strong in its modern stance and will preserve the intimate, open and gentle landscape that we so enjoy in the Rodings, along the river valleys, in the chalklands of the north-west and out to the estuarine territory to the east. Engaging villages, rural scenery of a pleasant subtlety and lovely period houses still embellish the countryside in much of the county. The variety of the Essex scene is little appreciated by those who, in their ignorance, still reproach the county as flat and uninteresting. There is a warmth and assimilability about rural Essex that is at once attractive and rewarding. Its history and architecture must fascinate and charm even the most demanding visitors. For those who live in the county it offers even more. Essex, in the totality of its scenic merits, its history, and the versatility of its architectural inheritance, can bear comparison with any other county in Britain. It is true that in the metropolitan reaches the old countryside has disappeared under the urban and industrial sprawl. But to the north the rural character of the old Essex survives in good measure and the New Towns add a further dimension of interest and are worthy representatives of the modern contribution to the county scene. Even in the metropolitan areas of Essex fragments of the rural past survive in the village centres miraculously preserved at Walthamstow and Rainham, and in the remaining timber-framed buildings and Norman and Gothic churches of the boroughs. The county may be thought by the uninitiated to epitomise William Cowper's oft-quoted remark that 'God made the country, man made the town'. It is the clay, the chalk and the sea, and its people that have made the county what it is. And in truth man made much of the county, too, in Essex, and has cultivated the fields and hills to advantage. It has all been contrived uncommonly well.

Since the previous paragraph was written for the first edition of this county history much has been done to reinforce the confident note that was struck in reference to the integrity of the Essex countryside. There have naturally been in the last twenty years unfortunate losses and trends that have threatened to dilute the historical traditions and eroded some of what was best in the Essex countryside. The impact of the supermarkets and the growth of car ownership has led to the demise of numerous shops and inns, public transport problems, the lack of affordable housing and the continued 'drift' from the land has changed the social idioms of village life. Declining congregations, the rising costs of the upkeep of ancient buildings, contemporary pastoral roles and other factors have led to redundant churches as at Wenden Lofts in the north-west, Little Oakley in Tendring, Wickham Bishops in mid-Essex and Langdon Hills in the south of the county. They become domestic dwellings, local museums or just close! All of this is symptomatic of the changes in the pattern and quality of rural life in our time. Yet, considered in a longer time-scale, rural life has improved dramatically. In a few centuries of progress rural conditions have risen from a state of scarcity to abundance; hunger and indigence in the Essex farmlands have been replaced by domestic comfort and relative affluence. The process has accompanied the development of monocultural farming economies and a tendency to much larger farms worked by few people. Subsistence economies have given way to the pressures of a market-oriented industry that supports the rising living standards of a society no longer, in the main, engaged in agricultural activity. Life in the countryside has never been static and there will be further changes.

In the course of a few score thousands of words we have followed the story of the county. From the earliest times Essex has always had close associations with London and has rarely stood aside from the broad current of English history. It is in Anglo-Saxon England that its true roots lie, though Essex today owes much also to the influence and experience of succeeding ages, and something to the fading and nebulous resonances of times yet more remote. In its historical and topographical setting we may see the county still as H.G. Wells described it as 'the essential England'. Although Essex does and should relish an individual integrity that history, geography and people have conferred upon it, its true validity lies only in the whole context of English life within which it has been nurtured and which, in return, the county and its people have enriched.

ESSEX HISTORIOGRAPHY

Reference note (1)

Essex historiography begins with a vicar of Great Waltham, Nicholas Tindal (1687-1774) though the earlier works of William Camden, John Norden and a few other topographers and cartographers contain material of relevance to Essex history. Tindal was working seriously, with the help of historical notes inherited from Thomas Jekyll (1570-1652), a lawyer of Bocking, and William Holman (1670-1730), a dissenting minister at Halstead. Their detailed research formed the basis for the first general histories of the county. Only those parts of Tindal's writings that covered the Braintree-Felsted area were ever published, in *c.*1732. Nathaniel Salmon, a clergyman of Bishops Stortford and an expert historiographer, appears to have drawn directly on Tindal's recorded research and indeed purchased Holman's manuscripts from Tindal in 1739. He published an incomplete history of the county from 1740 which, in common with other county histories of that period, was overly concerned with genealogy and the descent of the manors. His use of historical material was also deficient and his work is therefore of limited value though of interest to collectors.

The doyen of Essex historiographers was Philip Morant (1700-1770), who was latterly rector of St Mary-at-the-Walls, Colchester and of Aldham. He was born in Jersey, educated at Pembroke College, Oxford and incorporated as a Master of Arts at Sidney Sussex College, Cambridge: he became a Fellow of the Society of Antiquaries in 1755. Morant first entered the field as an Essex historian as Tindal's curate at Great Waltham and had access to that cleric's material when he later embarked on his own great works. Between 1748 and 1768 Morant published complete and detailed volumes of considerable scholarship containing a history of Colchester and then of the county of Essex. These fine books, though sometimes unreliable in detail in view of the limited resources available to Morant's generation of historians, are the first complete histories of the county and still find a legitimate place in the corpus of basic information to which later historians must turn. They were not written for general use and are lacking in the wider evaluation of historical events and the social and economic life of the county. However, although his role was to an extent to collate, reorganise and correct the work of his predecessors his name quite rightly remains pre-eminent in the field.

A history, although relying largely on Philip Morant's work, that is readable and meriting reference in this note was issued in parts between 1769 and 1772. The title of this work, ostensibly more popular in character, is *A new and complete History of Essex, by a Gentleman.* It appeared under the patronage of one Peter Muilman whose name is usually associated with the authorship of this county history. There is relevant information, too, in *The Environs of London* (1796) by yet another prolific parson, Daniel Lysons. From 1814 a pleasant and well-produced volume on south-west Essex was published by Elizabeth Ogborne (1763-1853) and attractively illustrated by her husband. A new standard was set in 1831 when Thomas Wright (1810-1877) began his serialised history of the county which was generously illustrated. It was not fully published until 1836 and was not superseded by D.W. Coller's (1805-1884) pleasing and useful *People's History of Essex,* published in 1861.

Not until 1903 when the first volume of the *Victoria History of the County of Essex* was published do we find county history written to modern academic standards. It was typical of the highest aspirations of Victorian Britain that work on this scale and level of scholarship should be commissioned to cover all of the counties of England. In the words of the Preface of the first volume on Hampshire, the *V.C.H.* traces 'county by county, the story of England's growth from its prehistoric condition through the barbarous age, the settlement of alien peoples, and the gradual welding of many races into a nation that is now the greatest on the globe'. Since then over 200 volumes have been completed. The first volume on Essex, which covered the Natural History and Prehistory of the County, Anglo-Saxon and Domesday Essex, was issued in 1903. A further volume which dealt with the Ecclesiastical, Political and Social Aspects of County History was published in 1907. Under W.R. Powell's editorship Essex historians have since been regaled with a superb volume on Roman Essex (1963), two bibliographies and territorial volumes covering the Ongar, Metropolitan Essex, Becontree (part) and other hundreds in south-west Essex in brilliant style and detail. Another superb work of scholarship is volume 9, a history of Colchester, which was published in 1994 under Janet Cooper's editorship.

Since the *V.C.H.* placed Essex history on such secure foundations no subsequent work can ignore it. Inevitably and rightly historical research has therefore tended to become more specialised and consequently narrower in scope and greater in depth. There have thus been a number of excellent local histories like John O' Leary's model *Book of Dagenham* (1937), G.H. Martin's *Colchester* (1959), *History of Harlow* (1969) edited by L.H. Bateman, Hilda Grieve's fine two-volume history of Chelmsford *The Sleepers and the Shadows* (1988 and 1994) and *A Village in Time* (Newport) compiled by a team led by Bernard Nurse (1995). Specialist work such as F.G. Emmison's erudite study of Elizabethan Essex which is based on the documentary riches of the county archives, J.E. Oxley's *The Reformation in Essex,* K.C. Newton's scholarly books on the manorial development of Thaxted and Writtle and volumes (see bibliography) published in relation to the millennium of the Battle of Maldon are now illuminating previously dark corners of county history into which general works cannot hope to probe.

There are several such general histories that ought to be mentioned here especially as there have been few that have attempted a comprehensive survey and the *V.C.H.* will not be completed for a long time yet. G.F. Bosworth's *Essex Past and Present* of 1898 and P.H.Reaney's *Essex* of 1928 are both short, serviceable essays, but not free from the constraints of conventional interpretation. A good concise history appeared in 1958 and was re-printed in 1994 in which A.C. Edwards gave us the benefit of his scholarship and experience at the Essex Record Office.

Essex in History (1977), now revised and reprinted, seeks to place the story of the county in a wider context of national and international history than its predecessors in this field. In doing so it presents a theme that, inspired by several thousand years of Essex history, heralds the millennium that is now imminent and which will itself, as the drama unfolds, open new chapters of life in the county for a future historian to record.

K.N.

ESSEX IN HISTORY—A BIBLIOGRAPHY

Reference note (2)

Many readers will wish to carry further their studies in particular aspects or periods of Essex history. This bibliography and the note on Essex historiography will serve as a guide to basic and certain specialist works; the county library services will provide access to much more. I would also commend the Guildhall Library which has a fine Essex collection and an unfailingly helpful staff. Interested readers should also join one of the excellent local history and archaeological societies that serve most localities in the county and such county organisations as the Friends of Historic Essex and the Essex Society for Archaeology and History, which will considerably enhance the scope of the material, experience and the knowledge that is otherwise available to the general public. The serious reader must necessarily learn how to make the best and appropriate use of the considerable resources of the archival material and scholarship at the Essex Record Office. Finally, all those interested in county history should use their eyes and feet more, for there is much to be derived from the Essex landscape that has yet to find its way into county literature.

Addison, W., *Essex Heyday* (1949)
Ashley, M., *England in the Seventeenth Century* (1967)
Black, J.B., *The Reign of Elizabeth* (1965)
Blair, P.H., *An Introduction to Anglo-Saxon England* (1956)
Blair, P.H., *Roman Britain and Early England* (1963)
Brown, A.F.J., *English History from Essex Sources, Vol. II: 1750-1900* (1952)
Brown, A.F.J., *Essex at Work 1700-1815* (1969)
Chisenhale-Marsh, T.C., *Domesday Book relating to Essex* (translation) (1864)
Clark, G., *The Later Stuarts* (1965)
Collingwood, R.G. and Myres, J.N.L., *Roman Britain and the English Settlements* (1937)
Cooper, W., *Harwich, The Mayflower and Christopher Jones* (1970)
Copley, G.J., *An Archaeology of South-East England* (1958)
Cox, J.C., *The Royal Forests of England* (1905)
Davies, G., *The Early Stuarts* (1959)
Dudley, D.R. and Webster, G., *The Rebellion of Boudicca* (1962)
Dudley, D.R. and Webster, G., *The Roman Conquest of Britain in A.D. 43-57* (1965)
Dunnett, R., *The Trinovantes* (1975)
Edwards, A.C., *English History from Essex Sources, Vol. I: 1550-1750* (1952)
Edwards, A.C., *A History of Essex* (1994)
Elsden-Tuffs, J., *Essex Coaching Days* (1969)
Emmison, F.G., *Elizabethan Life* (1970-1980)
Emmison, F.G., *Tudor Secretary* (1961)
Fisher, W.R., *The Forest of Essex* (1887)

Godman, E., *Medieval Architecture in Essex* (1905)
Godman, E., *Norman Architecture in Essex* (1905)
Gordon, D.I., *Regional History of the Railways of Great Britain* (1969)
Grieve, H., *The Great Tide* (1959)
Hardy, D. and Ward, C., *Arcadia for all* (1984)
Hockliffe, E. (ed.), *The Dairy of the Rev. Ralph Josselin 1616-1683* (1908)
Hodgkin, R.H., *A History of the Anglo-Saxons* (1952)
Longford, E., *Victoria R.I.* (1964)
Liddell, W.H. (ed.) and Wood, R.G., *Essex and the Great Revolt of 1381* (1982)
Macfarlane, A., *The Family Life of Ralph Josselin* (1970)
Mackie, J.D., *The Earlier Tudors* (1966)
Margary, I.D., *Roman Roads in Britain* (1967)
Morant, P., *The History and Antiquities of the County of Essex* (1768)
Morris, J., *Domesday Book: Essex* (text and translation) (1983)
Nicholls-Palmer, K., *The Knights of St John in Essex* (1991)
Neale, J.E., *Queen Elizabeth* (1947)
Neale, K.J., *Discovering Essex in London* (1970)
Neale, K.J., *Sir Thomas Smith and Hill Hall, Essex* (1970)
Newton, K.C., *Thaxted in the Fourteenth Century* (1960)
Newton, K.C., *The Manor of Writtle* (1970)
Oman, C., *The Great Revolt in 1381* (1906)
Oxley, J.E., *The Reformation in Essex* (1965)
Oxley Parker, J., *The Oxley Parker Papers* (1964)
Pevsner, N., *The Buildings of England* (Essex) (1965)
Pewsey, S. and Brooks, A., *East Saxon Heritage* (1993)
Plumb, J.H., *England in the Eighteenth Century* (1950)
Poole, A.L., *From Domesday Book to Magna Carta* (1955)
Reaney, P.H., *The Place Names of Essex* (1935)
Scarfe, N., *Essex* (1968)
Steer, F.W., *Samuel Tufnell of Langleys* (1960)
Taylor, H.M. and J., *Anglo-Saxon Architecture* (1965)
Thirsk, J., *Tudor Enclosures* (1958)
Thomas, N., *A Guide to Prehistoric England* (1960)
Scott-Watson, J.A. and Hobbs, M.R., *Great Farmers* (1951)
Stenton, D.M., *English Society in the Early Middle Ages* (1965)
Stenton, F., *Anglo-Saxon England* (1947)
Warren, C.H., *Essex* (1950)
Williams, B., *The Whig Supremacy* (1962)
Woodward, L., *The Age of Reform* (1962)
Young, A., *A General View of the Agriculture of the County of Essex* (1813)
Young, A., *A Six Weeks Tour through the Southern Counties* (1772)
Young, T., *Becontree and Dagenham* (1934)

General

The Anglo-Saxon Chronicle
Dictionary of National Biography
Essex Review
Essex Journal
Essex Naturalist
Publications of the Archaeology Section, Essex County Council
Publications of the Colchester Archaeological Trust
Publications of the Essex Record Office
Publications of the Local Historical Societies of Essex
Victoria County History of Essex

INDEX

175